Rick Steves ®

SNAPSHOT

St. Petersburg, Helsinki & Tallinn

CONTENTS

INTRODUCTION

This Snapshot guide, excerpted from my guidebooks *Rick Steves Scandinavia* and *Rick Steves Northern European Cruise Ports*, introduces you to the three great cities of eastern Baltic Sea: St. Petersburg, Russia's showpiece "window on the West," which was custom-built by the czars to impress the world; the slick Finnish capital of Helsinki, with a livable urban core, world-famous architectural gems, inviting harborfront market, and a knack for design; and the charming Estonian capital of Tallinn, with fine viewpoints, oodles of cobbles, and an irrepressible Estonian spirit. At these chilly northern latitudes, the summer travel season is short, but the charms are ample. Ogle St. Petersburg's opulent palaces, boulevards, and onion domes. Squeeze between Finns and squat on a wooden bench to sweat in a sauna. And browse the charms of Tallinn, one of Northern Europe's most atmospheric old towns. With its ties both to Scandinavian kings and to Russian czars of yore, you'll see how East meets West here in Europe's north. All three of these cities are well-connected by short and scenic boat trips.

To help you have the best trip possible, I've included the following topics in this book:

• **Planning Your Time,** with advice on how to make the most of your limited time

• **Orientation,** including tourist information (abbreviated as TI), tips on public transportation, local tour options, and helpful hints

• **Sights** with ratings:

    ▲▲▲—Don't miss

    ▲▲—Try hard to see

    ▲—Worthwhile if you can make it

    No rating—Worth knowing about

• **Sleeping and Eating,** with good-value recommendations in every price range

• **Connections,** with tips on trains, buses, and boats

Practicalities, near the end of this book, has information on money, phoning, hotel reservations, transportation, and more.

To travel smartly, read this little book in its entirety before you go. It's my hope that this guide will make your trip more meaningful and rewarding. Traveling like a temporary local, you'll get the absolute most out of every mile, minute, and dollar.

Счастливого пути..*Hyvä matkaa... Head reisi...*Happy travels!

RUSSIA

RUSSIA

Россия

 Enigmatic. Intimidating. Fascinating. Boasting some of the most spectacular cities, churches, and fortresses on earth, wrapped in a culture that's as monolithic and xenophobic as its onetime rival (read: us), Russia is an exciting frontier for adventurous Western travelers. Though no longer the great military and political power that it was during the Cold War, Russia remains a country of huge natural resources—energy, minerals, forests, rivers, and arable land.

Russia was poor and remote for centuries, with a good part of the population bound in serfdom until the 1860s. In the late 19th century, Russia began to industrialize, built closer ties to Europe, and fostered writers such as Tolstoy, Dostoyevsky, and Chekhov.

One of the new ideas that came to Russia from the West was communism. Led by Lenin and Stalin, the communist experiment lasted almost 75 years before it collapsed in 1991. Since then, despite widespread corruption, Russia has managed to build up something akin to a free-market economy. In urban shopping districts, you'll watch Russians perusing at least as many choices as American shoppers have.

Recently, Russia has taken baby steps toward making it easier for tourists to come on short visits to St. Petersburg, especially by ship. But a wildly fluctuating currency, still-improving service standards, limited knowledge of English, and a general lack of user-friendliness continue to challenge. And complicated, expensive visa requirements make Russia an uninviting destination for independent American travelers. However, the travel experience in Russia is slowly improving, year by year—particularly as the country has geared up for the world spotlight as the host country of the Winter Olympics in 2014 and the World Cup in 2016.

Traveling in Russia—or even just tuning into the news from there—leaves a strong impression of a place that, while massive and powerful, is still finding itself in the post-communist world. Yeltsin-era reforms and optimism have faded. Recent changes in the law have alarmed lovers of free speech, gay-rights advocates, and anyone who supports democratic ideals. And, more than a

Russia Almanac

Official Name: Russian Federation (Российская Федерация), or just Russia.

Population: Russia is a vast, multiethnic country of more than 142 million people, including a wide range of ethnic-Asian minority groups (one in five Russians is not ethnically Russian).

Latitude and Longitude: St. Petersburg sits at about 60°N and 30°E. It's nearly as far north as Canada's Northwest Territories and Yukon, and farther east than Istanbul.

Area: 6.6 million square miles, nearly double the size of the US.

Geography: The world's biggest country by area, Russia stretches from Europe all the way across Asia to Alaska. The European continent contains only about a quarter of Russia's land, but three-quarters of its population.

Biggest City: Moscow, Russia's capital, is home to 11.5 million people—making St. Petersburg, the second city, seem small with "just" 4.8 million.

Economy: Russia's Gross Domestic Product of $2.5 trillion makes it the world's seventh-biggest economy—though its per capita GDP ($17,700) ranks around 70th.

Currency: The Russian ruble (R, official RUB) has been in flux recently. Check the latest rates online.

Government: As a federation, Russia has 46 provinces (like the 50 US states)—which include oblasts, republics, and federal cities. The country is firmly led by President Vladimir Putin and his handpicked associate, Prime Minister Dimitry Medvedev.

Language: The native language is Russian, which uses the Cyrillic alphabet. For details, see page 18.

Flag: Russia's "Tricolor" flag consists of equal horizontal stripes (top to bottom): white, blue, and red.

The Average Russian: Lives only to age 59 and consumes four gallons of alcohol a year, much of it vodka.

decade and a half into his quasi-authoritarian rule, Vladimir Putin casts a long shadow over the world's largest country.

Today's Russia is wrestling with an ostensibly free-market economy that's dominated by the monopolistic instincts of the communist past, troubling concerns about ethnic diversity, and an increasingly stratified society (with a tiny and extremely wealthy upper class, a huge and desperate lower class, and little room in the middle). Bribery is an integral part of the economy—estimated at 20 percent of GDP. A corporate survey found it's harder to do business in Russia than in Bangladesh, Yemen, or Pakistan.

You'll see many "Asian" (most are actually Siberian) Russians, a reminder that this vast nation stretches from Norway to China. The friction between ethnic Russians and their eastern countrymen—which erupts violently in the form of periodic hate crimes—demonstrates that that gap between rich and poor has left a growing number of Russians desperate for scapegoats.

The Russian elite is wealthy and fashion-conscious. Upscale young women here dress very deliberately—taking seriously the task of looking like fashion photographs. They strut down city sidewalks, passing without a second glance the withered, sad-faced babushki selling a few paltry turnips from a tattered blanket.

Yes, Russia is challenging, both for Russians and for tourists. But it's also a richly rewarding destination for those willing to grapple with it. This following chapter focuses on St. Petersburg—Russia's "window on the West"—the country's northwestern outpost, peering across the Baltic Sea to Europe. In addition to advice on sightseeing, hotels, and restaurants, the you'll also find tips on the Russian language (see page 18) and cuisine (page 114).

Russian Survival Phrases

Russia comes with a more substantial language barrier than most of Europe. In general, young Russians know at least a little halting schoolroom English; hoteliers and museum clerks may speak only a few words; and older people speak none at all.

For help with decoding the Cyrillic alphabet, see the sidebar on pages 18-19.

English	Russian / Transliteration	Pronunciation
Hello. (formal)	Здравствуйте. / Zdravstvuyte.	**zdrah**-stvee-tyeh
Hi. (informal)	Привет. / Privyet.	pree-**vyeht**
Goodbye.	До свидания. / Do svidaniya.	dah svee-**dahn**-yah
Do you speak English?	Вы говорите по-английски? / Vy govoritye po angliyski?	vih gah-vah-**ree**-tyeh pah ahn-**glee**-skee
I (don't) understand.	Я (не) понимаю. / Ya (nye) ponimayu.	yah (nyeh) poh-nee-**mah**-yoo
Yes.	Да. / Da.	dah
No.	Нет. / Nyet.	nyeht
Please.	Пожалуйста. / Pozhaluysta.	pah-**zhahl**-stah
Thank you.	Спасибо. / Spasibo.	spah-**see**-bah
Excuse me.	Извините. / Izvinitye.	eez-vee-**nee**-tyeh
(Very) good.	(Очень) хорошо. / (Ochen) khorosho	(**oh**-cheen) kha-**roh**-show
How much?	Сколько стоит? / Skolko stoit?	**skohl**-kah **stoh**-yeet
one, two	один, два / odin, dva	ah-deen, dvah
three, four	три, четыре / tri, chetyre	tree, cheh-**teer**-yeh
five, six	пять, шесть / pyat, shest	pyaht, shyest
seven, eight	семь, восемь / sem, vosem	syehm, **vwoh**-sehm
nine, ten	девять, десять / devyat, desyat	**dyeh**-veht, **dyeh**-seht
Where is...?	Где...? / Gdye...?	guh-**dyeh**
...the toilet	...туалет / tualet	too-ahl-**yeht**
men	мужчины / muzhchiny	moo-**shee**-neh
women	женщины / zhenshchiny	zhen-**shee**-neh
(to the) right	(на) право / (na) pravo	(nah) **prah**-vah
(to the) left	(на) лево / (na) levo	(nah) **leh**-vah
beer	пиво / pivo	**pee**-vah
vodka	водка / vodka	**vohd**-kah
water	вода / voda	vah-**dah**
coffee	кофе / kofe	**koh**-fyeh
Cheers! (To your health)	На здоровья! / Na zdorovya!	nah zdah-**roh**-veh

ST. PETERSBURG

Санкт-Петербург

Once a swamp, then an imperial capital, and now a showpiece of vanished aristocratic opulence shot through with the dingy ruins of communism, St. Petersburg is Russia's most accessible and most tourist-worthy city. During the Soviet era, it was called Leningrad, but in 1991 St. Petersburg reverted to its more fitting historic name. Designed by imported French, Dutch, and Italian architects, this is, arguably, European Russia's least "Russian" city.

Palaces, gardens, statues, and arched bridges over graceful waterways bring back the time of the czars. Neighborhood markets bustle with gregarious honey maids offering samples, and brim with exotic fishes and meats, pickled goodies, and fresh produce. Stirring monuments—still adorned with hammers, sickles, and red stars—tower over the masses, evoking Soviet times. Jammed with reverent worshippers, glorious Orthodox churches are heavy with incense, shimmer with icons, and filled with hauntingly beautiful music. Topping things off are two of the world's premier art museums—the Hermitage and the Russian Museum—and one of its most opulent royal houses, the Catherine Palace.

St. Petersburg can challenge its visitors, most of whom have to jump through hoops to get a visa—and then struggle with not enough time, limited English, and an idiosyncratic (and not quite Western) approach to "service" and predictability. But most visitors leave St. Petersburg with vivid memories of a magnificent city, one that lives according to its own rules. While this place can be exasperating, it is worth grappling with. Beyond its brick-and-mortar sights, St. Petersburg gives first-timers a perfect peek into the enigmatic Russian culture.

Save time on a sunny day just to walk. Keep your head up: The upper facades are sun-warmed and untouched by street grime. While Nevsky Prospekt—the city's famous main boulevard—encapsulates all that's wonderful and discouraging about this quixotic burg, get beyond that axis. Explore the back streets along the canals. Stroll through the Summer Garden. Shop for a picnic at a local market hall. Go for a canal boat cruise. Step into a neighborhood church to watch people get intimate with an icon. Take a Metro ride anywhere, just for the experience. Climb St. Isaac's Cathedral for the view. When the Baltic Sea brings clouds and drizzle, plunge into the Hermitage or the Russian Museum.

PLANNING YOUR TIME

St. Petersburg is fantastic and gigantic. Two full days is a great start; with more time, you can squeeze in some of the out-of-town sights. A longer stay makes the visa hassle and expense more worthwhile.

Don't get uptight about timing your visit to the summer solstice for St. Petersburg's much-bandied **"White Nights."** While it's enjoyable—and a bit mind-bending—to watch the sun set after 11 o'clock at night, you can enjoy bright evenings here all summer long.

If you're arriving by **cruise,** you'll most likely have two days here. To make the most of your daylight sightseeing time, find out whether your cruise line offers an evening visit to the Hermitage.

ST. PETERSBURG IN ONE DAY

With just one day, you'll have to make some tough decisions. Devout art lovers should tour the Hermitage, then follow my self-guided Nevsky Prospekt walk. For a wider-ranging experience, skip the Hermitage and follow this ambitious plan (if you're not up for it all, omit the Russian Museum):

9:00	Follow my self-guided Nevsky Prospekt walk (about 2 hours), stopping in the Kazan Cathedral (30 minutes), Church on Spilled Blood (30 minutes), and Russian Museum (2 hours). Along the way, grab a quick lunch (30 minutes) and take some time to shop and linger (30 minutes).
15:00	Take a canal boat cruise.
16:00	Ride the Metro to the Peter and Paul Fortress, and tour the Romanov tombs at Sts. Peter and Paul Cathedral.
18:00	Walk back across the Neva, pausing at Strelka for a panoramic view.

ST. PETERSBURG

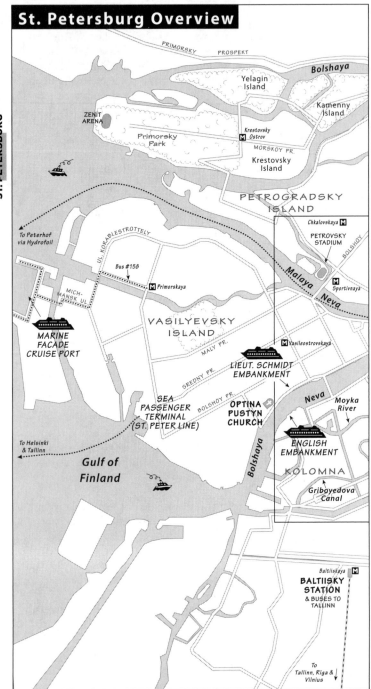

St. Petersburg Overview

PRIMORSKY PROSPEKT

Bolshaya

Yelagin Island

Kamenny Island

ZENIT ARENA

Krestovsky Ostrov Ⓜ

Primorsky Park

MORSKOY PR.

Krestovsky Island

PETROGRADSKY ISLAND

Chkalovskaya Ⓜ

PETROVSKY STADIUM

BOLSHOY

To Peterhof via Hydrofoil

UL. KORABLESTROTTELY

Malaya Neva

Ⓜ *Sportivnaya*

Bus #158

MICH-MANSK. UL.

Ⓜ *Primorskaya*

VASILYEVSKY ISLAND

Ⓜ *Vasileostrovskaya*

MALY PR.

MARINE FACADE CRUISE PORT

LIEUT. SCHMIDT EMBANKMENT

SREDNY PR.

Neva

Moyka River

BOLSHOY PR.

SEA PASSENGER TERMINAL (ST. PETER LINE)

OPTINA PUSTYN CHURCH

ENGLISH EMBANKMENT

To Helsinki & Tallinn

Gulf of Finland

Bolshaya

KOLOMNA

Griboyedova Canal

Baltiiskaya Ⓜ

BALTIISKY STATION & BUSES TO TALLINN

To Tallinn, Riga & Vilnius

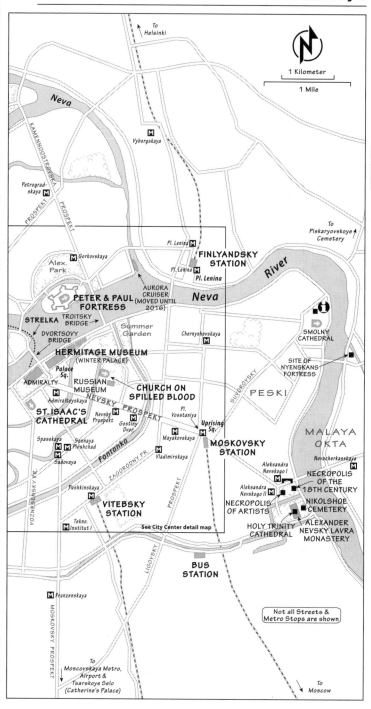

ST. PETERSBURG

Evening   Attend the ballet (seasonal), a concert, or the circus; explore some of the city's hipster dining and nightlife neighborhoods; or simply enjoy the city's famous "White Nights."

St. Petersburg in Two, Three, or More Days

Day 1

9:00   Follow my self-guided walk along Nevsky Prospekt to acquaint yourself with the city.

11:00   Visit the Kazan Cathedral and Church on Spilled Blood, and grab a quick lunch.

13:00   Tour the Russian Museum.

15:00   Take a canal boat cruise.

16:30   Visit St. Isaac's Cathedral.

18:30   Dinner.

Evening   Ballet, concert, circus, etc.

Day 2

10:30   Plunge into the Hermitage.

13:30   Grab a quick lunch, then walk across the Neva River to the Strelka viewpoint, continuing to Peter and Paul Fortress.

15:30   Tour the Kunstkamera and/or the Museum of Russian Political History; for a break, stroll through the Summer Garden.

18:00   Visit the Fabergé Museum.

19:30   Dinner.

Evening   See above.

Days 3, 4, and 5

With more time, do days 1 and 2 at a more relaxed tempo, with more time in the Hermitage or the Russian Museum—letting what you don't get to spill over to days 3, 4, and 5. Other choices are to visit other museums that interest you; ride the Metro to less-touristed parts of the city (such as the back streets of Vasilyevsky Island; see page 38); or go to Peterhof or Tsarskoye Selo for the day. WWII history buffs should consider a visit to Piskaryovskoye Memorial Cemetery.

GETTING TO ST. PETERSBURG

If connecting to St. Petersburg via Helsinki or Tallinn, bear in mind that St. Petersburg's time zone is one hour ahead of those cities.

By Sea: The only way to visit St. Petersburg without the bother of getting a Russian visa is to arrive by sea.

One option is to take a **cruise:** Many lines include a two-day stop in St. Petersburg on their Baltic itineraries. If you join an excursion into St. Petersburg with your cruise line, no visa is required (see sidebar on next page).

The other sea option is the **St. Peter Line ferry,** which departs from Helsinki every other night, year-round (and also has a once-weekly connection via Tallinn, plus two-day journeys all the way to Stockholm). Passengers sleep while the boat travels overnight from Helsinki to St. Petersburg; they then have a day to explore the city before sailing back to Helsinki (again overnight). As of this writing, paying €25 for the St. Peter Line "City Bus Tour" shuttle service from the port to downtown St. Petersburg allows you to see the city without a guide or a visa. However, requirements are constantly in flux, so confirm this is still possible before making plans. You can buy a one-way ticket on the St. Peter Line only if you have a Russian visa.

By Air: Many airlines serve St. Petersburg directly. Flying in and/or out of Helsinki rather than St. Petersburg itself is a viable option, as the Finlyandsky train station in St. Petersburg (where trains from Helsinki arrive and depart) is much easier to reach from the center than St. Petersburg's airport.

By Train from Helsinki: The 3.5-hour Allegro train trip through birch forests and past the old fortress city of Vyborg costs about €70-105 (price varies with demand, 4/day). Border formalities are carried out efficiently at your seat en route, and on-board currency exchange means you can hit the ground with cash in your pocket. Trains arrive at the Finlyandsky train station in St. Petersburg, which is right at the Ploshchad Lenina Metro stop (with an iconic Lenin statue out front).

By Bus: Buses from either Tallinn or Helsinki are easy and cheap, but not quick (from Tallinn—€25-30, about 10/day, 7 hours, www.luxexpress.eu; from Helsinki—€35-40, cheaper for students, 3-5/day, 8-9 hours, www.matkahuolto.fi). Buses arrive at the Baltiisky Vokzal train station in St. Petersburg (Metro: Baltiiskaya).

Orientation to St. Petersburg

St. Petersburg is gigantic and decentralized; you'll want to carefully plan your time to minimize backtracking. Most of the sights (and the dense urban core) are on the south bank of the Neva River; to the north are the historic Peter and Paul Fortress and the tidy, grid-planned residential zone of Vasilyevsky Island (with the cruise port at its western tip). The city—built over a swamp—is a horizontal one. Foundations for skyscrapers are too challenging.

Russian Visa Requirements

Note: *The following information was accurate as of 2015, but Russian visa regulations are notoriously changeable. Confirm everything stated here before you make your plans. For the latest requirements, see www.ricksteves.com/russianvisa.*

Do I Need a Visa?

To enter Russia, residents of most countries, including the US and Canada, are required to obtain a visa in advance. The only exception is for travelers arriving by sea (on a cruise ship or passenger ferry), who can be in the country for up to 72 hours without a visa. However, there's a catch: You must book a tour through a local organization.

If you're arriving on the **St. Peter Line ferry,** you will likely be able to pay for their "shuttle service"—an unguided, round-trip bus between the port and downtown, leaving you with free time to explore. This option, which exploits a loophole that could close at any moment, is the only way to see the city both unaccompanied and without a visa.

If you're arriving by **cruise** without a visa, things are a bit more restrictive: You must pay for a cruise-line excursion (or book a tour through a locally based company), and remain with your guide or escort the entire time you are on land—you'll have virtually no free time to explore on your own. An excursion is more expensive and completely scripted, but virtually effortless. If you're an adventurous traveler and want to experience the real Russia, consider obtaining a visa and exploring the city on your own. Note that if you go the visa route, you must start the application process well in advance.

How to Get a Visa

Getting a Russian visa is not exactly difficult, but it does take a few weeks to accomplish. If the steps outlined below make your head spin, skip down to "Third-Party Visa Agencies."

1. Before applying for a visa, you must first get an official document called a **"visa invitation"** (*priglashenie;* sometimes called a "letter of invitation," "visa sponsor," or "visa support letter") from a Russian organization recognized by the Russian Foreign Ministry. Visa invitations are typically issued either by a hotel or by a tour operator. If you're arriving by cruise, you'll need to arrange an invitation through a third-party agency—see below.) When you make a hotel reservation, ask the hotel to arrange for an invitation as well (they'll usually charge $15-30). If you're visiting more than one city in Russia, ask if your entire trip can be included on a single invitation, so that you don't have to get invitations from each hotel. You may find online agencies willing to issue invitations for a fee, but stick with the agency recommended by your hotel. Don't expect the invitation process to make sense; it feels (and is) bureaucratic. The organization that issues your invitation is legally responsible for you during your

stay in Russia, but in practice, you will never have any contact with them.

2. Fill out the **Electronic Visa Application Form** (available online at http://visa.kdmid.ru). Request a multiple-entry visa, which is valid for three years for $160, plus a processing fee of $33-103 (explained below). Note that your passport must be valid for at least six months beyond the date of your departure from Russia, and must have two adjacent blank pages to accommodate the visa.

3. Submit the invitation, the form, your passport, a passport photograph, and the processing fee (money order or cashier's check only) to the Russian Embassy. Applications are accepted anywhere from **30 to 60 days before departure** (the specific timeframe changes constantly, but you'll need a few weeks for the full process). There are Russian consulates in Washington, D.C., New York, San Francisco, Seattle, and Houston (for details, see www.russianembassy.org). You have three options for filing your application: You can deliver it to one of the consulates in person ($33 fee); you can mail it to a consulate ($103 fee); or you can submit your application through a third-party service ($33 in-person fee, plus the agency's add-on service fee)—see next.

Third-Party Visa Agencies: Various agencies specialize in steering your visa application through the process. They can also help you arrange visa invitations and navigate the confusing application. I've had a good experience with Passport Visa Express.com (www.passportvisasexpress.com).

In addition to the $160 visa price, visa agencies charge a service fee of about $80-110 (including the invitation fee). To ship your passport securely to and from the visa agency costs another $50 or so. Figure at least $350 total per person.

Entering Russia with a Visa: When you enter the country, the immigration officer will ask you to fill out a **migration card** in duplicate, listing your name, passport number, and other details. The officer will stamp both parts of the card and keep one. Don't lose the other half—it must be presented when you leave the country. (A digital version of this card is being phased in, but you'll still need to carry the hard copy.)

Once you arrive in Russia, it's wise to **register** your passport and visa with the local authorities. Usually your hotel will take care of this for you—they'll need a copy of your passport. You'll receive a confirmation slip, which you may need to show when you leave Russia. While this step is required only for stays of more than seven days, if you don't register, when you depart, you may be asked to show proof (such as hotel receipts) that you were in Russia for less than a week.

While in Russia, you are required to carry your original passport (not just a copy) with you at all times. Police in Russia can stop you at any time and ask to see your documents, though this seldom happens to tourists.

Don't go looking for a cutesy, cobbled "old town"; the entire city was carefully planned to fit within its three concentric waterways: first the Moyka (**Мойка**) River, then the Griboyedov Canal (**Канал Грибоедова**), and finally the Fontanka (**Фонтанка**) River.

The geographical center of the city is the Admiralty building, with a slender, golden spire that shines like a beacon (next to the river, Hermitage, and Palace Square). From here, bustling avenues (called prospekty) radiate out to the distant suburbs. The busiest and most interesting thoroughfare is Nevsky Prospekt (**Невский Проспект**). Almost everything you'll want to see is either along Nevsky or a few blocks to either side of it. Uprising Square (Ploshchad Vosstaniya, **Площадь Восстания**)—home to a tall obelisk and the Moskovsky train station—marks the end of the usual tourist zone.

Maps make St. Petersburg appear smaller than it is. What looks like "just a few blocks" can easily translate into a half-hour walk. The two-mile walk along Nevsky from the Admiralty to Uprising Square takes about an hour at a brisk pace. Make things easier on yourself by getting comfortable with the city's cheap and generally well-coordinated public transit. The Metro boasts frequent trains that zip effortlessly below clogged streets. A well-planned network of buses, trolley buses, and shared minibuses called marshrutki help you bridge the (sometimes long) gaps between sights and Metro stops; while a bit less user-friendly to the uninitiated, these can save tons of time when mastered.

A few terms you'll see on maps: *ulitsa* is "street," *ploshchad* is "square," *prospekt* is "avenue," and *most* is "bridge." Many street signs are conveniently bilingual. They usually list the house number of the building they're on, as well as the numbers of the buildings to either side (this is convenient, as buildings can be very large).

You may see free maps around town, but if you'll be navigating on your own, buy a good map at one of the bookstores listed later, under "Helpful Hints." I like the "city tourist map" by Discus, with labels in both English and Cyrillic.

TOURIST INFORMATION

The city TI has several branches. While they aren't as well-organized as many European TIs, the staff tries hard, speaks at least a bit of English, and may be willing to call around to help you with a question they can't answer. The most convenient branch is in the glass pavilion just to the left of the **Hermitage** (as you face it from Palace Square); the main branch is a few steps off **Nevsky Prospekt** (at Sadovaya 14, across from Gostiny Dvor—watch for the low-profile door and go up one flight of stairs; Mon-Fri 10:00-19:00, closed Sat-Sun, tel. 310-2231, www.visit-petersburg.ru or www.ispb.info). You'll also see TI kiosks in high-tourist areas such as St. Isaac's Cathedral, Peter and Paul Fortress, on Uprising Square (Ploshchad Vosstaniya) near Moskovsky train station, and at the airport (all generally open daily 9:00-19:00, but hours and services are unpredictable). The city also runs a 24-hour "Tourist Help Line," with English operators, at tel. 303-0555.

The bimonthly *St. Petersburg In Your Pocket* guidebook is good; look for free copies around town or browse it online at www .inyourpocket.com.

ST. PETERSBURG

ARRIVAL IN ST. PETERSBURG

For more details on each of the following, see "St. Petersburg Connections," at the end of this chapter.

By Train: All train stations have Metro stops. But if you're arriving with large bags, for convenience and peace of mind, pay the extra cost and arrange in advance with your hotel to be picked up at the station by a driver. Although a few newer Metro stations (such as Admiralteyskaya) are friendly to wheeled luggage, most have unavoidable flights of stairs (as do some train stations themselves). Those grabbing a taxi at the station without booking it in advance are likely to be overcharged (see "By Taxi," later).

By Plane: St. Petersburg's Pulkovo Airport is about 12 miles south of the center, and linked to downtown by a Metro/bus combination or taxi.

By Boat: St. Petersburg is a major stop for cruise ships and the St. Peter Line passenger ferry.

HELPFUL HINTS

Sightseeing Schedules: Opening times for St. Petersburg's museums and churches are very changeable—particularly the closed days, and days when sights are open late. When planning your visit, confirm hours online.

Take note of closed days: The Hermitage, Kunstkamera, and Peterhof are closed on Mondays, the Russian Museum and Tsarskoye Selo on Tuesdays, many religious sites (St. Isaac's, Church on Spilled Blood) on Wednesdays, the Museum of Russian Political History on Thursdays, and the Fabergé Museum on Fridays.

Don't Drink the Water: While new water treatment plants have improved quality in recent years, and most locals wash fruit and brush their teeth with tap water, they still don't drink it—and neither should you. Buy bottled water cheaply in grocery stores. St. Petersburg provides its residents with preheated water that's boiled at a station in the suburbs, then piped directly into city taps. Each summer, they close the plant for a week or two of cleaning—effectively cutting off the city's hot

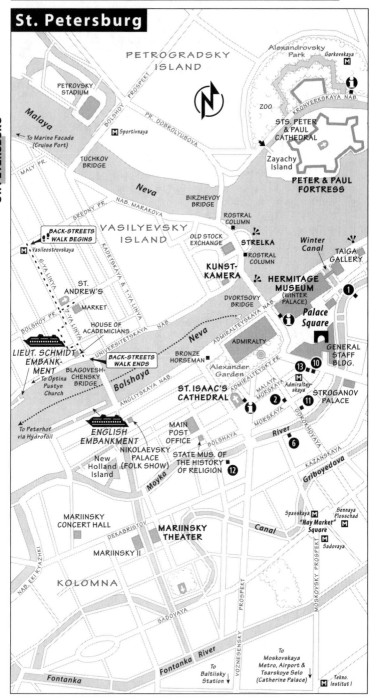

ST. PETERSBURG

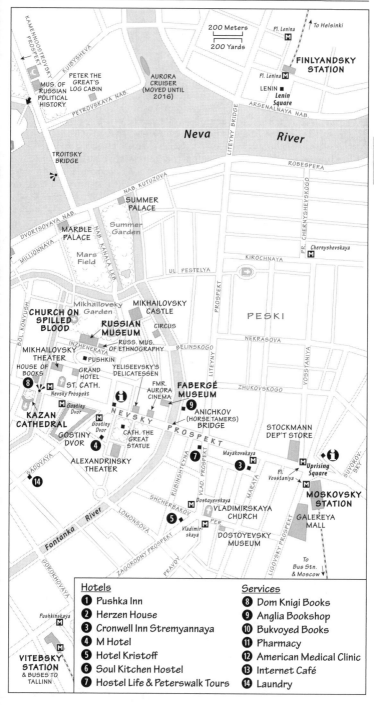

KAMENNOOSTROVSKIY PROSPEKT
KUYBYSHEVA
PETER THE GREAT'S LOG CABIN
MUS. OF RUSSIAN POLITICAL HISTORY
PETROVSKAYA NAB.
AURORA CRUISER (MOVED UNTIL 2016)
Pl. Lenina
To Helsinki
FINLYANDSKY STATION
Pl. Lenina
LENIN
Lenin Square
ARSENALNAYA NAB.

Neva River

TROITSKY BRIDGE
NAB. KUTUZOVA
LITEYNY BRIDGE
ROBESPERA
PR. CHERNYSHEVSKOGO
Chernyshevskaya

DVORTSOVAYA NAB.
MILLIONNAYA
SUMMER PALACE
MARBLE PALACE
Summer Garden
NAB. KANALA LEB.
Mars Field
UL. PESTELYA
KIROCHNAYA

BOL KONYUSH
Mikhailovsky Garden
CHURCH ON SPILLED BLOOD
MIKHAILOVSKY CASTLE
RUSSIAN MUSEUM
CIRCUS
PESKI
PROSPEKT

INZHENERAYA
RUSS. MUS. OF ETHNOGRAPHY
NEKRASOVA
MIKHAILOVSKY THEATER
PUSHKIN
BELINSKOGO
LITEYNY
VOSSTANIYA
HOUSE OF BOOKS
GRAND HOTEL
YELISEEVSKY'S DELICATESSEN
ZHUKOVSKOGO
ST. CATH.
Nevsky Prospekt
FMR. AURORA CINEMA
FABERGÉ MUSEUM
⑧
KAZAN CATHEDRAL
Gostiny Dvor
⑨
ANICHKOV (HORSE TAMERS) BRIDGE
GOSTINY DVOR
Gostiny Dvor
④
CATH. THE GREAT STATUE
N E V S K Y
P R O S P E K T
STOCKMANN DEP'T STORE
ALEXANDRINSKY THEATER
RUBINSHTEYNA
⑦
Mayakovskaya
③
Pl. Vosstaniya
Uprising Square
SUVOROV-SKY
SADOVAYA
VLAD. PROSPEKT
MARAYA
LIGOVSKIY PROSPEKT
⑭
SHCHERBAKOV
Dostoyevskaya
⑤
VLADIMIRSKAYA CHURCH
MOSKOVSKY STATION
River Fontanka
LOMONOSOVA
PER
Vladimirskaya
GALEREYA MALL
GOROKHOVAYA
ZAGORODNY PROSPEKT
PRAVDY
DOSTOYEVSKY MUSEUM
To Bus Stn. & Moscow
Pushkinskaya

VITEBSKY STATION & BUSES TO TALLINN

200 Meters
200 Yards

Hotels
① Pushka Inn
② Herzen House
③ Cronwell Inn Stremyannaya
④ M Hotel
⑤ Hotel Kristoff
⑥ Soul Kitchen Hostel
⑦ Hostel Life & Peterswalk Tours

Services
⑧ Dom Knigi Books
⑨ Anglia Bookshop
⑩ Bukvoyed Books
⑪ Pharmacy
⑫ American Medical Clinic
⑬ Internet Café
⑭ Laundry

ST. PETERSBURG

Learning the Cyrillic Alphabet

If you're going to Russia—even if just for a couple of days on a cruise—you'll have a much richer, smoother experience if you take the time to learn the Cyrillic alphabet. Once you know the basics, you can (slowly) sound out signs around town, and some of those very long, confusing words will become familiar. It's actually a fun pastime to try to figure out signs while you're walking down the street, waiting for a bus, or riding a long Metro escalator.

The table shows the Cyrillic alphabet (both capital and lowercase), and in the second column, the Roman equivalent. Notice that the letters fall—very roughly—into four categories: Some letters are basically the same sound as in English, such as A, E, K, M, O, and T. Others are easy if you know the Greek alphabet: Г—gamma (g) , Д—delta (d), П—pi (p), and Ф—phi (f). Some are unique to Russian; most of these are "fricative" sounds, like ts, sh, ch, or kh (Ж, З, Ц, Ч, Ш, Щ, Х). And the fourth category seem designed to trip you up: "false friends" that have a different sound than the Roman letter they resemble, such as В, С, Н, Р, Х, and У. It can be helpful to remember that the "backwards" Roman consonants are actually vowels (И, Й, Я).

The letter Ы, which sounds somewhat similar to the i in English "ill," looks like two letters but is treated as one. The "hard sign" and "soft sign" are silent letters that affect the pronunciation of the preceding consonant in ways you need not worry about.

Two important words which you'll often see are easy to confuse: вход means entrance, but выход is an exit. For more Russian words and phrases, see page 5.

water. For this reason, wealthier locals (and most hotels) have their own backup hot-water heaters.

Theft Alert: Russia has hardworking, often unusually aggressive pickpockets who target tourists. Be particularly aware anywhere along Nevsky Prospekt, in crowded shopping areas (such as Gostiny Dvor), and on public transport. Assume that any scuffle is a distraction by a team of thieves, and that anyone who approaches you on the street is trying to pull off a scam. Some thieves are well-dressed and even carry guidebooks to fool you. Thieves can be rough—they've even been known to detach and steal big camera lenses in one smooth motion. Keep anything precious close (wear a money belt for your passport, credit cards, and other valuables, leave the fancy jewelry at home, and don't be careless with cameras, smartphones, and tablets).

Pedestrian Safety: Russian drivers are shockingly forceful, zipping between lanes and around any obstructions. They drive fast, even on small downtown streets. Don't jaywalk: *Always* use crosswalks and look both ways before crossing—espe-

Cyrillic	Roman
Аа	a
Бб	b
Вв	v
Гг	g
Дд	d
Ее	ye, e
Ёё	yō
Жж	zh
Зз	z
Ии	i
Йй	y
Кк	k
Лл	l
Мм	m
Нн	n
Оо	o
Пп	p

Рр	r
Сс	s
Тт	t
Уу	u
Фф	f
Хх	kh
Цц	ts
Чч	ch
Шш	sh
Щщ	shch
Ъъ	hard sign
Ыы	y
Ьь	soft sign
Ээ	e
Юю	yu
Яя	ya

ST. PETERSBURG

cially along Nevsky Prospekt, with its eight lanes of traffic moving at terrifying speeds.

Online Translation Tip: If a website you want is available only in Russian, try using the Chrome browser (www.google.com/chrome), which can (roughly) translate the page for you.

Business Hours: Most shops, restaurants, and services are open the same hours seven days a week (the legacy of communism, which tried to do away with weekends). You'll see a surprising number of shops and restaurants open 24/7 (look for *24 Часа*).

"Sightseeing Tax" for Foreigners: You may notice that the admission price for Russians to various sights can be cheaper than the cost for foreigners. I've listed only the "foreigner" price, but if you happen to have a Russian passport, insist on the lower price.

Tipping: As in most of Europe, tipping here is less routine—and much less generous—than in the US. But if you're satisfied with the service, you can round the bill up 5-10 percent (more than that is considered excessive). Tip a taxi driver by rounding up the fare a bit (pay 300 R on an 280-R fare).

ST. PETERSBURG

Dress Code: In Orthodox churches, modest dress is expected (no shorts or bare shoulders; women are encouraged to cover their heads with a scarf).

Pharmacy: Look for the chain called **36.6**—as in the normal Celsius body temperature. The most central location is at Gorokhovaya 16, near the Admiralteyskaya Metro stop (open long hours daily).

Medical/Dental Services: The (entirely Russian-staffed) **American Medical Clinic** is near St. Isaac's Cathedral on the Moyka embankment (Naberezhnaya reki Moyki 78, tel. 740-2090, www.amclinic.com, info@amclinic.ru).

Internet Access: Most hotels, many cafés and restaurants, and even some museums have free Wi-Fi hotspots. If you need a terminal, you can get online at the Internet café at the back of the Subway restaurant at Nevsky Prospekt 11 (enter on side street and take stairs to second floor; Skype installed, open 24 hours, tel. 314-6705).

Laundry: Prachka.com is St. Petersburg's launderette chain. The most convenient branch is along Sadovaya Ulitsa, beyond the back end of Gostiny Dvor if coming from Nevsky. It's in the old Apraksin Dvor market complex: Walk along the street almost to the end and look for the small launderette in one of the basement stalls. Don't be put off by the run-down building—inside, it's all modern and computer-controlled (daily 10:00-22:00, Sadovaya Ulitsa 30).

Bookstore: The city's best-known bookstore, **Dom Knigi** ("House of Books," Дом Книги), is in the old Singer sewing machine building at Nevsky Prospekt 28 (by the Griboyedov Canal, across from Kazan Cathedral). It sells English novels and locally produced guidebooks and has a pretty second-floor café with a view over the Kazan Cathedral (daily 9:00-24:00). **Anglia Bookshop** (Англия), just off Nevsky Prospekt facing the Fontanka River (next to the horse statues on the Anichkov Bridge, at the end of my self-guided Nevsky Prospekt walk), has a fine selection of English-language books by Russian authors and about Russian history (Mon-Sat 11:00-20:00, Sun 12:00-20:00, Fontanka 38, tel. 579-8284). You'll also see the **Bukvoyed** (Буквоед) bookstore chain around town, with several handy branches along Nevsky Prospekt (generally daily 9:00-22:00).

Currency Fluctuation: The ruble is on a roller-coaster ride—mostly going down. Depending on economic conditions when you travel, you may find higher prices (in rubles) than those quoted here. Because of the currency instability, in some listings I've given prices in US dollars, especially for personal services and smaller vendors (walking tours, private guides, etc.) For current exchange rates, check www.oanda.com.

ATMs: The word for ATM is банкомат *(bankomat)*. They are most commonly *inside* banks, hotels, restaurants, and other establishments, though you will find a few out on the street. Locals advise using machines inside bank lobbies when possible.

Telephones: There are no pay phones in St. Petersburg. For international calls, your best bet is to use Skype or another computer-based service from your hotel or an Internet café.

Mail: Mailboxes are blue with "Почта России" in white lettering. The central post office, open 24 hours, is in a historic building a couple of blocks beyond St. Isaac's Cathedral at Pochtamtskaya Ulitsa 9 (look for the archway that crosses the street). The Russian mail service has a reputation for delivering things extremely slowly, if at all, but just for postcards—well, you can take the risk.

Convenience Stores: There are small stores in every neighborhood (often down a few steps from street level and open late or even 24 hours) where you can pick up basic necessities. Look for signs saying *Продукты* ("foodstuffs") or *Универсам* (Universam, meaning "self-service store"). In the very center, the 24-hour *universam* at Bolshaya Konyushennaya Ulitsa 4 (at the corner of Shvedsky Pereulok) is convenient and decent-sized.

What's With All the Weddings? It's a Russian tradition for bride and groom to visit about 10 different parks and monuments around town on their wedding day and have their photo taken.

GETTING AROUND ST. PETERSBURG

The best available English-language **journey planner** for St. Petersburg's public transportation is www.spb.rusavtobus.ru/en. Though not very user-friendly, it covers both the Metro and surface transport. The official Metro website (www.metro.spb.ru) is in Russian only.

By Metro: Compared to systems in many other European metropolises, St. Petersburg's Metro has fewer stations and lines. This means it's a longer walk between stations—but beneath the city you'll move at a shockingly fast pace. The system is clean, efficient, very cheap, and—with a little practice—easy to use (everything is clearly labeled in English). You'll marvel at one of the most impressive people-movers on the planet—at rush hour, it's astonishing to simply stand on the platform and watch the hundreds upon hundreds of commuters pile in and out of each train. It's worth taking at least once just for the experience.

You enter with a metal token (zheton, жетон), which you can buy for 31 R—either at the ticket windows, or from machines in station entrances (in Russian and English, easy to figure out: push button labeled Купить жетоны—"buy tokens," select the number

ST. PETERSBURG

A Timeline of Russian History

800s	Spurred by Viking trade along Russia's rivers, states form around the cities of Novgorod and Kiev. ("Russia" comes from a Viking word.)
988	Kiev converts to Christianity and becomes part of the Eastern Orthodox world.
1224-1242	Tatar (Mongol) hordes conquer Russia and exact tribute. But Russia succeeds where the Baltics fail: keeping the Germans out.
1465-1557	The Russian czars consolidate power in Moscow, drive away the Tatars, and form a unified Russian state.
1613	Foundation of the Romanov dynasty, which lasts until 1917. (For a full rundown of the Romanovs, see "Romanovs 101" on page 98.)
1703	Czar Peter the Great founds St. Petersburg as Russia's forward-looking capital and "window on the West." Russia expands southward and eastward under Peter and his successor, Catherine.
1812	Napoleon invades Russia and burns Moscow, but loses an army on the way home.
1855-1861	Russia loses Crimean War and decides to modernize, including freeing the serfs.
1905	Russia loses a war with the Japanese, contributing to a failed revolution later glorified by the communists as a manifestation of the workers' consciousness.
1917	In March, the Romanov czar is ousted by a provisional government led by Alexander Kerensky; in the October Revolution, the provisional government is ousted by the Bolsheviks (communists), led by Vladimir Lenin. A few months later, the entire Romanov family is executed.
1924	Lenin dies on January 26, and in his honor St. Petersburg is renamed Leningrad (it reverted to St. Petersburg again in 1991).
1924-1939	Josef Stalin purges the government and the army. Forced collectivization causes famine and tens of millions of deaths in Ukraine.
1939-1945	In World War II, Russia loses 20 million people to the Germans (including as many as a million in the Siege of Leningrad), but winds up with control over

of tokens you want, then insert money). A 10-journey pass is sold at ticket windows only (295 R, valid 7 days, cannot be shared). There are no day passes.

Signs in the Metro are fully bilingual, and maps of the system are posted widely. Each of the five lines is numbered and color-coded. It helps to know the end station in the direction you're traveling. Unlike most European subway systems, transfer stations

	a sizable chunk of Eastern and Central Europe.
1945-1962	At the peak of the Cold War, Russia acquires the atom bomb, and launches the first satellite and the first manned space mission.
1970s	During a time of stagnation under Leonid Brezhnev, the communist system slowly fails.
1985	Mikhail Gorbachev comes to power and declares the beginning of *glasnost* (openness) and *perestroika* (restructuring) in the Soviet system.
1991	Reactionaries try to topple Gorbachev. They fail to keep power, but so does Gorbachev. Boris Yeltsin takes control of the government and starts reforms.
1993	Reactionaries fail to topple Yeltsin. Weakened, Yeltsin manages to hang on to power until 1999, despite grumbling from the ultra-nationalist right and the communist left.
1999	On New Year's Eve, Yeltsin suddenly and inexplicably resigns, handing the country over to former KGB officer Vladimir Putin.
2000-2008	Putin serves as president.
2008-2012	The term-limited Putin becomes prime minster, keeping a close watch on the presidency of his handpicked successor, Dmitry Medvedev. (Cynical onlookers dub the arrangement a "tandemocracy.")
2012	Surprise! A conveniently timed change in the law allows Putin to return as president, while Medvedev swaps roles to become prime minster. Russian protesters and international observers grumble about "reforms" that shore up Putin's power.
2014	The Russian city of Sochi, on the Black Sea, hosts the Winter Olympics, amid controversy over Putin's laws against "gay propaganda." Soon after the Olympics, Ukraine's Crimea region (a highly strategic, traditionally Russian Black Sea peninsula) falls under Russian control, and warfare rages in eastern Ukraine between pro-Russian and pro-Ukrainian factions. US- and EU-driven sanctions, coupled with declining oil prices, cause the ruble to plummet on the international market.
2018	Russia hosts the World Cup.

(where two lines meet) have two names, one for each line. Some stations in the center have flood doors along the boarding area that open only when trains arrive. Trains run from about 6:00 in the morning to a little after midnight.

Though St. Petersburg's Metro is not as ornate as Moscow's, some stations are works of art. For a rundown of the best stations, see page 94. It's OK to take pictures in the Metro, but you can't use a flash.

Because bedrock is far beneath the city surface, the Metro is very deep. The Admiralteyskaya station is nearly 350 feet below ground. The escalator ride alone takes several minutes—long enough that people pull out ebook readers, play smartphone solitaire, or kiss.

Pickpocket Alert: Metro stations, especially at rush hour, are particularly high-risk for pickpocketing. While any line near a touristy sight is targeted, the busy green line—connecting the cruise port to the city center (Gostiny Dvor), then out to the Alexander Nevsky Lavra Monastery—is particularly plagued. A common strategy: A team of thieves spot a tourist. Then, as everyone loads into the train, the thief in front stumbles, your arms go out, the guy behind you grabs his target, the door closes...and it's just you without your wallet, zipping across town on the train.

By Bus and Trolley Bus: Buses and trolley buses (with overhead wires) are very quick, cheap, and convenient for getting around the center of town. They're useful for connecting locations not served by the Metro, and let you see the city instead of burying you underground (especially nice when zipping along Nevsky Prospekt). The system takes a little patience to figure out (it helps if you can sound out Cyrillic to decipher posted schedules); ideally, ask a knowledgeable local which bus number to look for.

Along the street, stops are marked by an A (for buses), a flat-topped M for trolley buses, and a K for *marshrutki* minibuses (explained later). Signs at bus stops—in Russian only—list the route number, frequency, and sometimes the names of the stops en route. (Tram lines, marked by a T, run only in the city's outer districts.)

All surface transport costs 28 R per ride; pay the conductor, who wears a reflective vest and will give you a thin paper-slip ticket. There are no transfers, so you pay again if you switch buses. Be sure to ask your hotel for a rundown of which handy buses stops are nearby.

The buses and trolley buses that run along Nevsky Prospekt (between its start, at Malaya Morskaya Ulitsa, and Uprising Square/Ploshchad Vosstaniya) are useful: buses #3, #7, #24, and #191, and trolley buses #1, #5, #7, #10, #11, and #22. Don't be afraid to make mistakes; if you take the wrong bus and it turns off Nevsky, just hop out at the next stop. Trolley buses #5 and #22 conveniently veer off from the lower end of Nevsky down Malaya Morskaya Ulitsa to St. Isaac's Cathedral and the Mariinsky Theater.

Marshrutki (**Minibuses**): These "share taxis"—operated by private companies—travel along set, numbered routes, prefixed with the letter K. You can wave them down anywhere along the way and ask to be dropped off at any point along the route. They're designed more for residents than for tourists, but can be useful for going to Peterhof, Tsarskoye Selo, or the airport.

By Taxi: Locals tend to avoid cabs, and you should use them only with caution. You won't see taxi stands in St. Petersburg, and you should walk away from cabbies who hail you down ("Taxi?"). But you can always call and order an **official taxi** by phone (you'll probably need a Russian speaker to help, as few dispatchers or cabbies speak English). Official taxis are a little more expensive and safer than those hailed on the street. Pay the fare on the meter, rounding up a little. Beware that congested city traffic can make a taxi ride slow. Official taxis typically have a set minimum fare—typically 350-400 R—which covers most trips within the city center.

Two reliable companies are **068** (tel. 068, www.taxi068.ru) and **Novoye Zhyoltoye** (New Yellow Taxis, Новое Жёлтое; tel. 600-8888, www.peterburg.nyt.ru/en). You can send in a form from the English-language section of either website to order a taxi, but you'll need to give a local phone number. The **Ladybird** taxi service (tel. 900-0504, www.ladybird-taxi.ru) has only women drivers and provides car seats for kids.

"Fishing for a Lada": Most Russians in need of a ride "fish for a Lada" (referring to the ubiquitous Soviet-era beater car). Immigrants (generally from Central Asia) cruise around town in sometimes well-worn cars as informal taxis. The local points to the pavement, the car stops, they agree on a destination and a price, and it's a win-win deal. For a tourist, the challenge is to communicate, as the driver will rarely speak a word of English; it also helps  to know roughly how much you should pay. This custom demands some common-sense caution (never get into a car with passengers). An average trip within the center will run about 200 R. Consider working out an hourly rate (generally around 1,000 R/hour).

Tours in St. Petersburg

Walking Tours

Peterswalk has been doing excellent, English-language walking tours of the city since 1996. I like this tour because rather than visiting the crowded, famous sights, you'll simply walk through the city and learn about contemporary life and culture ($22/person, 4 hours, mobile +7-921-943-1229, www.peterswalk.com, info@peterswalk.com). From April through October, the tour begins every day at 10:30 at Hostel Life, around the corner from Nevsky Prospekt 47 (near the Fontanka River—ring the bell at Vladimirsky Prospekt 1 and go up to the fourth floor; tour may run sporadically off-season—check website). Peterswalk also does bike tours, private guided tours, and visa-free tours for cruise travelers (see below).

Bike Tours

Peterswalk offers 3.5-hour weekend and late-night bike tours (mid-May-Sept Sat-Sun at 11:00, also mid-May-Aug Tue and Thu at 22:30, $40/person, starts at SkatProkat bike shop at Goncharnaya Ulitsa 7, near Moskovsky train station and Ploschad Vosstaniya).

Boat Tours in English

St. Petersburg is a delight to see from the water. Low-slung canal boats ply their way through the city, offering a handy orientation to major landmarks. After curling  through narrow, urban waterways, your boat pops out onto the wide Neva River and a grand panorama of the Hermitage, Admiralty, and Peter and Paul Fortress. Various companies advertise at touristy points near canals and offer essentially the same one-hour cruise, most with recorded or live narration in Russian. It's worth asking the various hawkers around town whether they have an English option. One that does is **Neptun** (Нептун), near the Hermitage (600 R one-hour cruise, 3/hour; recorded narration in English typically available at 13:00, 15:00, and 17:00; on Moyka embankment at #26, near recommended Troitsky Most restaurant—see map on page 112, tel. 924-4452, www.neptun-boat.ru).

Hop-on Hop-off Bus Tours

CityTour runs red, double-decker, hop-on, hop-off buses that make a circuit of major sights in the center, with recorded commentary. Buses start at Ostrovsky Square (near the statue of Catherine the Great, along Nevsky Prospekt) about every 30 minutes from 9:00 to

19:00; the full circle takes two hours (600 R all-day ticket, buy on board, tel. 718-4769, mobile +7-961-800-0755, www.citytourspb.ru).

Private Guides for Travelers with Visas
Each of the following guide organizations is smart, small, reliable, and committed to helping visitors enjoy and understand their city. I work with them when my tour groups are in town, and they are consistently excellent. If you have a visa, you can hire them privately for walking or car tours (generally $40/hour for up to 8 people on foot, 4-hour minimum). If you're coming on a cruise without a visa, see the next section.

Natalya German-Tsarkova: Natalya and her team of guides make touring the city easy and meaningful ($40/hour, $300/4 hours, $450/8 hours with car, up to 6 people; mobile +7-921-391-1894, www.original-tours.com, natalya.german@gmail.com).

Timofey Kruglikov's "Tailored Tours of St. Petersburg": Tim and his team of guides are passionate about art and history, and they're all Russian scholars ($40/hour, $70/hour with car, 4-hour minimum, www.tour-petersburg.com, info@tour-petersburg.com).

Peterswalk Private Guides: The most entrepreneurial and "Back Door" of these guide groups, Peterswalk offers daily public walks and bike tours (explained above) as well as private tours. Their passion is to be out and about in town, connecting with today's reality ($40/hour for up to 8 people, 4-hour minimum, mobile +7-921-943-1229, www.peterswalk.com, info@peterswalk.com).

Private Guides for Cruise Travelers Without Visas
The three outfits recommended above can also work with cruise passengers who don't have visas. For many cruisers, this is the ideal way to experience St. Petersburg: It's less hassle than getting a visa and offers more freedom than a typical cruise-line excursion.

You'll have to book well in advance to allow time for your guide to handle all the red tape (expect to provide your passport details). For two full eight-hour days of sightseeing with a guide and car, a couple can expect to pay around $550 per person. Larger groups are cheaper per person ($350/person for 4, $270/person for 6). The price typically includes admission fees. Your guide can pick you up at your cruise terminal, and bring you back there at the end of each day.

St. Petersburg Walks

Two self-guided walks take you through two sides of St. Petersburg: "A Stroll on Nevsky Prospekt" cuts through the bustling historical center of town, while my "Back-Streets Walk on Vasilyevsky Island" (see page 38) reveals a local neighborhood and an aspect of the city that most tourists never see.

ST. PETERSBURG

A STROLL ON NEVSKY PROSPEKT

Taking about two hours (not counting sightseeing stops), this walk, worth ▲▲▲, offers a fascinating glimpse into the heart of the city.

Nevsky Prospekt (Невский Проспект)—St. Petersburg's famous main thoroughfare—represents the best and the worst of this beguiling metropolis. Along its two-mile length from the Neva River to Uprising Square (Ploshchad Vosstaniya, Площадь Восстания), this superlative boulevard passes some of the city's most opulent palaces (the Hermitage), top museums (the Hermitage and Russian Museum),

most important churches (Kazan Cathedral, Church on Spilled Blood), finest urban architecture, liveliest shopping zones, lushest parks, and slice upon slice of Russian life.

This walk also gives you a taste of the smog, congestion, and general chaos with which the city perennially grapples. Pickpockets are brazen here (blurring the line between petty theft and mugging), as are drivers—it's essential to be watchful, remain calm, and cross the street only at designated crosswalks (and even then, use caution). If it's crowded and you're getting stressed, duck into a serene shopping gallery or café for a break.

As Nevsky Prospekt cuts diagonally through town from the Admiralty building (the bull's eye of this city's urban layout), it crosses three waterways. We'll focus on the first mile-and-a-quarter stretch to the Fontanka River—though you could carry on all the way to Uprising Square and beyond.

• *Begin your walk on the vast square facing the Hermitage.*

Palace Square to the Admiralty

The impressively monumental **Palace Square** (Dvortsovaya Ploshchad)—with the arcing, Neoclassical General Staff Building facing the bubbly, Baroque Hermitage—lets you know you're in an imperial capital. It oozes blue-blood class.

Take a moment just to let the grand scale of this space sink in. Like all of St. Petersburg, it was custom-built to impress—and intimidate—visiting dignitaries. If your trip also takes you to Estonia, ponder this:

The entire Old Town of Tallinn could fit comfortably inside the footprint of this square and palace.

The **Alexander Column** honors Czar Alexander I, and celebrates Russia's military victory over Napoleon in 1812. Along with Moscow's Red Square, this is the stage upon which much of early modern Russian history played out. On January 22, 1905, the czar's imperial guard opened fire on peaceful protesters here, massacring hundreds (or possibly thousands). By 1917, the czar was ousted. The provisional government that replaced him was in turn dislodged by the Bolsheviks' October Revolution—kicking off 75 years of communist rule.

• *As you face the Hermitage, exit the square over your left shoulder, toward the glittering dome. When you reach the corner, before continuing, look across the busy street.*

The **Alexander Garden** (Alexandrovsky Sad), with benches and jungle gyms, are a favorite place for families. It's the backyard of the **Admiralty** building—the stately structure with the golden spire. When Peter the Great was laying out his new capital in the early 18th century, he made the Admiralty its centerpiece—indicating the importance he placed on his imperial navy. From here, three great avenues fan out through the city; of these, Nevsky Prospekt is the main drag.

Before we head up the street, notice that **St. Isaac's Cathedral**—with that shimmering dome—is a 10-minute walk away (to the right, with your back to the Admiralty, at the far end of this park; for more on this church, see page 76).

• *Standing at the corner across from the garden, you're already at the start of Nevsky Prospekt. Use the crosswalk to reach the right side of the street and the first part of this walk.*

Admiralty to the Moyka River

A few steps down this first block, watch on the right for the shop marked **КОФЕ ХАУЗ**. Visitors are intimidated by the Cyrillic alphabet, but with a little practice (and the alphabet tips on page 18), you can decode signs easily—often surprising yourself when they turn out to be familiar words. In this case, Кофе Хауз is Kofe Haus...coffeehouse. This Moscow-based Starbucks clone is popular, but very expensive. Russia's deeply stratified society has an enormous lower class, a tiny upper class, and virtually no middle class. Trendy shops like this (where a latte costs double your hometown Starbucks) are filled with upwardly mobile urbanites, but the poorer locals around you could never dream of affording a drink here.

In the next block, halfway down on the right, the recommended **Stolle** (Штолле) is a chain restaurant good for a snack or light lunch. They specialize in savory and sweet pies.

ST. PETERSBURG

Look directly across the street at the building with 1939 above the door. On the pillar just to the right of the door, notice the small length of barbed wire and blue plaque. This is a monument to the **Siege of Leningrad,** as the city was named during the Soviet era. During World War II, Nazi forces encircled the city and bombarded it for 872 days (from September 1941 through January 1944). At the outset, the city's population, swollen with refugees, was at 3 million—but by the siege's end, a million or more people were dead, mostly civilians who succumbed to starvation. The assault claimed more lives than any other siege in world history. St. Petersburg's buildings were ravaged, but not the spirit of those who refused to surrender.

Here, the north side of the street was in the direct line of fire from Nazi shells, lobbed in from German positions southwest of the city. The blue sign reads, roughly, "Citizens: During artillery bombardment, this side is more dangerous."

About 30 yards down, on the right, the "Буквоед" sign marks an outlet of the **Bukvoyed** bookstore chain—a handy place to pick up a St. Petersburg map if you need one. At the next intersection, look left down Bolshaya Morskaya street to see the magnificent **yellow arch** of the General Staff Building. The archway opens to Palace Square—where we started this walk. To the right, the street leads to a handy branch of the **Teremok** (Теремок) Russian fast-food chain (see page 116) and, beyond that, to the square in front of St. Isaac's Cathedral.

• *Continuing one more block on Nevsky Prospekt brings you to the first of St. Petersburg's concentric waterways, the Moyka River. As you proceed straight across the bridge, stick to the right side of the street.*

Moyka River to Kazan Cathedral

Crossing the Moyka, you'll likely see many touts selling tickets for **canal boat tours.** While this is an excellent way to get your bearings in St. Petersburg, most offer commentary only in Russian. Confirm the language before you hop aboard (see page 26).

The river is lined with fine 19th-century architecture. The pink building with white columns (on your right as you cross the water) is the **Stroganov Palace.** The aristocratic family that resided here left their mark all over Russia—commissioning opulent churches, financing the czars' military agenda, and fostering the arts—but their lasting legacy is the beef dish, likely named for them, that has made "Stroganoff" a household name around the world.

Continue another long block, and watch across the street (on the left) for another chance to practice your Russian—though the distinctive logo may give it away: **САБВЭЙ** ("SABVAY" = Subway).

Just beyond Subway, looking left (across the street), notice the pretty, park-like street (Bolshaya Konyushennaya) flanked by beautiful buildings. On the left side is a sort of community center for **Dutch** transplants, while the building on the right is for **Germans.** Catherine the Great (r. 1762-1796), who—like Peter the Great—loved to promote the multiethnic nature of her empire, encouraged various cultural enclaves to settle in community buildings like these. Each enclave consisted of several apartment houses clustered around a church. You'll see another example as you proceed up Nevsky Prospekt, where the German **Lutheran Church of St. Peter and St. Paul** is set back between two yellow buildings (on the left). The church is a reminder that much of St. Petersburg was built by Lutherans: Dutch, Germans, Swedes, and so on. This is only one of the many

houses of worship built along this avenue under the auspices of the czars. Later, the aggressively atheistic communist regime repurposed churches all over the city; in this case, the church was turned into a swimming pool.

• *Coming up on the right is the Kazan Cathedral, with its stately semi-circular colonnade and grand dome.*

Kazan Cathedral to Griboyedov Canal

Built in the early 1800s and named for a revered Russian icon, **Kazan Cathedral** was later converted into a "Museum of Atheism" under the communists. It's since been restored to its former glory and is free to enter. To find the main entrance, go down Kazanskaya street (perpendicular to Nevsky, just before the church). Go in through what looks like a "side" door, and soak in the mystical Orthodox ambience. Inside you'll find a dim interior, a much-venerated replica of the icon of Our Lady of Kazan, a monument to the commander who fended off Napoleon's 1812 invasion, and lots of candles and solemn worshippers (for more on the cathedral's interior, see the listing on page 71). You'll exit

ST. PETERSBURG

Architectural Styles That Shaped St. Petersburg

St. Petersburg, devastated in the siege of World War II, has put tremendous energy into restoring its architectural treasures—and today it sparkles. While the mostly communist 20th century left the outskirts with lots of gargantuan "Stalin Empire"-style buildings, the center is remarkably dense with 18th- and 19th-century architectural gems. From 1712 until 1918, the city was the capital of Russia, and the impossibly wealthy Romanov czars and czarinas—who seemingly had more money than they knew what to do with—energetically left their mark. Today, their palaces and "rental property" (apartment blocks owned by wealthy aristocrats until the Revolution) line the city's waterways and boulevards.

During the glory days of St. Petersburg, this ornate architecture evolved in three phases:

Elizabethan Baroque (c. 1740-1760): Czarina Elizabeth (the daughter of Peter the Great) commissioned the French-born Italian architect Francesco Bartolomeo Rastrelli (1700-1771) to create buildings bursting with frilly Baroque energy. The Louis Teens of France (Louis XIV, XV, and XVI) had set the bar for pal-

aces that just screamed "your ruler is divine." And Elizabeth wanted to top them all. Elizabethan Baroque buildings feature white-stucco frills, lots of gold leaf and mirrors, and a "more is better" opulence; examples include the facades of the Winter Palace/Hermitage and the Catherine Palace at Tsarskoye Selo.

Catherine's Neoclassicism (c. 1762-1796): Catherine the Great, who ruled from 1762 until 1796, was disgusted by the Baroque excesses of Elizabeth. In Catherine's age, rulers looked back to the glories of ancient Greece and Rome for inspiration.

through the left transept, which pops you out into a delightful little **grassy park** facing Nevsky Prospekt. This is a good spot to sit, relax, and maybe buy a drink from a vendor.

It's appropriate that Nevsky Prospekt is lined with so many important churches. The street leads to the monastery that holds relics of Alexander Nevsky (1220-1263), an esteemed Russian saint who, as an influential prince, fought off encroaching German and Swedish foes—including in a pivotal 1240 battle on the Neva River, near what would later become St. Petersburg. (For more on the Alexander Nevsky Lavra Monastery, see page 78.)

• *Leaving the park, head to the intersection and cross over Nevsky Prospekt.*

She commissioned Scottish architect Charles Cameron (c. 1740-1812) to give the city a Neoclassical makeover, with stern, clean columns and arches as an antidote to Baroque baubles and frills. Examples of this style include many of the side-wings and other structures at the Catherine Palace grounds.

Russian Empire Style (c. 1801-1840s): As throughout Napoleonic Europe, Neoclassicism was put on steroids—it became bolder, more bombastic, and took on an even grander scale. Under Alexander I (r. 1801-1825), the Empire Style (which had been favored by Napoleon before his fall) had come to represent a connection between modern monarchs and the ancient

greats. Later, inspired by this French fashion, Czar Nicolas I (r. 1825-1855) commissioned the Italian architect Carlo Rossi to give the city a Neoclassical statement. Examples include the Russian Museum, the General Staff Building on Palace Square (the big yellow building facing the Winter Palace), and many facades lining the Neva. Rossi street—behind Ostrovsky Square (just off Nevsky Prospekt)—is called "the Street of Perfect Proportions," with buildings as high as the street is wide and a clean line of Neoclassical columns on each side.

Later Styles: Following these three styles, in the mid-1800s, Nicholas I—with his emphasis on orthodoxy, autocracy, and populism—embraced the eclectic "Historicist" style of mixing different historical styles; the shiny dome of St. Isaac's is a perfect example. And by the turn of the 20th century, the Bolsheviks were already on the rise—about to introduce a starkly different, boxy-concrete style that would dominate Russia virtually through the entire 20th century.

Scrutinize the distinctive oxidized-copper tower of the Art Nouveau building on the corner (at #28). At the base of the globe-topped turret is an unlikely symbol—an American bald eagle, wings spread wide, grasping a laurel wreath in its talon and wearing a stars-and-stripes shield on its breast. Architecture fans know this building as the Singer House (yes, the Russian headquarters of the American sewing machine company—the globe at the top proclaims Singer's

worldwide reach). Today it's home to **Dom Knigi** ("House of Books"). Up close, take a minute to examine the building's fine decorative details. Inside, the inviting bookshop has a delightfully atmospheric—if pricey—turn-of-the-century café on the second floor (daily 9:00-23:00).

• *The Singer building sits next to the Griboyedov Canal. Walk to the midsection of the intersection/bridge over the water (watch out for pickpockets in this highly concentrated tourist zone—they work in groups and can get physical all along Nevsky Prospekt).*

Griboyedov Canal to Gostiny Dvor

Looking down the length of the river, you can't miss one of Russia's most distinctive buildings: the **Church on Spilled Blood.** Dramatically scenic from here, it gets even prettier as you get closer. To snap some classic photos, work your way to the small bridge partway down the river. If you plan to visit this church, now's a good time; the **Russian Museum** is also nearby (the yellow building fronting the canal just before the church is a side-wing of that museum; we'll reach the museum's main entrance later on this walk). The church and museum are both described in more detail later, under "Sights in St. Petersburg." If you want to do some souvenir shopping, see if the handy (if touristy and overpriced) **crafts market** just behind the church is open. I'll wait right here.

Back already? Let's continue down Nevsky Prospekt (for now, stay on the left side). Just after the river is the **Small Philharmonic** (Малый филармония)—one of the "big four" cultural institutions in St. Petersburg (the others are the Great Philharmonic, the Mariinsky Theater, and the Mikhailovsky Theater). Consider taking in a performance while you're in town; on a short visit, the ballet is a popular choice (for details, see "Entertainment in St. Petersburg," later).

A half-block farther along, tucked between buildings on the left, you'll see the pale yellow facade of the Roman Catholic **St. Catherine's Church.** This is one of several "St. Catherines" that line Nevsky Prospekt— many congregations named their churches for the empress who encouraged their construction. This one has an endearing starving artists' market out front.

At the next corner, on the left, is the **Grand Hotel Europe**—an ultra-fancy (if dated) five-star hotel that opened in 1875. Its opulence attracted the likes of Tchaikovsky, Stravinsky, Debussy, and H. G. Wells as guests.

The hotel sits at the corner of Mikhailovskaya street. If you

detour one long block down this street, you'll find the main entrance of the **Russian Museum,** with a fantastic collection of works by exclusively Russian artists. (While the Hermitage's art collection is world-class, there's nothing "local" or Russian about it.) For a self-guided tour of the highlights of the Russian Museum, see page 62. Presiding over the park in front of the museum (Ploshchad Iskusstv, "Square of the Arts") is a statue of **Alexander Pushkin** (1799-1837)—Russia's leading poet, considered by many to have raised modern Russian literature to an art form.

Back on Nevsky, capping the red tower across the boulevard from the hotel, notice the black metal skeletal **spire**—like a naked Christmas tree. This was part of an early 19th-century optical telegraph system that stretched more than 800 miles from here to Warsaw (which was then part of the Russian Empire). Each tower in this line-of-sight chain across the empire winked Morse code signals at the next with mirrors.

• *Continue along Nevsky to the middle of the next block.*

In a gap in the buildings on the left, you'll see yet another church—the beautiful robin-egg-blue home of the local Armenian community. **St. Catherine's Gregorian Church** belongs to the Armenian Apostolic faith, one of the oldest branches of Christianity—founded in a.d. 301, when St. Gregory the Illuminator baptized the Armenian king. Approaching the

front door, look for the little shop window on the right, which sells breads, jams, and honey imported from Armenia to comfort homesick transplants here.

Now face across the street to confront the gigantic, yellow Gostiny Dvor shopping complex. We'll cross over later to take a

look, but for now, continue past the church. Keep an eye out on the left for #48 (look for the Пассажъ sign above the door; it's before the ramp leading to a pedestrian underpass). Step inside and climb the stairs into the gorgeously restored, glass-roofed **"Passazh" arcade,** an elite haven

ST. PETERSBURG

for high-class shoppers since 1846 (daily 10:00-21:00), making it one of the first shopping malls in the world. The communists converted the Passazh into a supermarket and, later, into a "model store," intended to leave foreigners with a (misleadingly) positive impression of the availability of goods in the USSR. These days it sells perfume, jewels, and decorative glass, giving off a genteel air as mellow music plays in the background.

• *At the end of the block, use the pedestrian underpass (which also leads to a pair of convenient downtown Metro stops—Nevsky Prospekt on the blue line, and Gostiny Dvor on the green line) to cross beneath Nevsky Prospekt: Take the ramp down, turn right, then turn right again up the next ramp.*

Gostiny Dvor to Fontanka River

You'll pop out of the underpass at **Gostiny Dvor** (which means, basically, "merchants' courtyard"—like a Turkish caravanserai).

Built in the 1760s, this marketplace is a giant but hollow structure, with two stories of shops (more than 100 in all) wrapping around a central courtyard. To see an undiscovered corner of Nevsky that most tourists miss, head upstairs: At the corner of the building nearest the underpass, go through the door and up the stairs, then find your way back outside to reach the tranquil, beautifully symmetrical arcades. Standing at the corner, the arches seem to recede in both directions nearly as far as the eye can see.

Looking out, take note of the open plaza in front of Gostiny Dvor. This is a popular place for **political protests**—which, in Putin's Russia, are barely tolerated. Article 31 of the Russian constitution guarantees the freedom of assembly—a right that seems always to be in question, especially since any protest must be officially registered. To push the boundaries, on the 31st of every month, peaceful demonstrators routinely seek government permission to stage a protest here, are denied, then stage the protest anyway—only to be dutifully arrested by riot-gear-clad cops. This "Strategy-31" movement tries to keep the issue of free speech alive in the consciousness of a Russia that seems willing to let that freedom lapse.

• *Go back into the underpass, and this time, stay on the right side of Nevsky Prospekt for one more block.*

You'll soon reach **Ostrovsky Square** (Ploshchad Ostrovskogo), a fine park anchored by a statue of **Catherine the Great.** While Peter the Great gets founding credit for this city, Catherine arguably made it great. A Prussian blue-blood (born in today's Poland),

Catherine married Russia's Czar Peter III, then quickly overthrew him in a palace coup. Throughout her 34-year reign, Catherine never remarried, but she is believed to have cleverly parlayed sexual politics to consolidate her power.

On the pillar below and to the right of Catherine is **Prince Grigory Potemkin,** one of the statesmen and military leaders with whom Catherine collaborated and consorted. Potemkin is the namesake of a fascinating story about how even a great ruler can be fooled. After Potemkin conquered the Crimean peninsula during the Russo-Turkish War, Catherine visited to survey her new domain. To convince her that "Russification" of the Crimea had been a success, Potemkin supposedly created artificially perfect villages, with stage-set houses peopled by "Russian villagers" custom-ordered from Centralsky Casting. To this day the term "Potemkin village" describes something artificial used to hoodwink a gullible target—a term as applicable to modern Russian and American politics as it was to Catherine's nation-building. In 1972, when President Nixon visited this city, Nevsky Prospekt itself was similarly spruced up to disguise the USSR's economic hardships. (Because Nixon viewed the street from a limo, the authorities only fixed up the bottom two floors of each facade.)

• *From the square, use the crosswalk to head back over Nevsky Prospekt.*

Just across from the park is the pleasantly pedestrianized street called Malaya Sadovaya. On the corner, **Yeliseevsky's delicatessen** occupies a sumptuously decorated Art Nouveau building (at #56).

Once the purveyor of fine food to the Russian aristocracy (like Dallmayr's in Munich), Yeliseevsky's was bumped down several pegs when the communists symbolically turned it into "Grocery Store #1." Now, in another sign of the times, it's been remodeled into an almost laughably over-the-top boutique deli with a small, expensive café—drop in to browse the selection of cheese and chocolates (daily 10:00-23:00, photography strictly prohibited).

A few steps beyond Yeliseevsky's, find the passage (at #60, just past the Teremok fast-food joint) leading to the Zara department store. The store fills a space once occupied by the historic

Aurora (Аврора) Cinema—one of the first movie houses in St. Petersburg. Entering, you'll step upon the original tiles and head up the grand staircase to the elegantly decorated main hall (daily 10:00-22:00).

• *Continue along Nevsky Prospekt for another block and a half, until you hit the Fontanka River.*

Fontanka River to Uprising Square

Of St. Petersburg's many beautiful and interesting bridges, the **Anichkov Bridge** is one of the finest. On pillars anchoring each end are statues of a man with a horse. The ensemble, sculpted in 1841 and known collectively as *The Horse Tamers*, expresses humanity's ongoing desire to corral nature. Watch the relationship between horse and man evolve: In one view, it's a struggle, with the man overwhelmed by the wild beast's power; in another, it's a cooperative arrangement, with the man leading the bridled and saddled horse. Looking over the Fontanka River, it's easy to take this as a metaphor for St. Petersburg's relationship to the water. To survive and prosper, the city had to tame the inhospitable, swampy delta on which it is built.

• *You've walked the most interesting stretch of Nevsky Prospekt, but if you'd like to see more of the city center, continue by foot or by bus down Nevsky for a half-mile until you reach **Uprising Square** (described on page 87; for bus numbers, see page 24).*

*Otherwise, you have several options. Just to the left along the Fontanka embankment is the exquisite **Fabergé Museum** (see page 69). To sightsee at the **Russian Museum, Church on Spilled Blood, Kazan Cathedral**, or **Hermitage**, walk back along Nevsky the way you came, or hop on a bus (see page 24 for buses that make the trip; note that a few trolley buses veer off from the end of Nevsky for **St. Isaac's Cathedral**, saving an extra 10-minute walk).*

*To easily reach the **Peter and Paul Fortress**, take the Metro: Backtrack to the underpass in front of Gostiny Dvor, find the Nevsky Prospekt station on the blue line, and ride one stop to Gorkovskaya—a short walk from the fortress.*

*Or, from the same Metro station, locate the Gostiny Dvor station on the green line, which you can ride one stop to the Vasileostrovskaya stop to begin my "**Back Streets Walk**," described next.*

Back-Streets Walk on Vasilyevsky Island

Tourists in St. Petersburg typically visit just a handful of famous sights and walk the grand Nevsky Prospekt. That's exciting, but if that's all you do, you'll miss the workaday city. This self-guided walk, worth ▲▲, is the remedy.

To start, ride the subway to the Vasileostrovskaya station (green line, first westbound stop after Gostiny Dvor). From this stop, you'll walk 15 minutes (passing a local market) to the riverfront, another 15 scenic minutes along the riverfront to the Strelka viewpoint, and 15 more minutes to either the Peter and Paul Fortress or the Hermitage and Nevsky Prospekt (in opposite directions).

• *Exiting the Metro station, you'll be kitty-corner from a palatial McDonald's. Turn right, then right again, and pause in the middle of the pedestrian street. You're smack-dab in...*

The Heart of the Island

This street, called Ulitsa 7-ya Liniya/Ulitsa 6-ya Liniya (улица 7-я Линия/улица 6-я Линия), is in the center of an upscale residential zone that stretches from the city center all the way to the massive Marine Facade cruise port. Carefully planned Vasilyevsky Island has 30 numbered north/west streets (called "lines") that cross its three big east/west thoroughfares (named "big"/*bolshoy,* "medium"/*sredny,* and "small"/*maly*). Each side of the street has a different number—in this case, 6 on the left, 7 on the right.

You're standing upon what was a canal—part of the planned town that was laid out in the 1720s, during Peter the Great's lifetime. Directly in front of the Metro station, just before the park-like center strip, notice the statue of a horse-driven tram. In the 19th century (after the canal was filled in), trams like this shuttled from river to river. The lowest buildings (on the left) date from the original 18th-century town.

Head to the center strip and stroll under the larch trees down this lively, colorful, traffic-free street—one of the oldest in the city. Gurgling fountains punctuate the walk. Look for food trucks parked on the sidewalk, selling cheap, tasty pastries. You'll pass several chain stores: mobile phones (Мегафон—that's "Megafon"); fast-food joints both Russian (Теремок) and American (Subway); and American-sounding chains that are actually Russian (Coffeeshop Company). Imagine this street under communism: less colorful...less tacky.

• *After one very long block, on the left you'll see a pink church.*

St. Andrew's Cathedral

While a church was first built here in the 1720s as part of the original street plan, the present building dates from the 1760s. Today this is a neighborhood church, where ordinary people stop by on the way home (visitors are welcome—no photos; women can borrow a scarf to cover their heads). Step inside for a totally untouristy Russian Orthodox experience (for more on the faith and the features of its churches, see page 72). Like most of St. Petersburg, this church echoes European styles—its Baroque exterior would be at home in Bavaria. But the interior is filled with Orthodox icons. Its iconostasis, or altar screen, survived communism. Discreetly notice the ritual: Women cover their heads, while sullen teens just flip up the hoods of their windbreakers. Upon leaving, worshippers turn back, face the church, and cross themselves. The reverence of these acts illustrates how faith has been reincorporated into Russian life in a huge way since the end of the atheistic communist era.

• *Continuing past the church, you'll reach a big intersection (Bolshoy Prospekt, "Big Avenue"). Cross the street, then detour a block to the left (cutting through the little park) to reach the yellow building with a big green* Рынок *sign over the gate. This is the neighborhood's...*

Farmer's Market

Poke through the gateway into the inner courtyard to find some open-air stalls, including a tasty tandoor bakery from Uzbekistan, the former Soviet republic in Central Asia (on the left as you enter the courtyard). Inside the market, wade through the clothing stalls to find the food—just follow your nose. (For strategies on enjoying a Russian market, see the sidebar on page 92.)

Backtrack to the street you were on (Ulitsa 6-ya Liniya), cross to the right side, and continue in the direction you were headed. After about 50 yards, pop into the historic, brick-and-stone **pharmacy** (on your right, Аптека). While open for business, it's like a little museum taking you back to 1908 (Mon-Fri 9:00-21:00).

• *Detour around the pharmacy (leaving the building, take three left turns) for a quick look at some...*

Back Streets

While these are a bit sterile, you can imagine how they originally served as a mews (stables). Throughout the town, formal parade entries to grand buildings face the front, while the rough "back entries" are for servants and the poor. With the 1917 Revolution, larger buildings were divided up to house many families—Doctor Zhivago-style. Partitions were put into staircases, and bathrooms were retrofitted into kitchens. Vast blocks were divided into a series of courtyards, with apartments becoming cheaper the deeper they were buried. Walking around town, you can see how fine 19th-century features survive on some buildings, and other buildings—shelled in World War II—were rebuilt more simply in the 1950s and 1960s. Continue walking around the old pharmacy block—exploring the unpolished back sides of 18th- and 19th-century buildings, and peeking into courtyards and playgrounds—

then turn left again to return to the main street.

• *Turn right, and notice the yellow building with sculpted heads over the windows, just before the river. This is the...*

House of Academicians

This was where big brains lived in the 18th century, and in Soviet times it functioned as a residential think tank. Each of the black plaques between the windows honors a great Russian scientist. The blue plaque by the door identifies the former apartment of Ivan Pavlov. If that name rings a bell, it's because he famously studied conditioned responses (and was the first Russian to win a Nobel Prize).

• *Continuing along, you'll pop out at the...*

Neva Riverbank

You're separated from the nicely pedestrianized embankment by a busy highway. (The nearest crosswalk is one very long block to your right, as you face the river.)

To your left, the **Annunciation (Blagoveshchensky) Bridge,** from 1850, was the first permanent bridge over the Neva.

Just to your right, notice the many **cargo ships** stacked up along the embankment. St. Petersburg is at the mouth of the Neva River, but its 342 bridges impede the progress of ships wanting to head upstream. The solution: Each night, from about 1:30 to 5:00 in the morning, drawbridges throughout the city center open, allowing cargo boats to proceed. Boats arriving during the day tie up here to wait their turn. From here, ships can go upstream and reach either the Arctic Sea (far to the north) or the Black Sea (far to the south) via a series of industrial canals built in Soviet times to connect the Neva with the great rivers of Russia's interior.

• *From here, you have two choices: Head right, to the Schmidt embankment and Optina Pustyn Church (described next), or walk left to the Strelka viewpoint, from where you can circle around to either the Peter and Paul Fortress or the Hermitage (described later, under "Sights in St. Petersburg").*

Schmidt Embankment

Turning right, the fine riverside promenade is lined with muscular Russian-made ships (note their ports of registry painted on their sterns). A stroll along here leads to the Schmidt embankment, where smaller, luxury cruise ships tie up. St. Petersburg is Russia's leading port, and looking downstream, you can see the huge cranes that are part of its big shipbuilding and shipping industry. Although marine shipping is still important to St. Petersburg, imagine when the town was newly founded in the early 18th century, and the only real access was by sea.

• *Across from the Schmidt embankment is a dazzling gold-domed church.*

Optina Pustyn

This is one of the many branch churches of the Eastern Orthodox Optina monastery. Step inside to enjoy one of St. Petersburg's most beautiful church interiors—with splendid frescoes, ornate icons, and shimmering gold (daily 8:00-20:00; tourists welcome but be discreet). Repurposed by the communists, this house of worship spent time as a hockey rink. Restorers even found a hard-hit puck still embedded in one wall. Now the building has reclaimed its sacred purpose, and its male choir is one of Russia's most beloved. Its café and bookshop face the busy embankment road.

Sights in St. Petersburg

Most of St. Petersburg's major sights and landmarks are in the central zone that radiates out from the south bank of the Neva River, starting with the city's most-famous sight—the Hermitage museum.

▲▲▲THE HERMITAGE (ЭРМИТАЖ)

Built by Peter the Great's daughter, Elizabeth, the Hermitage was later filled with the art collection of Catherine the Great. The

Hermitage's vast collections of just about everything—but especially its European masterworks—make it one of the world's top art museums, ranking with the Louvre and the Prado. Housed in the Romanovs' Winter Palace, the Hermitage (EHR-mee-tazh, officially the State Hermitage, Государственный Эрмитаж), is actually two top-notch sight-seeing experiences in one: an art gallery of European works and an imperial residence. Enjoy the Leonardos, Rembrandts, and Matisses while imagining the ostentatious lifestyles of the czars who collected them. Between the canvases, you glide through some of the most opulent ballrooms and throne rooms ever built. Warning: Dense crowds tarnish the Hermitage experience, and visiting early or late makes only a minimal difference. If you're particularly bugged by crowds, consider skipping the visit.

Cost and Hours: 400 R (students free), Tue-Sun 10:30-18:00, Wed until 21:00, closed Mon.

Information: Tel. 710-9625 (recorded info) or 710-9079, www.hermitagemuseum.org.

Ticket-Buying Tips: Handy **machines** in the main courtyard sell tickets without a line (available 10:00-16:00 only, clearly explained in English). It's also possible to buy a ticket in advance **online** for a slightly inflated price ($18/1 day, $26/2 days—bring email confirmation to exchange for ticket on-site, www.hermitage shop.org). You're not tied to a particular entry time. If you buy a ticket online or from one of the machines and want to add extras (such as a guided tour), go to the ticket windows inside, with typically shorter lines.

Getting In: Individual visitors enter through the courtyard that faces the grand Palace Square with the Alexander Column. From the column and square, you'll go through a passageway—if you bought tickets online, exchange your voucher for tickets at the kiosk here. Next you'll emerge into a large courtyard with **ticket machines** scattered around—use one of these if you didn't book ahead. You'll see a long **ticket line** at the far end of the courtyard, by the entrance door, but that's primarily for Russians (who qualify for a discounted price unavailable at the machines). With tickets in hand, skip the line and head right into the entry hall. There, line up at the security checkpoint to scan your ticket at the turnstile and enter the museum.

Tours: Immediately beyond the security checkpoint is a desk where you can rent an English audioguide (350 R, leave ID as deposit; less-crowded **audioguide** stand at top of main stairway). The audioguide has handy, digestible descriptions of the palace's historical rooms and of major paintings, but isn't worth the high price for a single traveler on a short visit. It's possible to customize your own tour with the museum's **audioguide app** (see the website). **Guided tours** are offered in the entry hall (300 R, times posted in courtyard).

Services: Pick up a free **map** at the information desk. Down the stairs from the entry hall is an **ATM**, a **cloakroom** (remember which of the 14 sections you use), a tiny **bookstore** (there are better ones later, inside the museum), and a crowded **WC** (there are more later). In the hall to the right, before you reach the stairway, are more **WCs**, a mediocre and crowded **café**, several gift shops, and a large **bookstore.**

Photography: You'll technically need a photo permit (200 R, sold in entry hall or at the machines)—but this rule is only loosely enforced.

Expect Changes to Modern Collection: The General Staff Building (the yellow building with the arch, across the square from the Hermitage) has been renovated into a gleaming exhibition space, and over time much of the Hermitage's modern art collection will relocate here. If Impressionist and Post-Impressionist art is your priority, confirm which building these works are in before buying your ticket.

Planning Your Time: Some people come to St. Petersburg just to see this amazing art-filled palace, especially because some of its riches (including a cache of Impressionist masterpieces) were for decades hidden away by the communist regime. Others don't want to spend time on painters whose work can easily be admired in New York, Paris, or Madrid. The first sort of person could spend days inside without exhausting the Hermitage's treasures; the second might bypass the place entirely in favor of the Russian Museum (described on page 61). For many visitors, a middle strategy works well: Plan on a three- to four-hour visit, focusing on one or two artistic periods as well as a few museum rooms important to Russian history. My self-guided tour fits this bill. If you're a serious museumgoer and want ample time here, consider the two-day pass.

Cruise-Line Evening Visits: If you're visiting St. Petersburg on a cruise, consider taking the evening Hermitage excursion-tour that's offered by many cruise lines. It's a more peaceful museum experience, saves your daylight hours for other activities, and is a good option if you don't mind a short and limited look at the collection's highlights.

● Self-Guided Tour

This tour will take you quickly through the Hermitage's highlights, divided into three parts: 1) historical rooms; 2) Old Masters (Leonardo, Raphael, Rembrandt, etc.), and 3) Modern Masters (Matisse, Chagall, Picasso, etc.). Very roughly, the first (ground) floor, where you enter, shows ancient art; the second floor has the historical rooms plus galleries covering the medieval, Renaissance, and Baroque eras (Old Masters); and the third floor is devoted to the 19th and 20th centuries (Modern Masters). Room numbers are posted over the doors to each room, but they're easy to miss in these opulent surroundings.

Length of this Tour: It should take about four hours—including one full hour just to fight the crowds and connect the dots.

Part 1: Historical Rooms

• *At the end of the entry area (the hall with the metal detectors and audioguide stand), head up the...*

Ambassador's Stairs: You are in the Winter Palace, the czar's official city residence, built by Italian architects (notably Francesco Bartolomeo Rastrelli) between 1754 and 1762 in the style called Elizabethan Baroque—named for the czarina who popularized it. At this time, all of St. Petersburg—like this staircase—drew on the talents of artists and artisans imported from Western Europe. The palace is designed to impress, astonish, and humble visitors

with the power of the Romanov dynasty. The stairway gives you a good feeling for the building's architecture, with its gilded ceiling showing the Greek gods relaxing in the clouds. A serious fire damaged the palace in 1837, but it was quickly restored. The museum occupies the Winter Palace plus two connected buildings, the Small Hermitage and the Large Hermitage, which were built in the late 18th century. The museum takes its name from these buildings, where the royal art collections were originally housed.

ST. PETERSBURG

• *At the top of the stairs, go through the door and pass through a series of large rooms—192, 191 (imagine grand balls of the czar in this room, with inlaid floors and three crystal chandeliers; today it generally hosts temporary exhibits), and 190 (with the tomb of Alexander Nevsky, adorned with two tons of silver)—to reach Room 189.*

The Malachite Room: This drawing room, which dates from just after the 1837 fire, is decorated with malachite, a green copper-based mineral found in Russia's Ural Mountains. After the first stage of the Russian Revolution in spring 1917, in which the czar was ousted, a provisional government led by Alexander Kerensky declared Russia a republic. This government took over the Winter Palace and met in the Malachite Room, overlooking the Neva River. Their last meeting was on November 7, 1917. That evening, communist forces, loyal to Vladimir Lenin and the Bolshevik Party, seized power of the city in a largely bloodless coup. (Although the Bolsheviks took over in November, back then Russia still used the old Julian calendar—so technically it was an "October" Revolution.)

• *At the end of the Malachite Room, turn left into Room 188, then Room 155, and find the long series of smaller rooms filled with Romanov portraits (Rooms 153 and 151), which returns you parallel to the way you came. At the end of the hall, turn right, directly into Room 193.*

Field Marshals' Hall: This hall was for portraits of Russia's military generals—perhaps so that the ruling family could keep names and faces straight. After 1917, the paintings were taken down and moved to other museums. But in recent years, the original portraits, dating from 1814 to the 1830s (and evoking the Russian victory over Napoleon and the French), have been returned to their places here.

ST. PETERSBURG

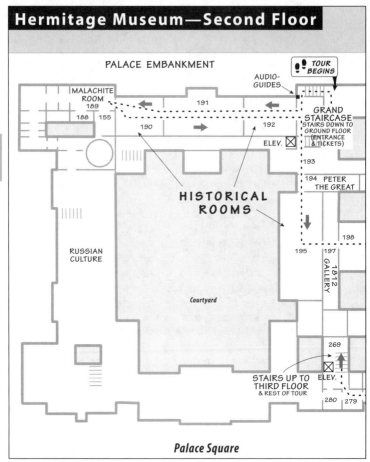

Hermitage Museum—Second Floor

PALACE EMBANKMENT

AUDIO-GUIDES

TOUR BEGINS

MALACHITE ROOM 189

188 155

191

190

192

ELEV.

GRAND STAIRCASE
STAIRS DOWN TO GROUND FLOOR (ENTRANCE & TICKETS)

193

194 PETER THE GREAT

HISTORICAL ROOMS

198

RUSSIAN CULTURE

195 197 1812 GALLERY

Courtyard

269

ELEV.

STAIRS UP TO THIRD FLOOR & REST OF TOUR

280 279

Palace Square

• *The next, very red room (194) is the...*

Memorial Hall of Peter the Great: This hall pays homage to Peter the Great, who founded this city a generation before the Winter Palace's construction. You see his portrait (with Minerva, the goddess of wisdom) and a copy of his throne. Above, on the wall to either side, are paintings commemorating his decisive victories over Sweden—at Lesnaya in 1708 and Poltava in 1709. (For more on the dynamic Peter, see the sidebar on page 88.)

• *Continue into the **Armorial Hall** (Room 195), a banquet hall with golden columns and sculptures of knights with spears in each corner, and take a left into the long, skinny Room 197, known as the....*

War Gallery of 1812: Opened in 1826, this hall displays over 300 portraits of the generals who helped to expel Napoleon from Russia in 1812 and chase him back to France. The Russian and French armies fought to a draw at the battle of Borodino, just

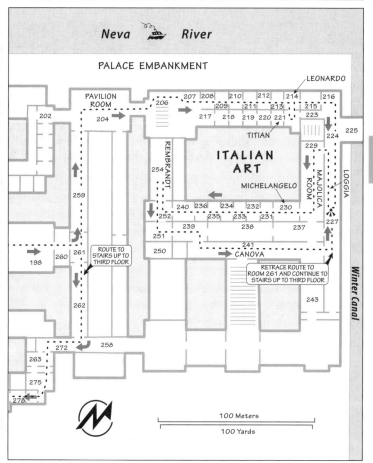

ST. PETERSBURG

west of Moscow, in September. The French troops were lured into Moscow, but the city was deliberately burned, Russian forces refused to submit to French control, and after some days, Napoleon's troops realized they were overextended and began to retreat through the deepening winter cold. Napoleon had entered Russia with 400,000 men, but only a tenth would make it back out. This crushing reversal ended his plans for European dominance.

The large portraits show the most important figures in Napoleon's defeat—practice your Cyrillic by reading the names. At the far-left end of the hall, the largest of all is an equestrian

portrait of Czar Alexander I (the czar who pushed out the French). To either side of him are the Austrian emperor Franz I (**Франц I**) and the Prussian emperor Friedrich Wilhelm III (**Фридрих-Вильхельм III**). Next comes Grand Duke Konstantin Pavlovich (**Константин Павлович**), the czar's unruly brother and heir to the throne; across from him is Field Marshal Mikhail Golenishchev-Kutuzov (**Голенищев-Кутузов**), the strategist of the battle of Borodino. To the other side of the doors are Britain's Duke of Wellington (**Веллингтон**) and Michael Barclay de Tolly (**Барклай де Толли**), a Russian general of Baltic German and Scottish descent. (A few generals weren't available for sittings, so they're remembered by squares of green cloth.)

At the end opposite Alexander, one painting depicts the battle of Borodino, while the other (Peter von Hess's Crossing the Berezina) shows Napoleon's troops retreating through the snow in rags and disarray, crossing a bridgeless river.

• *Back in the middle of this long hallway, proceed into Room 198.*

Throne Room: This grand hall, created in the early 1840s, was of great importance as the setting for official ceremonies and receptions in czarist times. The magnificent parquet floor, made from 16 types of wood, is original. The Soviets added to the grandeur by installing a huge map of the USSR inlaid with semiprecious stones (now gone).

• *From Room 198, pass through the smaller room beyond it (260) into Room 261; here, hang a left and pass through the looong Room 259 and little Room 203 before stepping into Room 204, the...*

Pavilion Room: You've left the Winter Palace and entered the original Small Hermitage (founded by Catherine the Great).

Consisting of two long and parallel galleries, this was where Catherine hung her original art collection in 1762. Admire the fine view of the interior courtyard. Decorated in the 1850s in French Renaissance style, the room contains the fun Peacock Clock, a timepiece made by British goldsmith James Cox and purchased by Catherine the Great. (The controls are in the large mushroom—a video shows it in action.) Across the hall, scrutinize the remarkably detailed inlaid floor.

• *You've seen the most important historical rooms in the Hermitage. At this point, it's best to focus on one or two artistic periods from among* *the Hermitage's vast collections. The basic options are to proceed directly into the **Old Masters** collection in the adjoining rooms (described next, in "Part 2" of this tour); or to skip forward several centuries and head upstairs to the fine **Modern Masters** collection (described later, in "Part 3").*

To find the modern section, head through the long and skinny Rooms 259 and 262, then turn right and loop through smaller Rooms 272-280 to find the stairs up to the third floor—watch on the right for Room 280. Once there, turn to "Part 3" of this tour. (Before following these directions, confirm that the modern collection is still in the building—it may be relocated to the General Staff Building, across Palace Square, by the time you visit.)

ST. PETERSBURG

Part 2: Old Masters

• *The Italian Renaissance works we'll see are on the same floor as the historic rooms. Just beyond the Pavilion Room and the Peacock Clock, proceed straight, cross the bridge between the hermitages, and then pass the top of the stairwell (with the huge, green malachite-and-bronze vase) to enter a long hallway. Here begins the Old Hermitage's collection of Italian art. While there's a lot to see, for now pass through Rooms 207-213 (but pause in Room 209, at the Fra Angelico fresco of Mary and Baby Jesus, and in Room 210, with some fine Della Robbia ceramic works)—until you emerge in the exquisite Room 214.*

Leonardo da Vinci

Considering that there are only about 20 paintings in existence by the great Renaissance genius, the two humble Madonnas in the Hermitage are world-class treasures. Leonardo da Vinci (1452-1519) reinvented the art of painting and influenced generations of artists, and these two small works were landmarks in technique, composition, and the portrayal of natural human emotion.

Paintings of mother Mary with Baby Jesus had always been popular in Renaissance Italy. But before Leonardo, large altarpieces typically showed the Madonna and Child seated formally on a throne, surrounded by saints, angels, elaborate architecture, and complex symbolism. Leonardo reinvented the theme in intimate, small-scale works for private worship. He deleted extraneous characters and focused on the heart of the story—a mother and her child alone in a dark room, sharing a private moment.

• *First up, on the wooden panel straight ahead as you enter the room is the...*

Benois Madonna (1475-1478): A youthful Mary shows Jesus a flower. Jesus (with his Casper-the-Friendly-Ghost-like head) inspects this wondrous thing with a curiosity and concentration that's wise beyond his years. Mary practically giggles with delight. It's a tender, intimate moment, but with a serious psychological

ST. PETERSBURG

undertow. The mustard flower—with four petals—symbolizes the cross of Jesus' eventual Crucifixion. Jesus and Mary play with it innocently, oblivious to the baby's tragic destiny.

This is one of Leonardo's earliest known works. In fact, it may be the first painting he did after quitting the workshop of his teacher, Verrocchio, to strike out on his own. The painting, which was often copied (including by Raphael), was revolutionary. The painstaking detail astonished Leonardo's contemporaries—the folds in Mary's clothes, Jesus' dimpled flesh, the tiniest wisps of haloes, Mary's brooch. How did he do it? The secret was a new technological advance—oil-based paints. Unlike the more common tempera (egg-based) paint, oils could be made nearly transparent. This allowed Leonardo to apply layer after layer to make the subtlest transitions of color, mimicking real life.

Also, Leonardo used different shades of light and dark color (chiaroscuro) to create his figures. For example, Mary's "blue" dress ranges from almost black navy-blue (the folds) to nearly white powder-blue (the raised areas). These color gradations create an illusion of three-dimensionality, with Mary's body rising cameo-like from the dark background. Leonardo accentuates the contrast between the shadowy "valleys" of the folds and the brightly lit "hills" to make the folds seem unnaturally deep.

• *Farther along the room is another panel, with the...*

Litta Madonna (1490-1491): Mary nurses Baby Jesus, gazing down proudly. Jesus stays locked onto Mary's breast but turns his eyes outward absentmindedly—dreamy-eyed with milk—to face the viewer, drawing us into the scene. The highlight of the painting is clearly Mary's radiant face, gracefully tilted down and beaming with tenderness.

At the time Leonardo created the *Litta Madonna,* he was living in Milan. In the same period he also painted his famous *Last Supper,* designed the largest bronze equestrian statue of the Renaissance, invented the hang-glider, and filled notebooks with sketches like the Vitruvian Man. Leonardo managed his own workshop, and this Madonna may have been done in collaboration with his prize student, Boltraffio. As was his practice, Leonardo made preliminary sketches to work out the various details of Mary's face and position of the baby's legs on his mother's lap (a surviving sketch of Mary's head is in the Louvre).

Compare the *Litta Madonna* and *Benois Madonna*—each is a slight variation on a popular theme. Both are set in dark interiors lit by windows looking out on a distant landscape (though the *Benois* landscape remains unfinished). Subconsciously, this accentuates the intimacy and tranquility of the setting. Both paintings were originally done on wood panel before being transferred to canvas (and retouched) a century ago. Both paintings are named for the family that at one point owned them. One difference is in the style. The *Litta Madonna* has crisper outlines—either because it was done in (less subtle) tempera or by a (less subtle) apprentice.

What they have in common is realistic emotion, and this sets all of Leonardo's Madonnas apart from those of his contemporaries. With a tilt of the head, a shining face, a downturned mouth, the interplay of touching hands and gazes, Leonardo captured an intimacy never before seen in painting. He draws aside a curtain to reveal an unguarded moment, showing mother and child interacting as only they can. These holy people don't need haloes (or only the wispiest) to show that sacred bond.

Before leaving this room, notice the palace architecture itself. The doors are inlaid with ebony, bronze, and tortoiseshell. The scenes decorating the fireplaces are delightful micro-mosaics.

• *The door across from the Benois Madonna leads to Room 221, where we'll find...*

Titian

Danae (1553-1554): One of art history's most blatantly sexual paintings, this nude has fascinated people for centuries—both for its subject matter and for Titian's bravura technique. The Hermitage's canvas is the second (or third) of five nearly identical paintings Titian painted of the popular legend.

It shows Danae from Greek mythology, lying naked in her bedchamber. Her father has locked her up to prevent a dreadful prophecy from coming true—that Danae will bear a son who will grow up to kill him. As Danae daydreams, suddenly a storm cloud gathers overhead. In the lightning, a divine face emerges—it's Zeus. He transforms himself into a  shower of gold coins. Danae tilts her head and gazes up, transfixed. She goes weak-kneed with desire, and her left leg flops outward. Zeus rains down between Danae's legs, impregnating her.

Meanwhile, Danae's maid tries to catch the divine spurt with her apron.

This legend has been depicted since ancient times. Symbolically, it represented how money can buy sexual favors. In medieval times, Danae was portrayed as being as money-hungry as the maid. But Titian clearly wants to contrast Danae and the maid. He divides the canvas, with Danae's warm, golden body on one side and the frigid-gray old maid on the other. Zeus rains straight down, enriching them both, and uniting the composition. *Danae* is a celebration of giving yourself to love.

• *Backtrack through the Leonardo room (214), continue through Rooms 215 and 216 (at the corner, with a love scene by Giulio Romano from Catherine's private erotica collection), and bear right. Pass straight through Room 224 to reach Room 227 and an homage to...*

Raphael

Loggia: This long, narrow hallway—more than 200 feet long, only 13 feet wide, and decorated with colorful paintings—is a rep-  lica of one of the painter Raphael's crowning achievements, the Vatican Loggia in Rome. (The original loggia, in the Vatican Palace, was designed by the architect Bramante—who also authored St. Peter's Basilica in Rome; Raphael and his assistants completed the loggia's fresco decorations in 1518-1519.)

In the 1780s, after admiring color engravings of the Vatican Loggia, Catherine the Great had this exact replica built of Raphael's famous hallway. It's virtually identical to the original, though the paintings here are tempera on canvas. They were copied from the frescoes in Rome (under the direction of Austrian painter Christoph Unterberger) and sent to St. Petersburg along with a scale model of the entire ensemble.

The Loggia exudes the spirit of the Renaissance, melding the Christian world (52 biblical scenes on the ceiling) and the Classical world (fanciful designs on the walls and arches). The ceiling tells Christian history chronologically, starting with the Creation and the expulsion of Adam and Eve and ending with Christ's Last Supper. For the walls, Raphael used the ancient "grotesque" style found in archaeological sites (or "grottos"): lacy designs, garlands, flowers, vases, and mythological animals. Raphael resurrected these motifs, which became extremely popular with European nobility. The complex symbolism, mixing the Christian and pagan, also intrigued the educated elite, and the Loggia has come to be called "Raphael's Bible."

• *When you're done in the Loggia, go back to the start of the hallway (Room 226) and turn left into Room 229, the* **Majolica Room.** *Here you'll find two authentic masterpieces by Raphael.*

Conestabile Madonna (c. 1504): The dinner-plate-size painting in the gilded frame just opposite the entrance is one of Raphael's first

known works, painted when he was still a teenager. Mother Mary multitasks, cradling Baby Jesus while trying to read. Precocious Jesus seems to be reading, too. Though realistic enough, the work shows a geometrically perfect world: Mary's oval face, Jesus' round head, and the perfect oval frame. The

influence of Leonardo is clear: in the tilt of Mary's head and position of Jesus' pudgy legs (similar to the *Litta Madonna*) and in the child's beyond-his-years focus on an object (from the *Benois Madonna*). The picture is remarkable for its color harmonies and its perfected forms—characteristics that Raphael would beautifully develop in his later works.

While you're in this room, look also for Raphael's somber **Holy Family** (c. 1507), another rare early work. It's also known as *Madonna with Beardless Joseph,* for obvious reasons.

• *At the far end of the Raphael room, hook right into Room 230. In the center of this gallery is a sculpture by...*

Michelangelo

Crouching Boy (c. 1530): The nude figure crouches down within the tight "frame" of the block of marble he came from. The statue was

likely intended to pose forlornly at the base of a tomb in the Medici Chapel in Florence, possibly to symbolize the vanquished spirit of the deceased's grieving relatives. Though the project (and this statue) were never fully finished, the work possesses Michelangelo's trademark pent-up energy.

• *We'll leave the Italian Renaissance now. Go back one room, turn immediately right, then right again at the blue vase. Head down the skylighted Rooms 247, 238, and 239 (with grand vases). At the last of these rooms (239), watch for the door on the left*

for the long, pastel-hazy, light-filled Room 241. Slow your pace and stroll through this gorgeous array of Neoclassical sculpture. Just after the doors, look for...

Canova

The Three Graces (1813-1816): The great Venetian sculptor shows the three mythological ladies who entertained the Greek gods at dinnertime. They huddle up, hugging and exchanging glances, their heads leaning together. Each pose is different, and the statue is interesting from every angle. But the group is united by their common origin—carved from a single block of marble—and by the sash that joins them. The ladies' velvety soft skin is Canova's signature element. Antonio Canova (1757-1822) combines the cool, minimal lines of Neoclassicism with the warm sentiment of Romanticism.

• *Go back into Room 239, then turn left into the smaller Room 251. Turn right and go through Room 252 and into the green-hued Room 254, with the best collection of Rembrandts outside the Netherlands.*

Rembrandt

The great Dutch painter is beautifully represented at the Hermitage. We'll tune into two works in particular.

• *As you enter the room, look to the left to find...*

Danae (1636): Compare this large-scale nude of the Greek demi-goddess to Titian's version, which we saw earlier. The scene  is similar—a nude woman reclines diagonally on a canopied bed, awaiting her lover (the randy god Zeus), accompanied by her maid (in the dim background). But Rembrandt depicts a more practical, less ecstatic tryst. Where Titian's Danae was helpless with rapture, Rembrandt's is more in control. She's propped upright and focused, and her legs aren't splayed open. Danae motions to her offstage lover—either welcoming him into her boudoir or warning him to be cautious. Historians note that Danae has the body of Rembrandt's first wife (the original model) and the face of his mistress (painted over a decade later).

Catherine the Great—herself no stranger to bedroom visitors—bought this painting in 1772 as one of the works that grew into the Hermitage collection. In 1985, a crazed visitor to the museum slashed the canvas with a knife and threw acid on Danae's face, causing significant damage to the painting. A heroic restora-

tion project repaired the canvas and retouched the melted paint.
• *At the far end of the room, look for...*

The Prodigal Son (c. 1669): In the Bible, Jesus tells this story of the young man who wastes his inheritance on wine, women, and song. He returns home, drops to his knees before his father, and begs forgiveness. Rembrandt recounts the whole story—past, present, and future—in this single moment, frozen in time. The Prodigal Son's tattered clothes and missing shoe hint at the past—how he was once rich and wearing fine clothes, but ended up penniless, alone, bald, and living in a pigsty. His older brother (standing to the right) is the present: He looks down in judgment, ready to remind their dad what a bad son the Prodigal is.

But the father's face and gestures foretell the story's outcome, as he bends down to embrace his son with a tenderness that says all will be forgiven. The father's bright-red cloak wraps around the poor Prodigal like loving arms.

Many artists have depicted this story. Most play up the drama and big emotions: the Prodigal's wild life of pleasure, the abject misery of his poverty, or the joyous celebration after he returns. Rembrandt is more subtle. He uses the tilt of the Prodigal's head against his father's lap to show his regret for all those wasted years. The father's lined face telegraphs the pain of loss, relief, love, and acceptance. He oh-so-gently places his hands on his son's shoulders, giving a blessing. The bystanders look on in total silence. Rembrandt's rough, messy brushstrokes and dark brooding atmosphere suggest the strong emotions going on below the surface.

The Prodigal Son is one of Rembrandt's last paintings. Some read Rembrandt's own life story into the painting: Rembrandt had been a young prodigy whose God-given talent brought him wealth, fame, and the love of a beautiful woman. Then he lost it all, and was even forced to sell off his possessions to pay his debts. His last years were spent in relative poverty and obscurity.

On the universal level, Jesus' parable was about how God, like a loving father, forgives even the worst of sinners. The painting resonates with anyone who's found themselves feeling lost, not living up to expectations, or estranged from a parent, family, or god. Note that Rembrandt shows us the scene from the Prodigal's point of view. That could be you or I rushing into the painting, to be received, forgiven, and enfolded in the warmth of a loving embrace.

• *It's a long haul from here up to the modern collection on the third floor.*

Follow these directions carefully: From Rembrandt, go back through Room 252 into Room 251, and continue straight ahead through Room 250, then the long Room 249. Emerging into Room 248, turn right and use the corridor (Room 258) to cut back across the three hermitages (crossing the bridge, then passing the garden). Carry on straight into Room 272, hook left, and do a loop through Rooms 272-280 to find the stairs (on the right, in Room 280).

Part 3: Modern Masters

The Hermitage has an impressive collection of paintings by Impressionist and Post-Impressionist masters. It's perfect for seeing how these artists—living in France in the late 19th century—influenced one another. The museum's core collection benefited greatly during the 1917 Russian Revolution. Many wealthy aristocrats with the taste and budget for these paintings fled the country. With not a hint of apology, the Soviet Union nationalized the collections you'll enjoy next so the proletariat could enjoy them. Remember: Some or all of this art may be relocated to the General Staff Building, across Palace Square. And in general, the art in these rooms is often shuffled around. Expect some changes to these descriptions.

Overview: So many canvases are crammed into these small rooms, it's hard to keep track of who's who. Here's a primer on just a few of the many famous names represented here: **Edouard Manet** (1832-1883) bucked the strict academic system to paint realistic scenes of everyday life, rather than prettified goddesses. Manet inspired his friend **Edgar Degas** (1834-1917) to sketch candid snapshots of the modern Parisian lifestyle—café scenes, workers, and well-dressed families bustling through Parisian streets. **Claude Monet** (1840-1926) and his close friend **Auguste Renoir** (1841-1919) took things another step, setting their canvases up outdoors and painting quickly to capture shimmering landscapes using a mosaic of bright colors. **Vincent van Gogh** (1853-1890), a moody Dutchman, learned this Impressionist technique from the bohemians in Paris, but infused his landscapes with swirling brushwork and an emotional expressiveness. Van Gogh's Post-Impressionist style was adopted by his painting partner, **Paul Gauguin** (1848-1903), who used bright patches of colors and simplified forms to re-create the primitive look of tribal art. **Henri Matisse** (1869-1954) went further, creating the art of "wild beasts" (Fauves), using even brighter colors and simpler forms than Gauguin. Gauguin had greatly admired a brilliant-but-struggling artist named **Paul Cézanne** (1839-1906), who also rejected traditional three-dimensionality to compose paintings as geometrical blocks of color. As the 20th century dawned, **Pablo Picasso** (1881-1973) broke Cezanne's blocks of colors into shards and "cubes" of color, all jumbled up, anticipating purely abstract art.

The Hermitage offers a unique chance to see this evolution—if you're inclined to look for it. If not, just switch off your cerebral cortex and simply browse, enjoying room after room of pretty, colorful, pleasant paintings by these modern masters. I've highlighted a few paintings that always catch my eye.

• *This floor's rooms are smaller—and more crowded. Sharpen your elbows and, from the top of the stairs, turn left into Room 314, turn left again, and do a loop through Rooms 332, 331, 330, and 323, and then right into Room 322. Finally, turn right into Room 321, where you'll find...*

Renoir

Later in life, Renoir—who, along with Monet, was one of the founding fathers of Impressionism—changed his style. He veered from the Impressionist credo of creating objective studies in color and light to begin painting things that were unabashedly "pretty." He populated his canvases with rosy-cheeked, middle-class girls performing happy domestic activities, rendered in a warm, inviting style. As Renoir himself said, "There are enough ugly things in life."

• *Now head into Room 320 and continue into Room 319, dominated by* **Monet***. Next up, Room 318 features lots of* **Cézanne** *(including Lady in Blue). And Room 317 is packed with works by...*

Vincent van Gogh

A self-taught phenom who absorbed the Impressionist technique before developing his own unique style, Vincent van Gogh struck out on his own in Arles, in the south of France, in 1888. For the next two years of his brief life, he cranked out a canvas nearly every other day. He loved painting the rural landscape and the colorful life of the locals.

• *On your left as you enter is...*

Arena at Arles (1888): Like a spontaneous photograph, this painting captures the bustle of spectators at the town's bullfighting ring. The scene is slightly off-kilter, focusing on the crowds rather than action in the ring. Van Gogh typically painted in a rush, and you can see it in the hurried lines and sketchy faces.

Memory of the Garden at Etten (*Ladies of Arles*, 1888): In the fall of 1888, Gauguin came to visit Van Gogh. The two friends roomed together and painted side by side. It was Gauguin who suggested that Vincent change things up and paint something besides Impressionist scenes of everyday life. The result was this startling canvas, in which Vincent portrayed a garden he remembered from his childhood. The vivid colors had special meaning to him, representing the personalities of his mother and sister. The style shows the influence of Gauguin—big swaths of bright colors, divided by thick black outlines.

• *On the facing wall are two more notable paintings.*

The Lilac Bush (1889): On December 23, 1888, a drunk and angry Van Gogh turned on Gauguin, threatening him with a knife. Then he cut off a piece of his own ear and sent it to a prostitute. Judged insane, Van Gogh checked into a mental hospital for treatment. There he painted this simple subject that bristles with life, a forest of thick brushstrokes charged with Van Gogh's strong emotions.

The Cottages (1890): Van Gogh moved north of Paris in 1890 to be under a doctor's care. The wavy brushstrokes and surreal colors of this work suggest an uncertain frame of mind. This was one of Vincent's last paintings. A few weeks later, he wandered into a field near these homes and shot himself, having spent his life in poverty and artistic obscurity. No sooner had he died than his work took wings.

• *The next room (316) has a wonderful collection of works by...*

Paul Gauguin

The Hermitage typically displays about a dozen paintings of the French Post-Impressionist Paul Gauguin, who famously left his

stockbroker job and family to paint full-time. Eventually he fulfilled his lifelong dream to live and work in the South Seas, especially Tahiti. He spent much of his later life there, painting island life in all its bright color and simplicity.

• *Just to the left as you enter the room is...*

Tahitian Pastorals (*Pastorales Tahitiennes*, 1892): This work, from Gauguin's first stay in Tahiti, captures the paradise Gauguin had always envisioned. He paints an island-dotted landscape peopled by exotic women doing simple tasks and making music. A lounging dog dominates the foreground. The style is intentionally "primitive," collapsing 3-D landscapes into a two-dimensional pattern of bright colors. In **Woman Holding a Fruit** (1893)—on the facing wall—a native girl enjoys the simple pleasures of life in all her naked innocence.

• *Continue straight across the bridge, peering down into a pastel-blue hall decorated with a whipped-cream can and Alexander's Wedgwood portrait at the end of the hall. Don't miss the wonderful view over Palace Square from the windows on your left. You'll head straight through Rooms 343-344 and into Room 345; the largest, most famous, and most important canvas here is by...*

Matisse

The Dance (1909-1910): Five dancers strip naked, join hands, and go ring-around-the-rosy, creating an infectious air of abandon.

 This large, joyous work was one of Matisse's personal favorites. It features his Fauvist colors—bright red dancers on a blue-and-green background. Meanwhile, the undulating lines that join the dancers create a pleasing design that anticipates modern, abstract art.

Other Matisse works in this room (and the previous one) trace his evolution from a realistic painter of still lifes to Impressionism to bright Fauvist colors to his semi-abstract works that pioneer modern abstract art.

• *Pass through Rooms 346-347 to reach Rooms 348 and 349, focusing on the works of...*

Pablo Picasso

In the year 1900, the 19-year-old Spaniard Pablo Picasso arrived in Paris, the world art capital. A relentless experimenter, Picasso would soon liberate himself from academic art traditions as he laid the basis for the new modern style. Besides groundbreaking examples of early Cubism and painted masterpieces from his Blue Period, the collection includes his playful ceramics. Be sure to enjoy these three paintings (all in Room 348):

• *On the left wall as you enter, between the windows, is...*

The Absinthe Drinker (1901): A woman sits alone in a grimy café, contemplating her fate, soothed by a glass of that highly potent and destructive form of alcohol. She leans on a table, deep in thought, with her distorted right arm wrapped around her protectively. All of the lines of sight—her unnaturally vertical forearm and the lines on the wall behind her—converge on her face, boxing her into a corner. The painting shows Picasso's facile mastery of the earlier generation of Impressionist and Post-Impressionists. It's a snapshot café scene like Degas, with the flat two-dimensional feel of Gauguin and the emotional expressiveness of Van Gogh. Notice the signature at top. Though his full Spanish name was Pablo Ruiz Picasso, by this time he has dropped his father's surname (Ruiz) and kept his Mom's to create that one-name brand that would become world-famous—Picasso.

• *Just to the left of the door you came in is...*

Two Sisters (1902): From Picasso's Blue Period, painted with a gloomy palette, this canvas looks sympathetically at people who, like Picasso, felt sad and alienated. The painting started with a sketch Picasso had made of two sisters—one a prostitute and one a nun. From that specific source, he developed a work of universal character.

• *On the facing wall is...*

Three Women (1908): This work (and the studies near it) shows how Picasso was rethinking how artists look at the world. He shattered reality into shards and cubes of color, then reassembled the pieces like a collage on canvas—the style called Cubism.

• *While there's much more to be seen, our tour is finished. If you're still craving more, the private apartments of Maria Alexandronovna (wife of Czar Alexander II; Rooms 289 and 304-307) are impressive, especially Room 304—the Empress' Drawing Room from the 1850s, with Catherine the Great's collection of gems and cameos. She claimed to be addicted to gems.*

Otherwise, make your way back down to the ground floor and plot your escape. Just follow signs with your new favorite word in the Russian language: ВЫХОД*..."exit." If you're looking for extra credit, you can head across the Palace Square for the special exhibits shown in the...*

General Staff Building

Designed in Russian Empire style as a headquarters for the Russian military, this building is now a palatial art gallery. It's currently being used for special shows of big-name modern artists and themed exhibits, but in time some or all of the Hermitage's 19th- and 20th-century painting collection will be relocated here. If and when that happens, these galleries, like those of its big sister across the square, will be worth [sss]—-and best of all, the art will become much easier to appreciate than in the cramped Hermitage attic. While things are in flux, your best source for what's where is the Hermitage website.

Most likely, you'll enter below the big yellow arch directly across from the Hermitage entrance (door on the left as you go under the arch). After the ticket desk, you'll find a lower level with a cloakroom, WCs, and other services, and—above that—a cavernous atrium with a wide, modern marble staircase leading up to the exhibition halls (200 R for special exhibits, Tue-Sun 10:00-18:00, Wed until 21:00, closed Mon).

MUSEUMS AND GARDENS NEAR NEVSKY PROSPEKT

Two adjacent, related museums—the Russian Museum, with a fine-art collection, and the Russian Museum of Ethnography—sit just beyond the Griboyedov Canal. Behind them is a pair of historic gardens, the Mikhailovsky and Summer Gardens. Farther down Nevsky, near the Fontanka River, is the dazzling Fabergé Museum.

▲▲▲Russian Museum (Русский Музей)

Here's a fascinating collection of Russian art, particularly 18th- and 19th-century painting and portraiture. People who are disap-

pointed that the Hermitage is mostly Western European art love the Russian Museum, since the artists shown here are largely unknown in the West. Much of the work reveals Russians exploring their own culture and landscape: marshes, birch stands, muddy village streets, the conquest of Siberia, fire-lit scenes in family huts, and Repin's portrait of Tolstoy standing barefoot in the woods.

This comparatively uncrowded museum adds depth to the experience you have as a visitor to St. Petersburg—the artists represented here saw the same rooftops, churches, and street scenes as you do. Their art brings you in touch with the country's turbulent political history and captures the small-town wooden architecture and forest landscapes that you won't see on a visit to this big city.

The museum occupies the Mikhailovsky Palace, built in the 1820s for Grand Duke Mikhail Pavlovich (a grandson of Catherine the Great). Though the interiors aren't as impressive as those at the Hermitage, original decorations in a few rooms give you a taste of how the Russian nobility lived.

Cost and Hours: 350 R, Wed and Fri-Mon 10:00-18:00, Thu 13:00-21:00, closed Tue, last entry 30 minutes before closing, photo permit-250 R, English audioguide-250 R.

Information: The museum is at Inzhenernaya Ulitsa 4, two blocks north of Nevsky Prospekt along Griboyedov Canal, near the Church on Spilled Blood. Tel. 595-4248, www.rusmuseum.ru.

Entering the Museum: The entrance is at the basement (servants') level, in the right-hand corner as you enter the main courtyard. Purchase your tickets, pick up a map (listing room numbers), and go through the security checkpoint. On the basement level, you'll find cloakrooms, a bookstore, a post office (handy if you need stamps), WCs, and a small café. For later, notice the back exit, which gives you the option of leaving through the gardens on the north side of the museum (from where you can bear left through the park to reach the Church on Spilled Blood). To reach the exhibits, take the stairs up one flight and show your ticket. Here, at the base of the grand staircase, you can rent the good audioguide, which interprets 300 of the museum's best works (or, for a quick visit, just use the self-guided tour, below).

Layout: The museum has 109 numbered rooms (find numbers over doorways), which lend themselves to a route in more or less chronological order.

◯ Self-Guided Tour

The museum's most exciting works cover the period from roughly 1870 to 1940. Russia was in ferment during these years—first with the end of serfdom and agitation for social change and equality; later with World War I, industrialization, and the beginnings of communism; and throughout with artistic currents such as Impressionism, Art Nouveau, and Modernism that came in from the West. I suggest a chronological tour through the collection, but pace yourself to spend the majority of your time with the most important works, near the end. Here are things to look for as you enjoy a sweep through Russian history via its art.

• *Head up the grand staircase and turn left into Room 1. We'll do a quick counterclockwise spin around this floor.*

Early Russian Art

Rooms 1-4: These rooms house Russian icons, the earliest dating back to the 1100s. Icons are a key part of Orthodox traditions of worship, and have roots in medieval Greece and Byzantium ("icon" means image or likeness in Greek). Just as it's best to see animals in the wild rather than in a zoo, icons are best seen in the context of the churches for which they were designed. These depictions of sacred people or events gave the illiterate faithful a way to "see" and communicate with the holy. You can follow the evolution of icon style from the 12th to the 16th century, finishing in Room 4, where some of the most recent icons are tainted by a European realism that kills the mysticism.

18th- and Early 19th-Century Russian Painting

Rooms 5-12: The grandest architecture in the museum is seen in these rooms, which overlook the gardens out back and display mostly 18th-century portraits. Notice the cultural revolution portrayed here: Following Peter the Great's reforms, the upper crust of Russia is clean-shaven, speaks French, and wears European clothes. There's a new outlook, and portraits mirror a society where people are showing off their individuality. You'll also see a few rare 18th-century Russian-made tapestries.

In Room 6, on the left wall, Ivan Nikitin's *Portrait of the Field Hetman* (1720s), with red-rimmed eyes, conveys an unusual degree of real personality. Peter the Great's court painter succeeded in showing this battle-worn officer ("hetman" means captain) not as a stuffed suit, but as a man proudly doing his duty for Russia despite being worn down by the horrors of war.

In the gaudy Room 10, Dmitry Levitzky's big portrait of Catherine the Great (*The Legislatress at the Temple of Justice,* flanked by smaller portraits of the leading figures in her court) is filled with symbolism and captures her cult of personality. Catherine gestures toward a pedestal with smoldering poppies—indicating that she was always alert, sacrificing repose for the betterment of her nation. Her orange-and-black sash indicates that Catherine established Russia's highest military honor, the Order of St. George. At her feet, an eagle perches on a stack of books, representing her respect for the word of law. And out the window on the left, see the wind-filled sails of a ship, suggesting Catherine's connection to the world and the expansion of the Russian realm. A similar, sculptural version of Catherine stands in the same room.

Room 11 is a great example of the Russian Empire style of Carlo Rossi, the architect who designed this building. Rossi's amped-up Neoclassicism, popularized by Catherine the Great's successor, Alexander I, pervades the city. Here you see the style at its cohesive zenith—from inlaid floor to furniture to architecture. (For more on Rossi—and other big contributors to the aesthetics of St. Petersburg—see the sidebar on page 32.)

Rooms 13-17: These rooms cover the Romantic era of the early 19th century. Room 14 is dominated by Karl Brullov's *The Last Day of Pompeii* (1833), a painting every Russian student knows well. It and paintings nearby (such as the dramatic shipwreck scenes) show the Romanticism of the age: They're emotional and theatrical, a reaction to the formal Neoclassicism of Catherine the Great. These Russian artists paint with confidence, no longer parroting European styles. Although inspired by European trends, they're confidently Russian now.

At the far end of Room 15 is Alexander Ivanov's *Appearance of Christ to the People* (completed before 1855), a variant of his masterwork of the same name (in Moscow's Tretyakov Gallery). The entire wall is filled with studies for this, his magnum opus, to which the artist dedicated 20 years of his career.

• *Continue back to the landing, head down the grand staircase, and turn left into Room 18.*

Late 19th- and Early 20th-Century Painting

Rooms 18-22: Paintings in Room 18, from the 1860s, show artists capturing real life. As across Europe, class awareness and social consciousness was growing, and artists began to use their work to question social inequalities. You can see an example of this "critical realism" in Vasily Perov's *Monastery Refectory* (1865-76), which shows fat monks scraping their plates clean while ignoring the hungry beggars at their feet.

Room 19 draws attention to Russian history in realistic paintings such as Nikolai Ghe's *Peter I Interrogating the Czarevich Alexei at Peterhof.* Without excessive pathos, we see the czar bluntly questioning his son—before putting in motion the inquisition that would condemn Alexei to death.

Rooms 20 and 22 focus on Romantic landscapes from the 1860s and 1870s that celebrate Russia's tranquil forests and seaside. In this period countries all across Europe experienced a resurgence of nationalism, and it showed in their art. Room 21 focuses on classical themes: the death of Nero, Christian martyrs in the Colosseum, and so on.

• *Now we'll jump forward to the museum's highlights. Proceed to Room 33 (if some rooms are closed, you may have to backtrack through later rooms to reach 33). But don't rush—there are some powerful canvases in the intervening halls that set the tone for what's to come.*

Rooms 33-34 and 54: Ilya Repin (1844-1930), who came from a modest background, often explored the rural lives of common people—he could be called an early Socialist Realist. His painting met approval during the Soviet period for its focus on the working class. He specialized in brilliant portraits that combined landscape settings with psychological insight and historical realism. A prime example is in Room 33—Repin famously painted Leo Tolstoy in peasant clothing, standing barefoot in the woods (1901).

In Room 34, find the painting that makes you want to sing the Volga Boat Song. With *Barge Haulers on the Volga* (1870-1873), Repin polished his local celebrity and gained renown in the West. Eleven wretched workers (called *burlaks*)—bodies groaning and with pain etched on their faces—are yoked like livestock for the Sisyphean task of pulling a ship against the current. The youngest *burlak* in the center, with inexplicable optimism, strikes a classically heroic pose. A steamship on the horizon emphasizes how cruelly outdated this form of labor is in the modern age. It's no wonder the Soviets embraced this painting as a perfect metaphor for the timeless struggle of the working class.

Also in Room 34, find *Seeing Off a Recruit* (1879), in which a young man hugs his mother as he prepares to let the army take him far away (25 years was a standard term of duty)—showing the sacrifice of military service in human terms that are still relevant today.

Rooms 36-37: One of Russia's foremost historical painters, Vasily Surikov (1848-1916) grew up in Siberia but later moved to European Russia. He excelled at creating dynamic battle scenes designed to spur Russian patriotism. In Room 36, his gigantic *Ermak's Conquest of Siberia* (1895) is a reminder that Russia has an uneasy relationship with its native peoples. Here, Caucasian-featured soldiers armed with guns cross a river by boat, meeting Siberian forces on the other shore armed with bow and arrow. In Room 37, Surikov's gigantic *Stepan Razin* (with the rowboat) commemorates the Cossack who led an uprising against the czar in 1670.

Room 38: Viktor Vasnetsov's *Knight at the Crossroads* (1882) evokes Russia's answer to Arthurian legend. A Russian knight on horseback, depicted in a natural landscape setting, ponders a stone with an inscription suggesting that any route he takes will present pitfalls. The skull and bones littering the grass and the ominous raven overhead drive home the somber message.

• *From here, backtrack to Room 35, and look for the door on the left that leads down into...*

Room 39: Vasily Vereshchagin (1842-1904) specialized in photorealistic paintings emphasizing two subjects: military scenes and exotic views of Eastern cultures (which he explored in his travels to the Balkans, Central Asia, and British India). Traveling with the military, he painted the  reality of war vividly, but got too close and became a casualty himself in the Russo-Japanese War in 1904. Because he took a warts-and-all approach to combat, many of Vereshchagin's warfare paintings were deemed too graphic or unsettling to be exhibited during his lifetime. *Shipka-Sheynovo* shows Russia's 1877 victory over the Ottoman Empire at the battle of Shipka Pass, in what's now Bulgaria. The victorious Russian general rides past cheering troops, but the composition is dominated by the grotesque corpses of soldiers scattered in the snow. Vereshchagin's evocatively detailed *At the Entrance to the Mosque* makes evident the artist's fascination with the Eastern cultures whose decline is documented on his other canvases.

• *As you pass through Rooms 40-43, notice how the sun-dappled canvases of the Russian Impressionists were clearly influenced by the French Impressionists.*

Room 45: *Seventeenth-Century Moscow Street on a Public Holiday* (1895), by **Andrei Ryabushkin,** is a semi-romanticized view of premodern Russian life: wooden houses, unpaved streets, women in headscarves and men in long beards, beggars, and the colorful, onion-domed St. Basil's Cathedral in the background.

Room 48: Here, in the small folk-art wing, you can get a glimpse of small-town Russia. It's worth perusal if only for its collection of village woodcarving. In addition, you'll see lace, lacquer boxes, pewter jewels, and folk dress (all described in English).

• *Now head back out to Room 48, turn left, and go down the corridor to reach a flight of stairs. Take this up to the top floor of the museum's Benois Wing (English descriptions in this wing for each room), housing most of the museum's 20th-century art. You'll begin in Room 66.*

More 20th-Century Art

Room 66: Mikhail Vrubel's *Bogatyr* (1898) was painted on the cusp of the new century. A massive, ogre-like knight errant sits on a fantastically fat horse. The decorative style borrows from the Art Nouveau movement, the theme echoes Russian myths and stories, and the surrealistic presentation anticipates expressionist painting. Vrubel (1856-1910) had a thing for demons and paintings beyond reality.

Rooms 69-70: Valentin Serov (1865-1911) made his name as the best Russian portrait painter of his day. Many Russian celebrities and aristocrats sat for him, eager for one of his freely brushed, technically adept portraits. It was said that his likenesses were so insightful that subjects could learn about themselves by viewing their Serov portrait.

Serov departed from his usual approach for his 1910 nude portrait of Ida Rubinstein, a famous Russian ballerina (in Room 70). Daring in its simplicity and starkness, the painting has the flatness and sharp outlines of Art Nouveau—evoking the works of Gustav Klimt.

Room 71: Although his bread and butter was book illustration, Boris Kustodiev (1878-1927) was also known for colorful paintings such as *Shrovetide* (1916). Here you see the inescapably recurrent theme in Russian paintings of winter: sleigh rides, snow-covered roofs, festivals, and fairy-tale churches, all under an achingly beautiful winter sky of swirling pink-and-blue pastels. The artist appreciated plump models (as evidenced by *Merchant's Wife* and *Merchant's Wife at Tea*). Just as we say a woman's figure is Rubenesque, Russians say someone is Kustodievesque.

Russian Abstraction, the Avant-Garde, and Socialist Realism

Rooms 72 to 85 take us farther into Russia's tumultuous 20th century. With the chaos and unprecedented destruction of World War I and the Bolshevik Revolution that followed, Russia was changing radically—as you'll see in the art displayed in these rooms. Zip through the first few rooms, seeing the Russian take on several modern European styles—Post-Impressionism, Cubism, Expressionism, Abstract Expressionism, and so on.

Rooms 78-80: Here you sense the 1920s. There was a feeling that a new world had been created; art and politics were parallel and complementary forces. But in 1928, with the strengthening of the idealistic communist movement under Stalin, there was a big change, as art became a servant of political ideology.

Rooms 80-83: The partition in the middle of Room 80 marks a major shift. Art from the early Soviet period glorified workers and the "dictatorship of the proletariat." Dubbed Socialist Realism, this government-sanctioned style had to be realistic and its content had to be socialist. Because the abstract cannot be controlled—it's open to free interpretation—it was not allowed. From 1928 on, art was acceptable only if it actively promoted socialist ideology. This was true for visual arts, literature, and even (as far as possible) for music.

In Room 80, Alexander Samokhvalov's *Militarized Komsomol* (1932-1933) conveys the Socialist Realist aesthetic: "realistically" showing everyday people who are, in an idealized way, eagerly participating in the socialist society. In this case, we see scouts learning how to scout—and potentially more than that, should the need arise.

In Room 81, you can see how art was used to build heroes, both in war and in the culture of sport.

The post-WWII canvases in Room 82 depict idyllic natural and peasant scenes, extolling the simple life held central in the Soviet worldview. These paintings make you want to sign up for a Russian-countryside summer vacation.

In Room 83, the Khrushchev-era art of the 1960s comes with a hint of spring—and a sense of the thawing that the summer of love (in 1967) blew across the Iron Curtain.

Rooms 84-85: It's subtle, but here you can feel change in the air. Rather than idealizing everyday Russian life, these works—from the later Soviet years—are clearly critical of it. In Room 85, Alexei Sundukov's *Queue* (1986)

is a perhaps too-on-the-nose depiction of the trials of a communist consumer. In the center of this room, Dmitry Kaminker's *The Oarsman* (1987), sculpted under perestroika, communicates the hopeless feeling of the last years of communism. This is dissident art, filled with political allegory, created not for the public but for an underground exhibition.

Then, in the late 1980s—just before the USSR fell apart—the Soviet leader Mikhail Gorbachev allowed a free art exhibit. This marked the end of Socialist Realism—and the end of real dissident art, because there was no longer any danger in showing it. The artistic spirit of the Russian people survived communism and came out of the closet.

▲Russian Museum of Ethnography
(Российский Этнографический Музей)
This branch of the Russian Museum offers an extensive, if dry, introduction to the various peoples of the former Soviet Union, reaching from Vilnius to Vladivostok. Fans of folk culture find it worthwhile, and anyone will be impressed by the diversity of one of the planet's biggest and most varied countries. The good, included audioguide (use the free Wi-Fi to download it) tells you more about each culture.

Cost and Hours: 350 R, Tue-Sun 10:00-18:00, closed Mon and last Fri of month, at Inzhenernaya 4—directly to the right as you face the main entrance of the Russian Museum, www.ethnomuseum.ru.

Visiting the Museum: Straight ahead as you enter, the grand, marbled, Neoclassical hall dedicated to Czar Alexander III feels like a Greek temple—with reliefs celebrating the ethnic diversity of "Russia" (i.e., anywhere that was once part of Russia). Flanking the lobby are two sprawling wings that offer a whistle-stop tour around the Russian realm of influence. Wander hall after hall of beautifully presented traditional costumes and tools from the Baltic Sea to the Bering Strait, and everything in between—the Caucasus, Volga region, Ural Mountains, Siberia, and the vast cultural fault zones where Russia touches Middle Eastern and Asiatic cultures. You'll also learn about the faiths of this pluralistic society—from Russian Orthodox Christianity, to Lutheranism, to Judaism, to Islam. (With an entire wing dedicated to Judaism—including a display of traditional garb that looks straight out of *Fiddler on the Roof*—this is the best place in town to learn about the Russian Jewish experience.) You'll see reconstructed log cabins, furniture, jewelry, handicrafts, archival photos, and more.

Summer Garden (Летний сад)
The zone behind the Russian Museum is filled with delightful parks and gardens. Directly behind the building, the inviting, tree-

filled Mikhailovsky Garden (Михайловский сад) leads (across the canal) into the geometrically regimented Field of Mars (Марсово поле) park, designed to showcase military parades. But best of all (just to the east, across another canal) is the Summer Garden (Летний сад), one of St. Petersburg's most enjoyable public spaces.

Cost and Hours: Free entry, garden open in summer daily 10:00-22:00; off-season Wed-Mon 10:00-19:30, closed Tue; fountains run Wed-Mon May-Sept only; audioguide-300 R.

Visiting the Garden: On a sunny day with some time to spare, there are few more enjoyable activities in St. Petersburg than strolling through the Summer Garden. The oldest garden in the city, it was laid out in 1710 under Peter the Great himself, right where the Fontanka River meets the Neva. It's laced with walking trails, studded with fountains and statues, and generously tree-shaded. Like St. Petersburg itself, it's the gorgeous result of the most talented artistic minds of the time—Dutch and French garden engineers helped to plot and populate the space with beautiful trees and hedges, and Venetian artists lined its walkways with stony sculptures.

Peter, impressed by the fountains he saw at Versailles, made sure that fine **fountains** enlivened this garden. They were destroyed by a flood in 1777, but recently restored. The original marble statues imported from Italy are now in museums, but fine copies ornament the grounds. You can see here Peter's passion for importing European culture. He opened the gardens "to all who were decently dressed."

The rich symbolism of the plantings is explained on English reader boards throughout. There's a small museum and café in the "Poultry Yard." And swans (which had been gone since the Revolution) are now back, gliding through the ponds as they did in Peter's time.

Along the Fontanka is Peter's own **Summer Palace** (Летний дворец). It's a strikingly modest mansion (from 1714), but still a step up from his original log cabin just across the river. It's easy to imagine Peter sitting back, relaxing, and gazing out over the waterways of his namesake city.

▲▲Fabergé Museum
(Музей Фаберже)

This sumptuous museum fills the beautifully restored Shuvalov Palace with the world's biggest collection of works by Carl Fabergé, jeweler to the czars. Opened in 2013, the museum is built around the collection assembled by the American publisher Malcolm Forbes (and later purchased by one of Russia's wealthy oligarchs). The undisputed highlight: 14 exquisite Fabergé eggs, including nine imperial Easter eggs. These jeweled fantasies—impossibly lavish, individually created "surprise"-loaded gifts given by the czars to their relatives and friends—represent the pinnacle of Romanov excess. Even those bored by treasury collections are wowed by the chance to get an up-close, 360-degree view of these incredible creations. The sight is a two-fer: Besides ogling the breathtaking treasury of priceless objects, you get to explore the halls of a grand canalside mansion, fueling fantasies of how the czars' aristocratic pals used to live.

Cost and Hours: 300 R, ticket office sells same-day admissions only—advance sales are online; Sat-Thu 9:30-20:45, closed Fri; dry audioguide-150 R; Fontanka 21, tel. 333-2655, www.fabergemuseum.ru.

Getting In: At this relatively new museum, logistics for your visit may be in flux (check their website for the latest). But as of this writing, you can visit with a **guided tour** before 18:00 (English tours generally run 2/day—otherwise you can join a Russian tour and pay for the audioguide; buy tickets online to be sure you'll get in, or call or email ahead to find out today's schedule—tel. 333-2655 or 3332655@fsv.ru). After 18:00, it's possible to visit **on your own** (with the help of the audioguide). On-your-own evening visit tickets go on sale at 17:45 (last ticket sold 1.5 hours before closing time).

Visiting the Museum: Ascend the grand staircase, under a gloriously stuccoed dome, and circle the collection counterclockwise. Each room is more amazing than the last.

From the **Knights' Hall**—filled with precious wine goblets, drinking horns, silver vessels, and military memorabilia—turn left into the **Red Room,** with silk walls and dark-stained walnut woodwork. Here you can get a close look at even more fine gold and silver work, from elaborate tankards to precious metals made to resemble wicker and cloth.

In the **Blue Room** are those 14 magnificent Fabergé eggs. They are displayed in chronological order, illustrating the evolution of their craftsmanship, inventiveness, and extravagance. Painstakingly crafted by court jeweler Peter Carl Fabergé (1846-1920), no two are alike. The variety of eggs and the surprises they hold is stunning: The first egg (commissioned by Czar Alexander III in 1885) held a golden yolk, which enclosed a golden hen concealing a diamond miniature of the royal crown and a ruby egg. Later eggs contain increasingly complex mechanisms: A miniature Jesus emerges from a tomb made of agates; a rose-colored egg contains a "bud," whose petals spring open with the press of a button to reveal a diamond crown. The coronation of Nicholas II (the last czar) is celebrated by an egg that reveals an astonishingly detailed miniature coronation carriage—complete with working wheels and suspension.

There's much more to see: snuff boxes, watches, belt buckles, paintings, and icons. If the door's open, peek into the spectacular **Concert Hall,** with a musicians' gallery up above. The **Gold Room** displays dozens of "cabinet gifts"—many of them *objets d'fantasie* (impossibly expensive knickknacks)—presented by people who curried favor with the Romanovs. In this room, also look for striking photos of the ramshackle palace before its long restoration. The **Gothic Room** is filled with exquisite icons, some dating back to the 1600s; the **Upper Dining Room** boasts a pristine collection of late 19th- and 20th-century paintings (including Renoir's Place de la Trinité); and the **White and Blue Room** shows off shimmering enamel, silverwork, filigree, and porcelain.

CHURCHES AND MONASTERIES

Russian Orthodoxy has revived since the end of communism. Duck into any neighborhood church, full of incense, candles, and liturgi-

cal chants. It's usually OK to visit discreetly during services, when the priest opens the doors of the iconostasis, faces the altar, and leads the standing congregation in chant. Smaller churches are usually free to enter (though you can leave a small donation, or buy and

light a candle) and full of Russians morning, noon, and night, and will give you more of a feeling for Russian religion than will church-museums such as St. Isaac's or the Church on Spilled Blood. For more on Russian Orthodoxy, see the sidebar on the next page.

▲▲Kazan Cathedral (Казанский Собор)

This huge, functioning house of worship, right along Nevsky Prospekt next to the Griboyedov Canal, offers an accessible Orthodox experience, although its interior is not very typical.

Reopened as a church after years as a "Museum of Atheism," the building has a sweeping exterior portico patterned after St. Peter's in Rome.

Cost and Hours: Free, daily 9:00-20:00, services generally at 10:00 and 18:00, Kazanskaya 2, www.kazansky-spb.ru.

Visiting the Church: Although the church faces Nevsky Prospekt, you'll enter through the west-facing main door, which is down a side street (Ulitsa Kazanskaya).

ST. PETERSBURG

The Russian Orthodox Church

The Russian Orthodox Faith

In the 11th century, the Great Schism split the Christian faith into two branches: Roman Catholicism in the west (based in Rome), and Eastern or Byzantine Orthodoxy in the east (based in Constantinople—today's Istanbul).

The Eastern Orthodox Church stayed true to the earliest traditions of the Christian faith, rejecting some theological issues accepted in the West (infallibility of the pope, and the doctrines of Purgatory and the Immaculate Conception, among others). *Orthos* is Greek for "right belief"—and if you believe you've already got it right, you're resistant to change.

The Eastern Orthodox Church is divided into about a dozen branches that are administratively independent even as they share many of the same rituals. Each branch is ruled by a patriarch (similar to a pope). The largest of these—with about half of the world's 300 million Orthodox Christians—is the Russian Orthodox Church.

Under communism, the state religion—atheism—trumped the faith professed by the majority of Russians. The Russian Orthodox Church survived, but many church buildings were seized by the government and repurposed (as museums, municipal buildings, sports facilities, and so on). Many more were destroyed. Soviet citizens who openly belonged to the Church sacrificed any hope of advancement within the communist system. But since the fall of communism, Russians have flocked back to their faith. (Even President Vladimir Putin, a former KGB agent and avowed atheist, revealed that he had secretly been an Orthodox Christian all along.) These days, new churches are being built and destroyed ones are being rebuilt or renovated... and all of them, it seems, are filled with worshippers. Today, three out of every four Russian citizens follows this faith.

Visiting an Orthodox Church

The doctrines of Catholic and Orthodox churches remain similar, but many of the rituals and customs are different. These become apparent when you step inside an Orthodox church.

Before entering an active church, women should cover their heads; women and men both must have their knees covered. (Churches that are tourist attractions may be more flexible.)

Watch worshippers arrive and go through the standard routine: Drop a coin in the wooden box, pick up a candle, say a prayer, light the candle, and place it in the candelabra. Make the sign of the cross and kiss the icon. You're welcome to join in.

Most Orthodox church decorations consist of icons: paintings of saints, packed with intricate symbolism and cast against a shimmering golden background. These are not intended to be lifelike, but to remind viewers of the metaphysical nature of Jesus and the saints. You'll almost never see statues, which, to Orthodox people, feel a little too close to the forbidden worship of graven images.

Most Eastern Orthodox churches have at least one mosaic or painting of Christ in a standard pose—as *Pantocrator,* a Greek word meaning "Ruler of All." The image shows Christ as King of the Universe, facing directly out, with penetrating eyes and a halo-cross behind his head.

While the sanctuary is visible in Catholic churches, it's hidden in Orthodox ones. Instead, you'll see an iconostasis: an altar screen covered with curtains and icons. The standard design of the iconostasis calls for four icons flanking the central door. On the right are Jesus and John the Baptist, and on the left are Mary and the Baby Jesus (together in the first panel), and then an icon featuring the saint or event that the church is dedicated to.

The iconostasis divides the lay community from the priests—the material world from the spiritual one. The spiritual heavy lifting takes place behind the iconostasis, where the priests symbolically turn bread and wine into the body and blood of Christ. Then they open the doors or curtains and serve the Eucharist to their faithful flock.

Notice that there are few (if any) pews. Worshippers stand through the service as a sign of respect (though some older parishioners sit on the seats along the walls). Traditionally, women stand on the left side, and men on the right, equally distant from the altar (because all are equal before God). The Orthodox faith tends to use a Greek cross, with four equal arms (like a plus sign, sometimes inside a circle), which focuses on God's perfection. Many Orthodox churches have Greek-cross floor plans rather than the elongated nave-and-transept designs that are common in Western Europe.

Orthodox services generally involve chanting (a dialogue that goes back and forth between the priest and the congregation), and the church is filled with the evocative aroma of incense, combining to heighten the experience for the worshippers.

Entering, let your eyes adjust to the low light. Built from 1799 to 1812 and now brilliantly restored, the cathedral seems to rival its model, St. Peter's—typical of this city so determined to be Western...only bigger and better. When Russia tunes into TV for Easter and Christmas services, the broadcast comes from this church. It's often packed with Orthodox visitors from throughout the country.

Straight ahead as you enter, appreciate the brilliant silver-arched iconostasis. Worshippers wait in a long line to kiss the church's namesake, the **Icon of Our Lady of Kazan** (left side of the iconostasis). Considered the single most important icon of the Russian Orthodox faith, the original icon was discovered by a young girl (directed by a vision of the Virgin Mary) in a tunnel beneath the city of Kazan in 1579. A monastery was erected on that site, and replicas of the icon were sent to other Russian cities—including St. Petersburg—to be venerated by the faithful. The original icon was stolen from Kazan in 1904 and went missing for nearly 100 years (it resurfaced in the Vatican and was returned to Kazan in 2005, although its authenticity has been questioned). Either way, this is a replica, but still considered holy.

The icon is important partly because it was invoked in many successful military campaigns, including the successful defense of Russia during Napoleon's 1812 invasion. (The painting above shows the icon in action as Russian soldiers liberate Moscow from a brief Polish occupation in 1612.)

In the left transept, find the statue and tomb of **Field Marshal Mikhail Kutuzov** (1745-1813), who led Russian troops during the Napoleonic conflict. On the pillars flanking the tomb up above, notice the original Napoleonic banners seized in the invasion, and the keys to the cities that Kutuzov's forces retook from Napoleon as they pushed him back to Paris.

▲▲▲Church on Spilled Blood (Спас на Крови)

This exuberantly decorative church, with its gilded carrot top of onion domes, is a must-see photo op just a short walk off Nevsky Prospekt. It's built on the place where a suicide bomber assassinated Czar

Alexander II in 1881—explaining both the evocative name and the structure's out-of-kilter relationship to the surrounding street plan. Ticket windows are on the north side of the church, facing away from Nevsky Prospekt. Go inside to appreciate the mysteriously dim interior, slathered with vivid mosaics.

Cost and Hours: 250 R, Thu-Tue 10:30-18:00, closed Wed; may be open later May-Sept (likely until 22:30) for 350 R; last entry 30 minutes before closing, audioguide-100 R, Kanal Griboyedova 2b, tel. 315-1636, http://eng.cathedral.ru.

ST. PETERSBURG

Background: Begun just after Alexander's assassination but not finished until 1907, the church is built in a neo-Russian, Historicist style. That means that its designers created a building that was a romantic, self-conscious, fairy-tale image of their own national history and traditions—similar to Neuschwanstein Castle in Bavaria. Psychologically, it seems fitting that the Romanovs, as they fought a rising tide of people power and modernity, would build a church as old school and traditionally Russian as their policies and approach to governance.

Alexander II, called "the Great Reformer," freed the serfs in 1861. He gave them land—but expected them to pay for it. The dumbfounded peasants responded by rioting, and the seeds of proletariat discontent were planted. (In this way, Alexander's liberal reforms unwittingly gave rise to the movements that would ultimately decapitate the dynasty.) Memorial plaques around the church exterior (translated in English) list Alexander's many reforms.

Jaw-droppingly beautiful as it was, the church had a short life as a place of worship. The very theme of the church—honoring an assassinated czar—was against what the Bolsheviks stood for, so it was looted with gusto during the 1917 Russian Revolution. To add insult to injury, during the communist era, the church was used for storing potatoes, and the streets around it were named for Alexander's assassins. (Out of about 300 churches in the city, only four continued to function during Soviet times.) The Church on Spilled Blood was damaged in World War II, when its crypt did duty as a morgue. Restored in the 1990s, today it serves mostly as a museum.

Visiting the Church: Enter the church and look up; Christ gazes down at you from the top of the dome, bathed in light from the windows and ringed by the gold balcony railing. The walls are covered with exquisite mosaics (nothing is painted) that show how Orthodoxy continues the artistic traditions of early Christianity. Walk up to the iconostasis (the partition at mid-church). Typically made of wood, this one is of marble, with inlaid doors. In the back of the church, the canopy shows an exposed bit of the cobbled street, marking the spot where Czar Alexander II was mortally wounded—where the czar's blood was spilled. Glass cases to the left show the painstaking restoration work.

ST. PETERSBURG

▲▲St. Isaac's Cathedral (Исаакиевский Собор)

The gold dome of St. Isaac's glitters at the end of Malaya Morskaya Ulitsa, not far from the Admiralty. St. Isaac's was built

between 1818 and 1858, and its Neoclassical exterior reminds Americans of the US Capitol building. Although the patriarch resides in Moscow, this is considered the leading church in the Russian Orthodox world.

Cost and Hours: Interior/ "museum"—250 R, Thu-Tue 10:30-18:00, May-Sept may be open later (likely until 22:30) for 350 R, closed Wed year-round; roof ("colonnade")—150 R, daily 10:30-18:00, May-Oct may be open until 22:30—or even later during "White Nights"; last entry 30 minutes before closing, Isaakievskaya pl. 4, tel. 315-9732, http://eng.cathedral.ru.

Getting Tickets: Bypass the line at the ticket window by using the machines (in English, bills only—no coins). When the main ticket window takes breaks, you can buy tickets at the group window around the corner, or at the machines.

Visiting the Church: Before entering, take a minute to appreciate the facade. The granite steps and one-piece granite columns were shipped here from a Finnish quarry 150 miles away. (Massive stonework like this, the grand embankments, and promenades throughout the city date from Catherine the Great's rule.) The enormous building sits upon swampy land, which challenged the French architect and required a huge stone foundation.

The **interior** has a few exhibits, but ultimately it's all about the grand space. Find the case in the nave showing models of the three churches that stood here before this one. Then simply appreciate the massive scale of this church— by some measures, the fourth-largest in Christendom. Notice the grand iconostasis, with its malachite veneer columns. Because the brutal winter weather is tough on paintings, most of what looks like paintings in the church are actually mosaics, which date from the first half of the 19th century. The large mosaic panels at ground level, while made to replace canvas versions on the walls and in the dome, remain parked on the floor.

A photo display shows how, during the "Great Patriotic War" (World War II), this church's crypt protected many of the Hermitage treasures. Today, aside from a small side chapel that was reconsecrated in 1994 (at the left end of the iconostasis), this building is not a functioning house of worship—it's technically a museum.

It's worthwhile to climb the colonnade stairway to the roof (262 steps) for the view. Every tenth step (heading up and down) is numbered in a countdown to your goal.

Nearby Sights: Between St. Isaac's Cathedral and the river stands one of the most evocative monuments in the city: the **Bronze Horseman.** This huge statue of a horseback Peter the Great stands atop a massive and symbolic rock inscribed, simply, "From Catherine II to Peter I, 1782." In 1782, Catherine the Great—who followed the reforms and approach to ruling of her predecessor—honored Peter with this monument. Famously mistranslated as "the Copper Cowboy," the Bronze Horseman sits atop a massive granite rock (dubbed the "Thunder Rock"). Moved here some eight miles from the Finnish Gulf, the enormous boulder originally sat in the legendary spot where Peter envisioned his gateway to the West. Many believe the Thunder Rock was a pagan stone sacred to Finnish tribes. By using the stone for this monument to Peter, considered the "great creator," Catherine was celebrating how Peter conquered the pagan world and nature.

A long block west of St. Isaac's is the **State Museum of the History of Religion** (Музей истории религии). This was the "Museum of Atheism" collection that filled the Kazan Cathedral during Soviet times. Curators were given great latitude to collect artifacts that reflect the place of religion and spiritual values in societies—things that communist leaders assumed would someday be regarded as curiosities of a bygone time (like the fetuses-in-jars of Peter the Great's Kunstkamera—see page 81). Since the end of communism, the collection has been moved to this big, dusty building, where you can see items representing a huge range of world faiths—from rough, hand-hewn pagan idols, to ancient Greek temple replicas, to glittering Orthodox icons. English information is sparse—borrow the English laminated sheets, or spring for the audioguide. It's worth a visit only for those with a special interest (300 R, free on Mon; Thu-Mon 10:00-18:00, Tue 13:00-19:00, closed Wed, audioguide-100 R, last entry one hour before closing, Pochtamtskaya 14, www.gmir.ru).

ST. PETERSBURG

▲Alexander Nevsky Lavra Monastery
(Александро-Невской Лавры)

Farther from the city center, this religious complex (a *lavra* is a special category of monastery) is of more interest to Russian Orthodox pilgrims than to curious sightseers. But it's famous, important, and offers a glimpse at a less touristy church complex than those downtown. Its park-like cemeteries and grounds offer a break from the bustle of the city.

Cost and Hours: You'll pay 130 R to enter the central zone of the complex but can visit the cathedral for free. The various cemeteries officially belong to the State Museum of Urban Sculpture, which charges a 200-R entrance fee. The grounds are open daily 6:00-23:00; the main church closes at 19:00, and other sights have shorter hours.

Getting There: It's easy to reach on the Metro—simply ride the green or orange line to the Ploschad Aleksandra Nevskogo stop.

Visiting the Monastery: From the Metro stop, cross the busy road to the yellow, green-domed Gateway Church. Passing through here, you'll follow a cobbled walkway that's flanked by walled cemeteries. On the right is the **Necropolis of Artists** (a.k.a. Tikhvin Cemetery), where you'll find the graves of Dostoyevsky, Tchaikovsky, and other Russian notables (to visit the cemetery, look for the "искусств" sign; 200 R to enter, posted map in Russian only but big names are individually signposted in English). On the left is the **Necropolis of the 18th Century** (a.k.a. Lazarev Cemetery), with military heroes, politicians, and other VIPs (covered by the same 200-R ticket).

Then you'll proceed straight ahead across the bridge and into the monastery complex. Looking around the walled complex, notice that each corner of the main courtyard is anchored—like a medieval watchtower—by a turreted steeple. Like many religious sites in Russia, this one was badly neglected during communism, and restoration work is ongoing. You'll stroll through a restful garden and along a large, heavily wooded cemetery known as the **Communist Plot** (no pun intended). After the Bolshevik Revolution made Russia an atheistic state, fallen heroes of that revolution—including Eino Rahja, Lenin's close associate—were interred here, as if to drive home the victory of communism over faith.

Looming up at the center of the complex is the yellow **Holy Trinity Cathedral,** with a Catholic-feeling Baroque interior (dating from Catherine the Great's time). Inside, in the right transept under a red-velvet canopy, is the silver sarcophagus of Alexander Nevsky—the 13th-century saint who defended Russia from would-be invaders. (While this cathedral was supposedly built on the site of Nevsky's most famous battle, contemporary historians believe it took place elsewhere. Nevsky's original, even more elaborate sarcophagus is now on display in the Hermitage.) To the left of the main altar, look for the icon called "She Who Is Quick To Hear." It's an icon of Mary (in its own frame, with a semicircular top) in a red tunic, holding her right hand open in an offer of divine help. It's believed that this icon is particularly receptive to prayerful requests; observe the long line of the faithful patiently waiting to press their foreheads against it.

Behind the cathedral is the even larger **Nikolskoe Cemetery,** with later (largely 20th-century) graves of Russian luminaries.

SIGHTS NORTH OF THE NEVA RIVER

From the waterfront side of the Hermitage, you can spot several sights across the river that are worth visiting. But you'll have to allow plenty of time; while these places appear close, it takes a while to reach them by foot.

▲▲Strelka Spin-Tour

To reach the Peter and Paul Fortress from the Hermitage, you'll cross the Dvortsovy Bridge and then pass a strategic viewpoint, called Strelka. For a sweep-ing 360-degree view of St. Petersburg's core, head down to the park that fills the knob of land at water level (between the two pink columns).

You're standing on a cor-ner of the large **Vasilyevsky Island**—one of the many islands that make up St. Petersburg. (A nickname for the town is "City on 101 Islands," although an official count is elusive.)

Literally meaning "Little Arrow," **Strelka** sticks out into the very heart of the Neva River and St. Petersburg. The park filling the point is one of the sites around town where newlyweds are practically obligated to come for wedding pictures. They toast with champagne, then break their glasses against the big granite ball (watch your step).

To begin your spin-tour, face the can't-miss-it **Hermitage,** just across the Neva—the Winter Palace of the czars and today a world-class art museum. The sprawling complex has several wings:

ST. PETERSBURG

the main green-and-white structure, as well as the yellow and mint-green sections beyond it. No wonder it could take days to fully see the place.

Now begin spinning to the left. The Art Nouveau **Trinity Bridge** (Troitsky Most)—one of St. Petersburg's longest and most beautiful—was built in 1903, its design having beat out a submission by Gustav Eiffel. Before the 1850s, no permanent bridges spanned the Neva; one crossed only on pontoon bridges (in the summer) or a frozen river (in winter). It wasn't unusual for St. Petersburgers to get stranded while waiting for a deep freeze or a thaw. Just beyond the bridge (on its right end), you can faintly see the trees marking the delightful **Summer Garden**—the private garden for Peter the Great's cute little Summer Palace, and now a public park and a wonderful place for a warm-weather stroll (for details, see page 68).

On the left side of the river, you'll see the stoutly walled **Peter and Paul Fortress,** with its slender golden spire (for details, see page 82). St. Petersburg was born here in 1703, when Peter the Great began building this fortress to secure territory he had won in battle with the Swedes. Are there any sunbathers on the sandy beach out front?

Scanning the waterfront, think for a moment about how strategic this location is, at the mouth of the Neva River. Although very short (only 42 miles), the Neva is an essential link in a vital series of shipping waterways. It connects the Gulf of Finland to Lake Lagoda, which feeds (via a network of canals) into Russia's "mother river," the Volga—Europe's longest river, which cuts north-to-south through the Russian heartland all the way to the Caspian Sea. A series of Soviet-era shipping canals connects the Volga to the Moskva River, the Black Sea, and the Danube. That makes the Neva the outlet for all Russian waterways to all of Europe and beyond. In other words, you could sail from Iran to Volgograd to Istanbul to Budapest to Moscow to Lisbon—but you would have to go through St. Petersburg.

Turning farther left, you'll spot the first of the two giant, pink **rostral columns** that flank the Strelka viewpoint. Inspired by similar towers built by ancient Greeks and Romans to celebrate naval victories, these columns are decorated with anchors and studded with the symbolic prows of ships defeated in battle. Once topped by gaslights (now electric), the pillars trumpet St. Petersburg's nautical heritage. (A similar column stands in the middle of New York City's Columbus Circle.) Facing Strelka is the white-columned **Old Stock Exchange,** bordered by yellow warehouses.

Just to the left, the turreted pastel-blue building is Peter the Great's **Kunstkamera,** a sort of ethnographical museum built around the czar's original collection (described next).

"Kunstkamera" and "Hermitage" are both European words and concepts that Peter the Great imported to class up his new, European-style capital.

Circling a bit farther to the left, the yellow buildings at the end of the bridge (just right of the Hermitage) are the **Admiralty,** the geographical center of St. Petersburg and the headquarters of Peter the Great's imperial navy.

• *Now that you're oriented, take your pick of the following sights: You can head one direction to the Kunstkamera, or the other to the Peter and Paul Fortress and beyond.*

▲**Kunstkamera** (Кунсткамера)

Peter the Great, who fancied himself a scientist, founded this—the first state public museum in Russia—in 1714. He filled it with his

personal collections, consisting of "fish, reptiles, and insects in bottles," scientific instruments, and books from his library. In the 19th century, Russian travelers returning from the Americas added a rich array of artifacts—and, amazingly, those original collections remain in this same building. The anthropological and ethnographic collections include the best exhibit on northern Native Americans that you'll find on this side of the Atlantic. While many tourists dismiss the Kunstkamera as a "museum of curiosities," locals are proud of its scientific tradition and its impressive collections.

Cost and Hours: 250 R; Tue-Sun 11:00-19:00, closed Mon and last Tue of month, last entry at 18:00; Universitetskaya Naberezhnaya 3, enter around the left side as you face the steeple from the riverfront; tel. 328-1412, www.kunstkamera.ru.

Visiting the Museum: While the displays are quite old-fashioned, there's ample English information. There are two floors (plus the tower) of mostly geographically arranged exhibits: North America, Japan, and Sub-Saharan Africa on **level 1,** and the rest of Asia, India, the Middle East, Polynesia, and temporary exhibits on **level 2.** For each culture, you'll see clothing, tools, ceremonial objects, models of traditional houses and vessels, and photography.

But most tourists are drawn to the **"First Scientific Collections of the Kunstkamera"** (on level 2)—especially Peter's stomach-turning exhibit on teratology, the study of deformities: a grand hall packed with jars of two-headed human fetuses pickled in formaldehyde, a double-headed calf, skeletons of a human giant and conjoined twins, and Peter the Great's own death mask and personal effects. Not for the faint of heart, this might be Europe's most offbeat—and nauseating—sight. As strange and titillating as it seems, this collection is based in sound science: Peter wanted to understand the scientific underpinnings of deformity to dispel the small-minded superstitions of his subjects.

Finally, climb to the top floor for a peek at the venerable **meeting room** of the St. Petersburg Academy of Scientists, with lots of historic artifacts. This temple of reason recreates the atmosphere of a scientific institution of the 18th century. Basking in this space, appreciate the idealism of Peter the Great, whose drive to introduce a European-style Age of Reason in his very traditional homeland was the impetus for the creation of this museum—and of St. Petersburg itself.

▲▲Peter and Paul Fortress (Петропавловская Крепость)

Founded by Peter the Great in 1703 during the Great Northern War with Sweden, this fortress on an island in the Neva was the

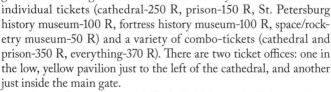

birthplace of St. Petersburg. Its gold steeple catches the sunlight, and its blank walls face the Winter Palace across the river. While it's a large complex, the most important parts are easy to see quickly: Wander the grounds, dip into the cathedral to visit the tombs of the Romanovs, and maybe do a little sunbathing on the beach. For those wanting to delve into history, the grounds also have museums about city history, space exploration, and the famous-to-Russians former prison.

Cost: It's free to enter and explore the grounds. The sights inside are covered by individual tickets (cathedral-250 R, prison-150 R, St. Petersburg history museum-100 R, fortress history museum-100 R, space/rocketry museum-50 R) and a variety of combo-tickets (cathedral and prison-350 R, everything-370 R). There are two ticket offices: one in the low, yellow pavilion just to the left of the cathedral, and another just inside the main gate.

Hours: Grounds open daily 6:00-22:00; cathedral and prison daily 10:00-19:00, last entry 30 minutes before closing; smaller museums Thu-Mon 11:00-19:00, Tue 11:00-18:00, closed Wed.

Tours and Information: The 250-R audioguide provides more information (www.spbmuseum.ru). You'll find pay WCs scattered around the grounds.

Getting There: Footbridges at either end of the fortress's island (Hare Island/Zayachy Ostrov) connect it to the rest of St. Petersburg. Getting there is easy: Just set your sights on the skinny golden spire. The main entrance is through the park from the Gorkovskaya Metro station. The other entrance is at the west end—a scenic, 20-minute walk from Palace Square and the Hermitage. Cross the bridge (Dvortsovy Most) by the Hermitage, angle right past the Strelka viewpoint (worth a quick stop to enjoy the view—described earlier), then cross the next bridge (Birzhevoy Most), turn right, and follow the waterline to a footbridge leading to the fortress' side entrance.

Background: There's been a fortress here as long as there's been a St. Petersburg. When he founded the city, in 1703, this was the first thing Peter the Great built to defend this strategic meeting point of the waterways of Russia and the Baltic. Originally the center of town was just east of here (near the preserved log cabin where Peter the Great briefly resided).

Self-Guided Tour: Pick up a map when you buy your ticket to navigate the sprawling complex. Begin at the cathedral, marked by the golden spire.

Sts. Peter and Paul Cathedral: The centerpiece of the fortress and—until modern times—the tallest building in the city, this church is the final resting place of the Romanov czars, who ruled Russia from 1613 through 1917.

The cathedral was designed by a Swiss-Italian architect who, like so many others, was imported by Peter the Great to introduce European culture to Russia. With the Bolshevik Revolution in 1917, mobs of workers and sailors ransacked the place—taking out their anger against the Romanov dynasty, desecrating the tombs, and looting everything they could. It's been a museum since 1922, and was extensively renovated in the last decade. Today, people are understandably caught up in the allure of the glamorous Romanov dynasty: White-marble monuments mark the graves of czars and czarinas, who are buried 10 feet below floor level.

Entering the church, pick up a floor plan identifying each member of the dynasty. I'll cover just a few highlights.

Start by facing the main altar, with its glittering iconostasis and its traditional Orthodox imagery painted in the Russian Baroque style. From here we'll circle clockwise to visit the most important tombs. The tombs to the right (as you face the altar) include perhaps the two greatest czars. On the right, in front, is **Peter the Great** (1672-1725). Marked by his bronze bust, the founder of the city was the first czar to be buried here. He's surrounded by other 18th-century rulers, including **Catherine II "the Great"** (1729-1796, back left).

Now turn 180 degrees and walk straight back to the opposite end of the church. To the left of the entry door is a small chapel containing the tombs of the much-romanticized family of the final Romanov czar: **Nicholas II** (1868-1918), his wife, Alexandra, and their four daughters and one son. The czar abdicated in

March 1917, and was imprisoned with the rest of his family. The Bolsheviks murdered them all on the night of July 16, 1918. The family was shot at point-blank range with handguns. Because the daughters had diamonds sewn into their dresses, some of the bullets deflected at crazy angles—to be sure they were dead, the assassins bayoneted them. Originally buried in an unmarked grave, the remains of most of the family members were only rediscovered in 1991, and reburied here in 1998.

Persistent legends surround the fate of the Romanov daughter **Anastasia,** who was rumored to have escaped the execution. In the decades since the massacre, different women emerged claiming to be the long-lost Anastasia—most famously Anna Anderson, who turned up in Berlin in the 1920s. But very recent DNA testing has positively identified the remains of the real Anastasia (found only in 2007 and now interred here), while similar tests disproved Anderson's claim.

In the middle of the church, about a third of the way from the main door to the iconostasis, on the left, is **Maria Fedorovna** (1847-1928). This popular Danish princess (known as Dagmar in her native land) moved from Copenhagen to St. Petersburg, married the second-to-the-last czar (Alexander III, next white tomb), gave birth to the last czar (Nicholas II), and fled the October Revolution to live in exile in Denmark. After her death, she was buried with her fellow Danish royals at Roskilde Cathedral; in 2006, her remains were brought back here with great fanfare to join her adopted clan. Hers is one of the most popular graves in the church.

History Exhibit: Exit through the gift shop (to the left of the main altar), but before leaving, turn right from the shop into a hall with a visual and well-described history of the church and the Romanov dynasty, complete with a family tree and portraits. At the end of this corridor is a collection of tombs of other Romanovs including late 20th-century family members—grand dukes and grand duchesses—reminding us that many Romanov cousins long outlived their ancestors.

Tower Climb: To climb the spire for a grand view, find the stairs and buy a special 150-R ticket just inside the cathedral entry.

The Grounds: Strolling the grounds, you'll get an up-close look at the stout brick wall surrounding the island. From the cathedral, head out through the gateway for a peek at the river. You can also circle around the fortress exterior to find the delightful sandy beach huddled alongside the wall—an understandably popular place for St. Petersburgers to sunbathe on balmy days, and for newlyweds to snap wedding portraits.

There are two ways to **climb up onto the wall** encircling the fortress. The "Neva Curtain Wall" (facing away from the river) is included in the comprehensive combo-ticket; the more scenic "Neva Panorama" (on the river side) has a separate 250-R ticket.

Trubetskoy Bastion Prison: The czars incarcerated political prisoners here in the late 19th and early 20th centuries. While famous among Russians as the place that held many of its revolutionaries, it's difficult for most Americans to appreciate. You'll wind your way through long, somber hallways past cells marked with plaques (in Russian and English) identifying former inmates. You may recognize

the names of Fyodor Dostoyevsky, Leon Trotsky, Maxim Gorky, and Lenin's brother, Alexander Ulyanov. The Soviets closed the prison, disdaining it as a symbol of czarist oppression, and then made it a museum in the 1920s.

More Official Museums: Three other museums are worth considering for those fascinated by St. Petersburg's past. The **History of St. Petersburg, 1703-1918** exhibit, in the Commandant's House, fills two floors with an excellent, chronological survey of this grand city, displaying artifacts, maps, models, paintings, and costumes—but with minimal English. It's engaging if you already know a bit of local history, but otherwise challenging to appreciate. The **History of the Peter and Paul Fortress** exhibit features old architectural drawings and maps, a replica of the angel weathervane that tops the cathedral spire, and some English descriptions. And the forgotten **Museum of Space Exploration and Rocket Technology** is a surprisingly extensive collection honoring the ingenuity that allowed this nation to kick off the space race with the 1957 launch of Sputnik (a replica of which you'll see here). There are old photos of scientists, newspaper headlines, desks and lab equipment, rocket bases, and space capsules—but virtually no English information.

Unofficial Attractions: The fortress grounds are scattered with tacky, privately run attractions: a miniatures museum, furniture collection, medieval torture exhibit, the "secrets of Da Vinci," and so on (each with its own ticket and hours). Geared toward Russian tourists, these have less historical oomph than the sights noted earlier.

▲Museum of Russian Political History
(Музея политической истории России)

This is the city's best exhibit about Russia's communist period. Across the moat from the Peter and Paul Fortress, it's partly housed in a mansion where Lenin had an office, and sprawls through several attached buildings. The eclectic collection is best appreciated by someone with a cursory understanding of modern Russian history. The core exhibit—"Man and Power in Russia, 19th-21st Centuries"—is modern and freshly presented, employing historical artifacts, photography, archival footage, sound clips, and touchscreens. Some English information is posted, and you can borrow descriptions in most exhibits, but it's worth investing in one of the audioguides (each with a different focus—ask about your options).

Cost and Hours: 150 R, Fri-Tue 10:00-18:00, Wed 10:00-20:00, closed Thu and last Mon of month, last entry one hour before closing, audioguides-200 R each, Kuybysheva 2-4 but enter around the corner facing the park at Kronverkskiy Prospekt 1, tel. 233-7052, www.polithistory.ru.

Visiting the Museum: As you enter, pick up a floor plan and start with the core exhibit. On the ground floor, the story kicks off with Czar Alexander II's freeing of the serfs in 1861. This gave Russian peasants personal freedom and an allotment of land—but they were obligated to pay for it. Saddled with indebtedness for land that most felt was rightfully theirs, defiant serfs reacted with acts of rebellion, creating a fertile breeding ground for the principles of communism.

Upstairs, the story continues with the Bolshevik Revolution, civil war, and Stalin's Great Terror of 1937-1938 (liquidation of independent farms, mass executions, and 1.7 million arrests). Khrushchev's "Secret Speech" to the Soviet politburo in 1956 dismantled Stalin's odious legacy, and Gorbachev's introduction of *glasnost* and *perestroika* in the 1980s brought the Soviet Union farther out from the shadows. You'll see Gorbachev's televised 1985 speech acknowledging the failings of the communist economy, and the stunning New Year's Eve 1999 announcement that Vladimir Putin was taking over the government from Boris Yeltsin. From this floor, you can cross into the attached mansion to see Lenin's office, with a painting of him addressing the crowds from this room's balcony. Other side exhibits (some in Russian only) delve into other facets of the 20th- and 21st-century Russian experience. For example, back on the ground floor, halls 1-9 are a confusing labyrinth of USSR-era propaganda, and replicas of home interiors from that age—from a humble cottage to an urban flat.

Nearby: Next door to the museum, look for St. Petersburg's huge and impressive **mosque**. Remember that Russia is a sprawling, multiethnic nation, where more than 6 percent of the population is Muslim. Built in the early 1910s, the building was converted into a warehouse under communism, but has since been restored.

▲Peter the Great's Log Cabin

The oldest surviving building in St. Petersburg is the log cabin that served as Peter's first "palace" when he arrived to oversee the building of his great city in 1703. (He was only Peter I then, not becoming "Great" until 1721.) Peter was fighting Sweden (then a major European power), and with the foundation of St. Petersburg here, on former Swedish soil, he was making it clear: This was Russia...and Russia now had a gateway to the Baltic Sea, and thus to Europe. All the buildings in the original settlement in the swamp were made of wood. This one (actually a log cabin contained within a bigger, modern brick structure, in a tidy riverfront park) is just six sparsely, yet evocatively, furnished rooms with an attached exhibit on the birth of St. Petersburg.

Cost and Hours: 200 R, Wed and Fri-Mon 10:00-18:00, Thu 13:00-21:00, closed Tue, Petrovskaya Naberezhnaya 6, tel. 232-4576.

▲Cruiser Aurora

The Soviet Union created a thrilling and inspirational mythology about the revolution that created it. According to popular history, that uprising kicked off with a shot from the battleship *Aurora*, a signal to revolutionaries to storm the Winter Palace. Usually positioned on the Petrogradskaya embankment, the Aurora is currently under renovation elsewhere in the city until sometime in 2016). State-of-the-art when built about 1900, the Aurora fought in the Russo-Japanese War (1904-1905). Later, its guns defended Leningrad during the Nazi siege in World War II; when it looked like the Germans might take the city, the Soviets sunk the Aurora rather than let this relic of the Revolution fall into their hands. After the war, the much-adored ship was salvaged and substantially rebuilt. It's remained a symbol of the Revolution with an almost religious significance for pilgrims from throughout Russia. This is a first stop for many Russians touring St. Petersburg, and it's fun to make the scene here with them. The gun on the bow with the brass plaque tells the story. When it returns to the Petrogradskaya embankment, the cruiser will likely open for tours once again (for details, see www.aurora.org.ru).

METRO SIGHTS

While most visitors to St. Petersburg stick to the big central sights, some of the most interesting landmarks are just an easy Metro ride away.

Uprising Square
(Metro: Ploshchad Vosstaniya/Red and Green Lines)

This intimidatingly gigantic transit hub is a showcase of Russia's bigger-is-better city planning aesthetic. Admire the round subway-

Peter the Great

Every so often, an individual comes along who revolutionizes an entire people. While Russia has had more than its share of those figures, perhaps the most dynamic and influential was Peter the Great.

During the four decades he ruled Russia (1682-1725), Czar Peter I transformed his country into a major European power.

Even more self-assured than your average monarch, Peter gave himself the nickname "Peter the Great"—and it stuck. He stood well over six feet tall, and he ruled Russia with a towering power and determination. Full of confidence and charm, Peter mixed easily with all classes of people and at times even dressed cheaply and spoke crudely.

Peter grew up at court in Moscow. In a formative episode, the newly crowned, 10-year-old Peter witnessed a bloody palace coup that sidelined him in a co-rulership for years. But Peter's exile put him in proximity to Moscow's German community, a source of bold new ideas that jolted his worldview. He was particularly taken with the Protestant work ethic, and was fascinated by the idea that humans could conquer nature. He saw this mindset as a refreshing antidote for the fatalistic Russian Orthodox outlook.

Peter came into his own as sole ruler in 1689, and quickly began making up for lost time. He became the first czar in a century to travel to Europe in peacetime, making an epic journey to

station entryway—classically Soviet in design. Moskovsky train station across the square is the architectural twin of St. Petersburg Station in Moscow. (Locals joke that, after too much vodka, many have stepped out in the other city and thought they'd never left home.)

On top of the big building facing the station, a sign still reads **Город-Герой Ленинград** ("Hero City Leningrad")—a tribute to the residents of this city—then called Leningrad—who withstood a nearly 900-day Nazi siege. The star-topped obelisk in the center of the traffic circle also commemorates the "Hero City." (In Soviet times, star-tipped spires like this were centerpieces of cities throughout Eastern Europe.) Even though the city is now officially "St. Petersburg," the name "Leningrad" is still used when referring to the siege out of respect to the people whose valor and suffering saved the city. Each May 9 (the date World War II ended), you'll see hammers, sickles, and the word Leningrad (Ленинград) all over St. Petersburg.

The **Ploshchad Vosstaniya Metro station** itself is a great example of the decorative art that enforced an esprit de corps dur-

Holland and England, great maritime powers from whom Peter wanted to learn everything he could about shipbuilding, technology, navigation, and seamanship. He even went undercover for a stint in an Amsterdam shipyard, sleeping in a humble cupboard bed.

Upon his return, Peter began implementing reforms to give Russia a fresh start. To encourage his subjects to be more enterprising, he created a 14-level "table of ranks," designed to reward hard work rather than simple hereditary. He did away with symbols of the old world, such as long beards, literally shaving the beards right off of his advisors' faces.

Internationally, Peter the Great refashioned Russia's army to resemble Western models, and he founded the Russian navy. He started the Great Northern War with Sweden to ensure that Russia would have access to the Baltic Sea for trade and strategic purposes. He built an entirely new capital in St. Petersburg and established a shipbuilding industry there. He reorganized the government and introduced new taxes to support his foreign policy.

Although Peter is revered by many Russians today, his reign was not without scandal. A heavy drinker with a short temper, Peter was known to lash out against even his closest advisors. He had his own son killed and exiled his first wife to a convent.

Despite his cruelties, Peter left a positive imprint on Russian history. When Peter took the throne, Russia was a backwater, stuck in the Middle Ages. By the time he died, his country had become a European powerhouse.

ing Soviet times. The Metro—started in the 1930s, interrupted by World War II, and completed in the 1950s—has a kind of time-warp feel. Enjoy this station's circa-1952 art lining the tracks deep underground, with bronze reliefs stoking the mythology of Lenin and the Revolution. See if you can find a rare surviving Stalin (most depictions of him were purged throughout the communist world after his death and the denunciation of his reign of terror).

▲Lenin Square (Metro: Ploshchad Lenina/Red Line)

Soviet history fans love this square across the Neva, marked by a dramatic **statue of Lenin** erected in 1925, just a year after his death. The square and statue stand in front of the Finlandsky train station, where Lenin arrived home on April 3, 1917, after years of political exile.

Imagine the intrigue: During Lenin's exile in various European capitals, the Germans supported him, knowing he was like a revolutionary time bomb that would one day explode in the heart of their enemy, Russia. During the height of World War I, Germany transferred Lenin back to Russia in a diplomatically sealed train—with millions in gold to fund the revolution that the Germans hoped would cripple the Russian war machine.

When Lenin arrived, the czar had just abdicated, leaving an overwhelmed and clueless provisional government. The Bolsheviks declared their own government, creating two parallel governments. The stage was set for revolution. Lenin immediately prepared his "April Theses"—which, like Mao's Little Red Book, became a cult volume among his followers. Something of a how-to for successful revolution, this collection of speeches and principles laid out Lenin's vision for seizing power.

Don't miss the towering mosaic of Lenin in the exit hall of the Metro station. Lenin's return and role in the Bolshevik Revolution was embellished and pumped up for propaganda purposes, becoming part of the Bible-like lore of Soviet society.

▲Monument to the Heroic Defenders of Leningrad (Metro: Moskavskaya/Blue Line)

This monument is located in the middle of a huge traffic roundabout, where people arriving from the airport are forced to see it—and remember the sacrifice this city made during World War II. It's hard to imagine the horror, suffering, and importance of the Siege of Leningrad, also known as "The Battle of 900 Days." Hitler intended to literally wipe the city off the map...and the people of Leningrad knew it. The city survived, and May 9, 1945, was Victory Day. To mark the 30th anniversary of that victory, on May 9, 1975, this stirring monument was inaugurated. The 160-foot-tall granite obelisk with the dates *1941-1945* marks the spot where the USSR's 300,000-strong, ragtag, mostly volunteer army held the line—facing off against 700,000 Nazi troops at the edge of the city. In the sculpture at its base (called *The Victors*), a worker stands by a soldier. In the two sculptural groups flanking the obelisk, it may be soldiers who are leading the charge, but everyone pitches in—civilians make artillery shells, carry beams, and bid farewell to their soldier sons. Standing strong here, on what was the front line, the monument symbolizes the unity of the people and the army in the struggle against the enemy. With the music of Shostakovich or Rachmaninoff playing, visitors ponder the nearly one million people who died defending the city. In the monument's lower level, see Leningradites cradling the bodies of their fallen comrades. Walking by 900 lamp lights (symbolizing the 900 days of suffering the battle brought), you enter an underground exhibit with a powerful 10-minute movie showing life and death during the siege.

Cost and Hours: Monument—free and always open; exhibition—120 R, open Thu, Sat, and Mon 10:00-18:00, Tue and Fri 10:00-17:00, closed Wed.

Getting There: It's a 10-minute walk from Metro: Moskavskaya (where a huge, dynamic statue of Lenin, his jacket flapping in the breeze, dominates a square in front of a hammer-and-sickle-adorned building). Exit the Metro toward the airport, then look for the monument's obelisk at the end of Moskovsky Prospekt (use the pedestrian underpasses on Moskovsky Prospekt). If you're going to the palaces at Tsarskoye Selo—you'll pass right by here on your way.

Nearby: In the 1920s and 1930s, communist authorities expected that the city center would wither and die from its overripe, post-imperial malaise. So they built this district to the south (toward Moscow), which they expected to emerge as St. Petersburg's new city center. As a part of this futuristic communist utopia, apartments in this area were originally designed without kitchens—they believed that eventually food would be prepared at a central canteen, setting women free from the "enslavement" of the family kitchen. But the canteens never came to fruition, and women ended up cooking anyway, in staggered shifts in cramped communal kitchens.

▲▲Back-Streets Walk on Vasilyevsky Island (Metro: Vasileostrovskaya/Green Line)

For a glimpse at a more authentically Russian neighborhood than many tourists see, ride the Metro to Vasileostrovskaya and follow my self-guided walk on page 38.

▲Vladimirskaya Neighborhood (Metro: Vladimirskaya/Red and Orange Lines)

The neighborhood around this Metro stop is a good one for a peek at workaday St. Petersburg. In addition to an incense-filled church, a lively market, and a museum in the home of one of the greatest Russian writers, a quick trip here lets you browse through a commercial district with very little tourism.

Vladimirskaya Church: While other churches are grander and more famous, the Church of Our Lady of Vladimir—which sits adjacent to the Metro station—is simply alive with worshippers and affords a good opportunity to see a Russian Orthodox community in action. If a service is going on, you're welcome to stand and observe. For more on Russian Orthodox churches, see page 72.

Kuznechny Market: This neighborhood market sits a half-block behind the church (facing the church, go around to the right about 50 yards and look for the clock on the wall marking the market's low-key entrance; Mon-Sat 8:00-20:00, Sun 8:00-19:00). This

Exploring Russian Famer's Markets

When visiting Russia, wandering through an authentic farmer's market (*rynok,* рынок) can be a highlight—even if you're not shopping. I've recommended a few markets that are handy to sightseeing, but not overrun by tourists: The best and most convenient is at Kuznechny Pereulok 3, across from the Vladimirskaya Metro station (see previous page); another good option is described on my "Back-Streets Walk of Vasilyevsky Island" (see page 38); and a bigger, more sprawling market zone hums around Sennaya Ploshchad (see next page).

When entering a market, survey the variety of offerings at the stands: pickled items, smoked and salted fish, honey, cheeses, fresh cream, dried fruits, spices, oils, and lots of produce (much of it trucked in from warmer-climate Central Asian republics).

In the honey (*myod,* мёд) section, a chorus line of white-aproned babushki stands ready to let you dip and test each kind (with each sample, they'll say, *Pozhaluysta*—"please"—meaning "here you go"). Russians consider honey medicinal and are connoisseurs, treating its many varieties like the French treat cheese or wine. While the

is where locals go to find everything they need to stock the fridge. Don't miss the chance to sample the honey. For tips on exploring a farmer's market like this one, see sidebar above. Just beyond the market is the Dostoyevsky Museum, described next.

Dostoyevsky Museum (Музей Ф. М. Достоевского): Although many of the furnishings are gone, a visit to this six-room apartment gives you a feel for how the famous writer lived (160 R, Tue and Thu-Sun 11:00-18:00, Wed 13:00-20:00, closed Mon, at Kuznechny Pereulok 5, one block from Metro: Vladimirskaya). The 200-R audioguide provides more background on the displayed objects, as well as general information about St. Petersburg at the turn of the 20th century.

Dostoyevsky, his second wife, and their three children lived here for the last two and a half years of his life, while he wrote *The Brothers Karamazov.* Unlike Pushkin, an aristocrat who lived in the wealthy part of town near the czar's palace, Dostoyevsky came from a middle-class background and wrote about the lives of the art of fine honey suffered through the communist age, it's still in the Russian DNA. It's fun to try the various honeys and interact with the honey maids. Smile. Buy something ($20/kilo).

Fruit sellers shout *"Molodoi chelovyek!"* (young man) and *"Devushka!"* (young lady) as they entice you toward their piles of oranges, tomatoes, cucumbers, and pears. A handy term is *polkilo* (полкило)—"half kilogram," about a pound.

In the herbs section, you can sniff massive bunches of fresh coriander (*kinza,* кинза) and wade through a lifetime supply of horseradish (*khren,* хрен). Since many herbs have similar names in English and Russian, the labeled bins provide a good opportunity to practice your Cyrillic. If you wonder about the staggering variety of pickled veggies, this is part of the vodka culture. To Russian men, pickles and vodka are inseparable.

In the meat section, you may see some lamb. While traditional Russian cuisine doesn't make use of lamb, many of the market workers are Muslim—"internal immigrants" from Central Asia and the Caucasus. Some of the tanks of fish are not for eating: Live sturgeon produce black caviar (a small tin goes for $180/100 grams—that's $1,180/kilo). Red caviar is the budget choice ($120/kilo, or $12/small tin). Also in the fish section, you'll typically find display cases with fragrant smoked fish.

And finally, clinging to the market's perimeter are little cottage-industry shops that fill a practical, if unglamorous, niche—get your remote control fixed, cheap.

poor—the writer himself was constantly short of money (he shifted around to as many as 20 different places in St. Petersburg, trying to stay afloat).

The museum appeals to Dostoyevsky fans, or to anyone curious to see a middle-class, late-19th-century apartment. Visiting is quick and simple. Black display cases contain lots of old photos and original editions of the author's books. Photos and etchings provide historical context for Dostoyevsky's era. You'll also visit the family's "memorial flat." In the study, you'll see the writer's desk, hat, cup of tea, and a clock permanently stopped at the hour of his death.

Sennoy Market and Dostoyevsky Neighborhood (Metro: Spasskaya, Sadovaya, and Sennaya Ploshchad/ Purple, Orange, and Blue Lines)

There's only one place in St. Petersburg where three Metro lines meet, and the vast square where the stations empty out (called Sennaya Ploshchad) is the site of one of the city's biggest markets. In the old days, Sennoy Market—literally "Hay Market"—was where livestock were sold. Today it's filled with modern, workaday shops and market stalls. Delving into the surrounding streets, you'll find vendors from all over Russia and neighboring regions—especially the Caucasus and Central Asia—selling exotic goods. More chaotic and less convenient than some of the smaller neighborhood markets I describe, this could be a rewarding stroll for adventurous picnic-shoppers.

The surrounding area is sometimes called the "Dostoyevsky Neighborhood." For a time, the young Dostoyevsky lived near here, just across the canal from the bustling square and market zone. Much of *Crime and Punishment* is set in these streets, making it a popular area for Dostoyevsky pilgrims to explore.

▲Ornate Metro Stations

In the idealistic communist days, a few Metro stations were hand-picked to be highly decorated, in an attempt to bring some sorely needed opulence to the masses. Often, the decor has themes from the communist era (work on the system started in the 1940s). While Moscow has the most remarkable Metro stations, St. Petersburg has a few palatial examples. The best is **Avtovo** (Автово), with crystal chandeliers, stirring mosaics, and stately columns. **Pushkinskaya** (Пушкинская) is sleeker, with dramatic lighting effects that draw your gaze to a statue of the great Russian writer. **Kirovsky Zavod** (Кировский Завод) has an elegantly dark-hued atmosphere, with stout, gray marble columns, checkered floors, and a stern bust of Lenin. **Narvskaya** (Нарвская) has more of a communist bent, with sleek marble-clad walls, reliefs celebrating workers and soldiers, and lots of stylized hammers and sickles.

OUTER ST. PETERSBURG

While the following sights are well worth a visit, they're out on the edge of town and time-consuming to reach. On a one- or two-day visit, focus on sights in the city center instead. But with a third day or a special interest, the trek to outer St. Petersburg is rewarding.

With limited time, visiting both Peterhof and Tsarskoye Selo is overkill. If choosing between them, consider these factors: **Peterhof** is easier to reach (thanks to a handy, if pricey, hydrofoil connection from downtown). While its palace interior is small and less thrilling, Peterhof does boast particularly grand gardens, with canals, waterfalls, and fountains populated by gilded statues. **Tsarskoye Selo** is a bit trickier to reach by public transit, but its palaces and parks are stunning—especially the Catherine Palace, with a peerless interior that includes the famously sumptuous Amber Room.

▲▲Peterhof (Петергоф)

Peter the Great's lavish palace at Peterhof (sometimes still called by its communist name, Petrodvorets/Петродворец) sits along the Gulf of Finland west of the city. With glorious gardens, this is Russia's Versailles and the target of many tour groups and travel poster photographers. Promenade along the grand canal, which runs through landscaped grounds from the boat dock up to the terraced fountains in front of the palace. You can visit the museum inside the palace if you want, but it's more fun to stay outdoors. Children love to run past the trick fountains—sometimes they splash you, sometimes they don't.

Cost and Hours: Park—500 R, open daily in summer 9:00-20:00, last entry 17:45; Grand Palace museum—550 R, Tue-Sun 10:30-18:00, until 19:00 in summer, closed Mon, May-mid-Oct open longer hours on Sat (10:00-21:00, last entry at 19:45); audioguide-500 R, www.peterhofmuseum.ru. Consider investing in the good 100-R guide-booklet that helps you locate each fountain.

Getting There: In summer, "Meteor" **hydrofoils,** run by competing companies, leave for Peterhof from docks to either side of the busy bridge by the Hermitage (first boat leaves around 10:00 and every 30 minutes thereafter, last boat returns from Peterhof at 18:00—or at 18:30 or 19:00 in summer, ask before you buy your ticket), 30-40-minute trip, 650-700 R one way, 1,100-1,200 R roundtrip, plus 500 R entry to the palace grounds; hydrofoils stop running in even mildly strong winds). Of the hydrofoil companies, only one has a good English website (www.peterhof-express.com, tel. 647-0017). These are enclosed hydrofoils—not a romantic cruise—but the trip does include a fascinating glimpse of the outer reaches of this city: burly shipyards, the brand-new Zenit Arena soccer stadium (purpose-built for the 2018 World Cup), the concrete communist apartment blocks at the far end of Vasilyevsky Island, and the massive cruise port.

If it's windy, in winter, or to save money, you can take **public transportation:** Ride the Metro to the lavishly decorated Avtovo station, cross the street to the right, and find a gang of marshrutka minibuses with signs for *Peterhof.* For variety, consider riding the minibus to the top end of the gardens, enjoy the half-mile stroll downhill through the grounds, and return via hydrofoil.

Visiting Peterhof: From the hydrofoil dock, stroll about a third of a mile up the straight-as-an-arrow **Sea Canal** to reach the spectacular **Grand Cascade.** The striking waterfalls and geysers take a backseat to 150 shimmering gold statues of classical and mythological figures. Many are replicas of ancient, marble originals. In the central pool, a musclebound Samson pries open the jaws of a furious lion. Out spurts a rocket of water 65 feet into the air. Taking nearly a century to complete, this elaborate fountain is one of the most impressive waterworks in existence. Peter the Great built a canal from a spring 12 miles away just to power these fountains.

Great Palace: Perched atop the Grand Cascade, up the grand staircase, sits the Great Palace. (Don't miss the stunning view of the fountain and canal from the terrace in front of the palace.) If you've already seen the Hermitage or the Catherine Palace, this interior may feel like a rerun—but if it's your best chance to bask in imperial luxury, it's worth seeing. After buying your tickets, you'll slip on booties to protect the floors and pass a model of the long, skinny, gilded palace. Then follow the one-way route: Head up the grand staircase, slathered in white stucco and gold leaf, and step into the sumptuous ballroom. Like much of the palace (and other Romanov residences), this was designed in Elizabethan Baroque style by the Italian architect Francesco Bartolomeo Rastrelli.

The delicate gold-wrapped wood carving frames a ceiling painting of Mount Parnassus, with Empress Elizabeth as Juno. The Chesme Hall's cycle of large paintings celebrates Russian naval victories over the Ottomans in the late 18th century. Then you'll proceed into the center of the complex: the turquoise Throne Room, then the Audience Hall, whose glittering gold decor, zig-zag inlaid floors, and reflective mirrors make the entire room twinkle like a diamond. The White Dining Room (whose table is set for an imperial feast, with Wedgwood tableware) leads to the two Chinese Lobbies, offering a change of pace. Like many big-wigs of his age, Peter the Great was fond of *chinoiserie*—porcelain and other decorative objects from Asia. From here, you'll proceed through the Picture Hall (part of Peter the Great's original palace, decorated floor-to-ceiling with imperial portraits), another Chinese Hall, the Partridge Room (with exquisite silk wallpaper), the Divan room (with an extra-cushy, powder-blue chaise lounge reminiscent of today's sectional sofas), and various dressing rooms, studies, and ceremonial halls. Finally you'll circle around to the Spare Apartments—which, because they were designed to impress visiting dignitaries, are even more sumptuous than the private apartments. Finally you'll reach the Oak Study of Peter the Great, which feels tasteful and homey thanks to its restrained carved-wood walls.

The Grounds: Explore the sprawling gardens. Behind the palace are the tidy, geometrical **Upper Gardens.** The much larger **Lower Gardens**—spreading out in both directions from the Sea Canal—are packed with fountains, pavilions, and other delights. The zone immediately flanking the Sea Canal is more rugged, but the deeper you go in either direction, the more manicured the grounds become. To the west (left, as you face the water), things are more geometrical, leading to the Great Marly Pond and

Golden Hill cascade (a stony version of the Grand Cascade). To the east (right), you'll find the orangery, Triton fountain (with a fancy terrace restaurant), Chessboard Hill Cascade (with colorful, water-spouting dragons at the top), and Monplaisir Palace, Peter the Great's original—and aptly named ("My Pleasure")—summer home along the water. The handy east-west pedestrian boulevard called Marly Avenue helps you connect the two zones easily.

ST. PETERSBURG

Tsarskoye Selo (Царское Село)

About 15 miles south of St. Petersburg is the charming small town of Pushkin. Back when Peter the Great started construction of a summer palace here, it was called Tsarskoye Selo—literally "Czars' Village." The site features a spectacular cluster of over-the-top-opulent Romanov palaces, pavilions, and gardens, built by Peter and his heirs (mostly in the 18th century). The main attraction is the Catherine Palace, famous for its breathtaking Amber Room. The adjacent Catherine Park—with manicured gardens, fanciful pavilions, and other decorative flourishes—surrounds the sprawling Great Pond. And just next door is the Alexander Palace—"modest" (relative only to the other sights here) and more endearingly lived-in (likely closed for renovation for the next few years, although the gardens surrounding it remain open).

Getting There: Tsarskoye Selo is most easily reached with a **guide,** who can provide door-to-door service and an efficient, highly focused tour of just the highlights (for private guide services, see page 27). If you prefer to linger at your own pace (you could easily spend the day here), it's also possible by **public transportation** (figure about an hour each way from downtown): From the Nevsky Prospekt stop downtown, ride the blue Metro line toward Kupchino, and get off at Moskovskaya (the third-to-last stop). Exit the platform at the back end of the train (follow signs that read "Bus to the airport"). Surface onto the large Moskovskaya Square, with a huge Lenin statue, his jacket flapping behind him. There's a bus stop behind Lenin's back (directly in front of the huge building with the hammer and sickle on top), where minibuses depart constantly for Pushkin. Look for buses marked *Tsarskoye Selo, Palaces, Parks,* or Пушкин (Pushkin)—or just ask around for "Pushkin?" Tell the driver you want to get off at "DVOR-ets" ("palace"). You'll ride the bus for about 30 minutes (50-70 R one-way), and hop off along Satovaya street. From here, head up the street (with the fenced garden on your left) to reach the golden domes and the Catherine Park entrance.

Note that to reach Tsarskoye Selo, you'll pass by the towering Monument to the Heroic Defenders of Leningrad (described on page 90)—which is an easy walk from the Moskovskaya Metro stop.

ST. PETERSBURG

Romanovs 101

As you tour the many imperial sights in and near St. Petersburg, this cheat sheet will keep you oriented to the Romanov czars and czarinas who built this city and ruled it until the Bolshevik Revolution in the early 20th century. The Romanov dynasty began in 1613 with Mikhail Romanov—but I'll start with his more famous descendant...

Peter I "the Great" (1689-1725): Dynamic and reform-minded, Peter was the founder of modern Russia. He famously moved the capital city from Moscow to St. Petersburg. (For more on Peter, see the sidebar on page 88). When Peter died, his wife Catherine (1684-1727) became empress; at her death, the throne passed to Peter's grandson from a prior marriage...

Peter II (1715-1730): He ruled only two years before dying of an illness. Because the teenaged Peter II lacked an heir, the throne reverted to Peter the Great's half-brother's daughter...

Anna (1693-1740): After a decade as czarina, Anna died of kidney disease. Her infant nephew, Ivan VI, was quickly deposed in a palace coup to install Anna's cousin...

Elizabeth (1709-1762): The overindulged daughter of Peter the Great and Catherine I, Elizabeth was raised in the lap of luxury at the Catherine Palace (which she later bathed in the frilly Elizabethan Baroque style). She never married, so the throne passed to her cousin Anna's son...

Peter III (1728-1762): He ruled just six months before being assassinated in a palace coup to install his wife...

Catherine II "the Great" (1729-1796): A German aristocrat who had married into the Romanov clan, Catherine enjoyed a very successful 34-year reign. She never remarried, but maintained (suspiciously) close relations with a trusted circle of mostly male advisors. The practical Catherine eschewed Baroque excess and popularized a more restrained Neoclassicism. (For more on Catherine, see page 36.) Catherine wasn't fond of her only son, whom she was unable to prevent from succeeding her.

Paul I (1754-1801): Catherine's son ruled only five years before a palace coup assassinated him to install his son...

▲▲▲Catherine Palace

Arguably Russia's single most enjoyable palace to tour (and that's saying something), the Catherine Palace lacks the staggering scale and world-class paintings of the Hermitage, but gives you much more insight into the dynamic czars and czarinas who ruled Russia. (For more on the Romanov family tree, see the sidebar on page 98.)

Alexander I (1777-1825): Alexander's grandmother Catherine aspired to make him the czar that she believed her son, Paul, could never be. Alexander enjoyed a long (nearly 25-year) but melancholy reign, while pursuing a more dynamic version of his grandma's Neoclassicism, called the Russian Empire style. When Alexander fell ill and died, he made way for his much younger brother...

Nicholas I (1796-1855): During his 30-year reign, Russia had high points (territorial expansion) and low points (the loss of the Crimean War). Upon his death, the throne passed to his son...

Alexander II (1818-1881): Alexander "the Liberator," who was czar for a quarter-century, boldly freed the serfs in 1861—but also instituted a convoluted land-redemption process that caused peasant uprisings (foreshadowing the eventual fall of the czarist regime). A left-wing terrorist group assassinated Alexander II in St. Petersburg (at the site of the Church on Spilled Blood). The throne passed to his son...

Alexander III (1881-1894): During his uneventful 15 years as czar, Alexander reversed some of his father's reforms and continued the Romanov trends of the 19th century: exuberant imperial decadence coupled with crippling societal ills. The empire was in decline, leaving a mess for Alexander III's son...

Nicholas II (1868-1918): This czar and his family have been much romanticized for their lavish lifestyle and tragic end. Seduced by the trappings of imperial life, and unwilling to grapple with the realities of a changing world, they retreated to Alexander's Place (in Tsarskoye Selo) and sought solace in the advice of the charismatic and enigmatic mystic, Rasputin. Nicholas oversaw Russia's failed foray into World War I (resulting in millions of Russian deaths) and was ultimately deposed by the February Revolution in 1917, setting the stage for the rise of Vladimir Lenin's Bolsheviks.

On July 17, 1918, Nicholas and his family (including his larger-than-life daughter, Anastasia) were executed by a firing squad—ending more than three centuries of Romanov rule from St. Petersburg.

Cost and Hours: 400 R, 550 R if purchased in advance online; open Wed-Mon 10:00-18:00 (during May-Sept, individuals can enter only 12:00-16:00—see below), closed Tue year-round; off-season also closed last Mon of month; audioguide-150 R, tel. 466-6669, http://eng.tzar.ru.

Crowd-Beating Tips: In peak season (May-Sept), individuals may enter the Catherine Palace only from 12:00 until 16:00, and tickets can sell out. To be sure you'll get in, reserve a ticket online (550 R, up to 4 tickets per order, includes entry to Catherine Park); you'll receive an email voucher that you'll exchange for a ticket at the booth near the Palace Church gate (look for onion domes, open Wed-Mon 12:00-16:00; must show ID). You may have to wait to enter until enough visitors are assembled to create a group. During the busiest times, you'll be required to join a (likely Russian-only) guided tour. Without a voucher, your best option is to line up at the palace as early as possible.

Background: Peter the Great and his wife, Catherine I, built the original palace at Tsarskoye Selo starting in 1717—when St. Petersburg itself was still in its infancy. In the following decades, the palace was rebuilt and expanded many times, most notably by Peter and Catherine's daughter, Elizabeth, who wanted to make it Russia's answer to Versailles. Most of what you see today was designed by the Italian architect Francesco Bartolomeo Rastrelli in Elizabethan Baroque style. Later, Catherine the Great left her own mark on the palace, expanding and renovating in the more restrained Neoclassical style (with the help of Scottish architect Charles Cameron). Because the palace had been turned into a museum (and carefully documented) after the Bolshevik Revolution, conservators could authentically restore it from the damage it suffered in World War II.

Self-Guided Tour: This "highlights" tour of the one-way route through the palace introduces you to some of the dynamic figures who shaped Russia, and it's a great way to trace the evolution of imperial aesthetics. (For a primer, see "Architectural Styles that Shaped St. Petersburg" on page 32.)

First you'll need to pay to enter the grounds (or exchange your voucher for an entrance ticket). To get oriented, make your way to the five shimmering, skinny, golden onion domes that mark the **Palace Church.** The church is attached by a skybridge to the yellow, Neoclassical **Lyceum of Tsarskoye Selo,** a prestigious, Eton-like boarding school for elites. The writer Alexander Pushkin was one of many important Russians who studied here.

• *If you need to, join the line of people waiting to buy palace tickets. Once inside, slip on a pair of provided booties (to protect the floors) and head up the Grand Staircase, following Tour's Beginning signs to our first stop.*

Great Hall: This, the largest room in any Russian palace (more than 9,000 square feet), is multipurpose: Its textbook Elizabethan Baroque interior works as a throne room, a ballroom, or a grand dining hall. The architecture, clearly inspired by the Hall of Mirrors at Versailles (with 300 mirrors, and lit by up to 7,000 candles for big events), exaggerates the spaciousness. It was here that Peter the Great and Catherine hosted extravagant masquerade balls to show off their beautiful daughter, Elizabeth. The lights would dim and a spotlight would be shone on the future czarina for her big entrance.

As a teenager, Elizabeth was spoiled, demanding, and lazy

(she reportedly endeavored to be productive for one hour each day, and devoted the other 23 to leisure). Later in life, as czarina, she was an insomniac—wracked by guilt over the palace coup that murdered her nephew to put her on the throne. She enjoyed having many servants around to keep her company, so the bigger the palace, the better. Elizabeth is also the ruler most responsible for the Catherine Palace's current appearance—she brought in the Italian architect Rastrelli to do the building in the lush style that came to be known as Elizabethan Baroque. Near the end of her reign, the aging Elizabeth became fiercely jealous of her nephew's bride, who would ultimately succeed her as Catherine the Great.

• *Next you'll pass into a series of...*

Baroque Apartments: This section of the palace represents the peak of Elizabethan Baroque. First, in the **Cavaliers' Dining Room,** ogle the dining table set with precious porcelain, and notice the oversized, delicately painted stove in the corner—you'll see more of these throughout this wing. "Cavalier" was one of the levels in Peter's "table of ranks," which tied noble privileges to one's rank within the bureaucratic hierarchy. In service to the crown, aristocrats and military officers could climb the 14 rungs of this carefully designed social ladder.

Continue into the White Dining Room—set with original Meissen porcelain—then through the crimson and green Pillar Rooms, and into the **Portrait Hall.** On the right wall, find Catherine I, the palace's namesake and the first empress of Russia. On the left wall is Catherine's daughter, Elizabeth. The mannequin in the middle of the room wears one of Elizabeth's original gowns, with the huge skirt and train that were the fashion of the time.

• *Next up is the highlight of the entire palace. Take a deep breath and brace yourself for the crowds of the...*

Amber Room: Wow. Utterly magnificent, the biggest amber box in the world is slathered with six tons of petrified tree resin. Frederick the Great of Prussia commissioned this work in the early 1700s, then shipped the panels here as a gift to the Romanovs. Later, the architect Rastrelli expanded the room with even more lavish decorations.

In 1944, the Nazi army completely dismantled the original Amber Room and shipped the pieces to Germany; it's never been seen again. Years later, in 1979, Soviet authorities set about to re-create the original room, relying mostly on black-and-white photographs. This replica is painstakingly accurate—although the exact shades of yellow and brown had to be guessed at. A few decades (and an estimated $350 million) later, Vladimir Putin unveiled the new Amber Room in 2003.

The space is particularly astonishing when you realize how difficult amber is to work with: Its brittleness demanded the highest possible skill to successfully shape each miniscule puzzle piece into the exquisite mosaics you see. The four color "paintings" represent the five senses—it was thought that amber was pleasing to the full range of human sensory experience.

• *Linger over the details until you can't take the crowds anymore. Then proceed through...*

More Baroque Apartments: In the **Picture Hall,** almost all the 114 paintings are original (they were squirreled away in Leningrad during the siege). There are no big-name artists or subjects here. Rather, the paintings are hung according to the "tapestry" approach: arranged purely according to size, shape, composition, and color scheme, creating a sort of mosaic wallpaper.

Next, in the **Small White Dining Room,** you'll see some paintings of this palace after its expansion in 1757 to (roughly) its current shape. In the next several rooms, appreciate the handmade silk on the walls and the Russian-made blue "Delftware" porcelain (suggesting Peter the Great's affection for all things Dutch).

• *Now we move forward in time to the early 19th century, to see the...*

Private Apartments of Czar Alexander I: You'll begin in the **Drawing Room of Alexander I,** where, on the left wall, you'll see a painting of the room's namesake and Catherine the Great's grandson: Alexander I. Alexander agreed to the palace coup that assassinated his father (Paul I), then went on to rule Russia for the first quarter of the 19th century. He succeeded in expanding Russia's territory (adding Finland and Poland to the realm), and was the czar who turned back Napoleon's forces (but only after the French had burned Moscow in 1812).

In the same room, portraits flank the door on the back wall (left to right): Catherine I and Peter the Great, then their daughters Anne and Elizabeth I. Because these portraits are not by official court painters—who took their subjects' egos into consideration—they are likely more true-to-life than most. The big portrait on the right wall is Catherine the Great, pointing at a stack of books that represents her respect for law.

• *Soon you'll cross into a section of the palace with an entirely different style.*

Catherine the Great's Neoclassicism: Beginning with the **Green Dining Room,** we leave the Elizabethan Baroque of the mid-1700s and transition into Catherine the Great's Neoclassicism of the late 1700s. The practical empress was unimpressed by architectural Baroque gaudiness and frilly excess: Notice that the stucco curlicues, gold leaf, and stylized shells have given way to subdued pastels, understated reliefs, and clean, white columns. Catherine imported the Scottish architect Charles Cameron, who had extensively studied the ancient Roman ruins of Pompeii, to remake parts of the palace in the so-called Palladian style in vogue in Italy. Evoking ancient Greek and Roman culture, Neoclassicism eventually evolved into the more beefed-up Russian Empire style of the early 19th century. Another feature that Cameron imported (from the British Isles) was the fireplace—notice that throughout this section, you'll see these rather than tall, sealed stoves.

Continue through the **Blue State Drawing Room,** then the **Chinese State Drawing Room**—its walls decorated with fanciful scenes of Chinese life.

Loop around the end of this wing, passing through a series of smaller, wood-clad rooms that belonged originally to Czar Paul I, and later to his son and successor, Alexander I. **The State Study of Alexander I**—the pink room with Doric columns—shows how this ruler jazzed up Catherine's Neoclassicism to its logical next stage, Russian Empire style.

• *Usually, you'll head downstairs now to exit. But at certain times—especially in the winter—you'll have access to a few more rooms. Either way, you have the option to buy a separate ticket that lets you tour an exhibit on...*

The History of the Romanovs: These rooms, with relatively dull interiors displaying uniforms, furniture, paintings, and other historical artifacts, are organized roughly chronologically—ruler by ruler, from the time of Peter the Great to Alexander II. Opt for this underwhelming-to-most exhibit only if you can't get enough of the Romanovs.

• *Our palace tour is over. Head outside and take some time to relax in the...*

▲▲▲Catherine Park

You could spend hours—or days—exploring the sprawling grounds around the Catherine Palace. While it's possible to enter some of the landmarks noted below (for separate admission fees), it's perfectly enjoyable to simply go for a walk in the park.

Cost and Hours: 120-R admission fee collected May-Sept 9:00-17:00, free at other times; open daily 7:00-21:00.

Visiting the Park: Facing the visitors entrance of the palace are delightful, French-style geometrical gardens. Tucked in the woods at the far end of these gardens is the Rastrelli-designed **Hermitage,** a retreat used to host special events to impress visiting dignitaries. To encourage relaxation without the intrusion of servants, the pavilion was fitted with tables that would disappear into the floor, then reappear set for dinner.

To the right as you face the Hermitage is the **Cold Baths Pavilion** (where the czars would take the waters); extending beyond that is the long, elegant Neoclassical **Cameron Gallery**—named for the Scottish architect who designed it.

Beyond the end of the Cameron Gallery, you reach the man-made **Great Pond.** Catherine the Great enjoyed spending time here, where she could see her fanciful pavilions on the island and, on the far side, a **Turkish bath** in a mosque-like building—a reminder of Catherine's dream of bringing Constantinople into the Russian Empire. Another reminder of this priority is the **Chesme Column,** rising up from the island in the middle of the pond, celebrating a Russian military victory over the Ottomans. Looking to the left around the pond, you'll see the white, Rastrelli-designed, Baroque pavilion called **"the Grotto."**

Stretching beyond the banks of the Great Pond sprawl acres of more rugged, English-style gardens.

• *With ample time, you could circle all the way around the Catherine Palace to see the manicured courtyard that served as its main entrance for aristocratic visitors. This entrance also faces the...*

▲Alexander Palace and Park

Forever disappointed with her son Paul, Catherine the Great took Paul's son Alexander from him almost the moment he was born, and built this residence where he could be raised to be the perfect czar. Later, Czar Nicholas II (the last Romanov ruler) favored the Alexander Palace in the winter, when the Winter Palace in town was too cold for his taste. It was in this palace that the mystic Rasputin first met the family of Nicholas II, and where he attended the czar's hemophiliac son, Alexei. The palace interior is under renovation, to create a museum of the Romanovs. When open, it will offer visitors the chance to see the apartments where Nicholas II and his family (and Rasputin) lived in the waning days of imperial rule. But even if the interior isn't open, you can still explore the park around it. Its rugged, thickly wooded grounds are dotted with whimsical pavilions, fanciful bridges, a faux-Chinese village, and a pointy-steepled Gothic chapel.

Cost and Hours: Park entrance free and open long hours daily; palace interior likely closed for renovation, but if open generally 300 R, Wed-Mon 10:00-19:00, last ticket sold two hours before closing, closed Tue and last Wed of each month, audioguide-100 R.

More Palaces near Tsarskoye Selo

The third big residence (after Catherine's and Alexander's) in the neighborhood, **Pavlovsk Palace** belonged to Catherine's son, Paul, with whom she had severe political differences. Built around 1777 and named for the heir who resided here ("Pavel" in Russian), Pavlovsk—about four miles southeast of Tsarskoye Selo—was effectively a way for Catherine to "exile" her son internally. While Catherine designed her own palace as a space for serious politics, Paul viewed his as a rustic retreat—a place to escape, rather than engage, the travails of the day. After he became czar, Paul built yet another palace, **Gatchina,** a faux-medieval castle about 18 miles farther from the city. While Pavlovsk and Gatchina are interesting, they're also-rans compared to the main sights at Tsarskoye Selo.

▲Piskaryovskoye Memorial Cemetery
(Пискарёвское Мемориальное Кладбище)

This is a memorial to the hundreds of thousands who died in the city during the Nazi Siege of Leningrad in World War II. The cemetery, with its eternal flame, acres of mass grave bunkers (marked only with the year of death), moving statue of Mother Russia, and many pilgrims bringing flowers to remember lost loved ones, is an awe-inspiring experience even for an American tourist to whom the Siege of Leningrad is just another page from the history books.

Cost and Hours: Free, daily 9:00-21:00, until 18:00 in winter, www.pmemorial.ru.

Getting There: The memorial is northeast of the city at Nepokorennykh Prospekt 72. From downtown, take the red Metro line (catch it at Uprising Square, near the end of Nevsky Prospekt) and ride it toward Devyatkino, getting off at the Ploshchad Muzhestva stop. Exit to the street, cross to the eastbound bus stop, and take bus #123 to the sixth stop—you'll see the cemetery buildings on your left.

Shopping in St. Petersburg

With vivid cultural artifacts for sale at reasonable prices, St. Petersburg is an obvious shopping stop for many tourists.

The famous Russian **nesting dolls** called *matryoshka* are one of the most popular items. The classic design shows a ruby-cheeked Russian peasant woman, wearing a babushka and traditional dress, but don't miss the entertaining modern interpretations. You'll see Russian heads of state (Peter the Great inside Lenin inside Stalin inside Gorbachev inside Putin), as well as every American professional and college sports team you can imagine—each individual player wearing his actual number. Other popular gifts include **amber** pieces and delicately painted **wooden eggs.**

High-quality **porcelain** is sold at numerous outlets of the Imperial Porcelain Factory (Императорский Фарфоровый Завод, sometimes referred to by its Soviet-era name, Lomonosov), which made fine tableware for the czars (there's one at Nevsky Prospekt 60, www.imp.ru).

You'll find colorful Russian **shawls** and **scarves** as well as tablecloths and **linens** at Pavloposadskie Platki (Павлопосадские платки, at Nevsky Prospekt 87 and elsewhere around town, www.platki.ru)—including entertaining themed patterns that memorialize events from Russian history and the lives of favorite saints.

St. Petersburg's major sights have excellent **museum gift shops,** such as those in the Hermitage and at the Russian Museum.

Big, glitzy **souvenir shops** (like the one facing the Moyka, just off Palace Square) offer a wide variety of items, but the prices are inflated to cover a 30 percent kickback for tour guides—even if you're on your own. Other, similar shops are typically located near major sights—consider popping in to Galeria Naslediye (Галерея Наследие) to check out the selection of *matryoshka,* imitation Fabergé eggs, and amber (between the Hermitage and the Church on Spilled Blood on the Moyka embankment at Naberezhnaya reki Moyki 37, www.souvenirboutique.com).

An affordable outdoor souvenir market behind the Church on Spilled Blood recently closed; ask around in case it's reopened elsewhere. You could check for lower prices among the souvenir shops inside the Gostiny Dvor complex—the section on the ground floor right along Nevsky has some decent souvenir stalls (it's OK to bargain hard here).

Hipster Design: St. Petersburg has a lively and youthful arts scene. Scattered around the city are big, decaying buildings that have been taken over by designers and turned into creative spaces. One of the easiest to reach is Taiga (Тайга), which faces the Neva River embankment just down from the Hermitage. It's sleepy through the mid-afternoon, then picks up on the evening (daily 13:00-21:00, www.space-taiga.org). In the middle of the complex, Grønland café fills the courtyard with picnic tables, ping pong, vegetarian food, and a dilapidated vibe. To get inside, buzz the bell at the front door (facing the embankment), or circle around the right side and up Moshkov street to let yourself in the door at #2.

Entertainment in St. Petersburg

▲▲Ballet

St. Petersburg is synonymous with classical ballet. Durable masterpieces like "Swan Lake" were first staged at the city's Mariinsky Theater, and many of the world's star dancers, past and present (Anna Pavlova, Rudolf Nureyev, Mikhail Baryshnikov), have trained and performed here.

The best venues in St. Petersburg for ballet are the Mariinsky Theater and the Mikhailovsky Theater. Ballet season at both theaters runs from mid-September to mid-July. Both theaters have storied histories, classic opera-house interiors (the Mariinsky's is a bit more opulent), and well-designed websites that allow you to buy tickets online in advance, in English (you may first have to create a registration account). Same-day tickets are often available (though not for the most popular ballets).

Although the historic Mariinsky (formerly Kirov) company is the most famous, there are other ballet troupes in town. Some companies stage summer performances especially for tourists (but usually not with their "A-list" dancers).

The **Mikhailovsky Theater** is conveniently located, at Ploshchad Isskustv 1, by the Russian Museum, a block off Nevsky (box office open daily 10:00-21:00, tel. 595-4305, www.mikhailovsky.ru).

The **Mariinsky Theater** (formerly the Kirov Theater) has grown into a complex of buildings southwest of St. Isaac's Cathedral, at Teatralnaya Ploshchad. Two separate but associated buildings face each other across a canal near "Theater Square": The original, traditional Mariinsky Theater; and the brand-new, sleek, and state-of-the-art Mariinsky II opera house. A couple of long blocks to the west, on Pisareva street, is the modern, lower-profile Concert Hall. Be clear on which venue you're attending (box office open 11:00-19:00, tel. 326-4141, www.mariinsky.ru). Buses take you right to Theater Square. Alternatively, you can take the Metro to Sadovaya and walk about 20 minutes.

Opera and Classical Music

Besides ballet, the Mariinsky and Mikhailovsky theaters host world-class opera and musical performances. Your best bet is to peruse their websites to see what's on; unfortunately, the theaters go dark in August.

Folk Music and Dancing

Every night, a hardworking troupe puts on a touristy, crowd-pleasing Russian folklore show at the Nikolaevsky Palace (near the Neva embankment, southwest of St. Isaac's Cathedral). The show

ST. PETERSBURG

kicks off with a men's a cappella quartet, followed by two different dance groups. The experience includes some light snacks and drinks. Popular with big bus groups, it's a rollicking introduction to Russian folk clichés. As seating is first-come, first-served, be sure to arrive early (nightly shows at 19:00, box office open daily 11:00-21:00, Ploshchad Truda 4, tel. 312-5500, or reserve by email at office@folkshow.ru or online at www.folkshow.ru).

▲Circus

The St. Petersburg circus is a revelation: Performed in one intimate ring, it has the typical tigers and lions but also a zany assortment of other irresistible animal acts (ostriches, poodles) as well as aerial acrobats (no nets), impossibly silly clowns, and more. Its performers have been staging their shows since 1877 in the stone "big top" on the edge of the Fontanka River. It's just east of the Russian Museum; some maps label it "Ciniselli Circus" after the Italian circus family that first built the place. Like many other entertainment options in town, the circus shuts down in summer—the season typically runs from September through May (tickets 500-2,000 R, box office open daily 11:00-19:00, tel. 570-5390 or 570-5411, www.circus.spb.ru).

Nightlife

St. Petersburg is becoming known for its after-hours scene. While the lineup of trendy cocktail bars is always changing, one reliable choice is **Bar 812,** with a stylish but unpretentious, youthful vibe and pricey, creative concoctions (nightly 18:00-late, Zhukovskogo 11, www.bar812.ru). A couple of blocks away is **The Hat,** a tight, youthful jazz bar. Things get rolling after 23:00, when local musicians gather for standing-room-only jam sessions. More famous jazz musicians often drop by here after their main gigs elsewhere to join in the fun. There's no food, but the bartenders specialize in whisky and bourbon (nightly 19:00-late, Belinskogo 9). **48 Chairs** is a more upmarket jazz bar and restaurant, on the happening Rubinshteyna street just off Nevsky Prospekt. It's sophisticated and dressy, with handsome striped decor and pricey food and cocktails (live jazz nightly after 21:00, Rubinshteyna 5, tel. 315-7775, www.48chairs.ru).

Sleeping in St. Petersburg

Accommodations in St. Petersburg are expensive, but there are lots of options in the city center in all price ranges. There's no reason to stay in Soviet-era behemoth hotels, and you don't need to pay for a five-star luxury hotel to feel secure and get friendly service.

If you search for St. Petersburg accommodations online,

you'll find many small "hotels" with just five or ten rooms. These typically occupy a single floor of an apartment building that has been remodeled into rooms for paying guests (websites may not be upfront about this). Bear in mind that such places are usually too small to have a 24-hour reception, and the front desk, if there is one, is not directly accessible from the street. You'll have to enter a code, buzz yourself into an entryway (which may be quite dingy), then take the building's rattletrap elevator to the hotel floor. This makes for an authentic cultural experience, but can unnerve first-time visitors, who may feel more comfortable at a larger establishment.

I've listed professionally run, midsize hotels in appealing locations, as well as cheaper youth hostels. All of my hotel listings have helpful, English-speaking staff on duty around the clock and a reception area accessible directly from the street (although not necessarily on the ground floor). If negotiating for a price, note that many offer a discount for nonrefundable bookings. Some hotels may tack on a surcharge for stays during the "White Nights" (summer solstice). For hotel locations, see the map on page 16.

Visa Tips: Choose accommodations that can also organize your visa invitation. If you're traveling to several destinations in Russia, try asking just one hotel to send an invitation for the entire trip. For more details, see the "Russian Visa Requirements" sidebar on page 12.

When you arrive at a hotel, the desk staff will register you with the local authorities and give you a confirmation form, which you should keep with your passport and migration card.

HOTELS

These listings are on side streets close to Nevsky Prospekt. The first two (Pushka Inn and Herzen House) are in the heart of downtown, near the Hermitage, and provide eager service in fluent English—at a cost. M Hotel is a little farther along Nevsky, and the Cronwell and Kristoff farther yet.

$$$ Pushka Inn does everything right—for a steep price. It has 33 rooms in a handsome building set in a quiet bend of the Moyka River, just steps from the Hermitage and not far from the Admiralteyskaya Metro stop. The word *pushka* means "cannon" and is also a play on the name of the writer Pushkin, who lived down the street (May and July-Oct: Sb-5,300 R, Db-9,000 R, Qb suite-12,200 R; prices rise in June and drop Nov-April, visa invitation-750 R, air-con, elevator, pay guest computer, Wi-Fi, Naberezhnaya Reki Moyki 14, tel. 644-7120, www.pushkainn .com, pushka@pushkainn.ru).

$$$ Herzen House has 29 well-located rooms in a nicely remodeled building in a busy downtown neighborhood, two blocks

Sleep Code

Abbreviations (country code: 7, area code: 812)
S = Single, **D** = Double/Twin, **T** = Triple, **Q** = Quad, **b** = bathroom

Price Rankings

$$$ **Higher Priced**—Most rooms 6,000 R or more.

$$ **Moderately Priced**—Most rooms between 4,000-6,000 R.

$ **Lower Priced**—Most rooms 4,000 R or less

Unless otherwise noted, English is spoken, credit cards are accepted, rooms are non-smoking, breakfast is included, and Wi-Fi is generally free. Prices change; verify current rates online or by email. For the best prices, always book directly with the hotel. For current exchange rates, check www.oanda.com.

from the Admiralteyskaya Metro stop. The reception is on the fourth floor—there's a restaurant at ground level and another hotel on the intervening floors (July-Sept: Sb-6,100-6,600 R, Db-7,000-7,600 R; prices rise mid-May-June and drop Oct-March, check website for frequent discounts, ask about 20 percent discount for nonrefundable bookings, extra bed-800-1,500 R, visa invitation-1,000 R, air-con, elevator, guest computer, Wi-Fi, Bolshaya Morskaya Ulitsa 25, tel. 315-5550, www.herzen-hotel.com, info@herzen-hotel.com).

$$$ Cronwell Inn Stremyannaya, tidy but slightly dated, offers 49 rooms on a pleasantly quiet street paralleling Nevsky Prospekt, close to the Mayakovskaya Metro (May-July: Sb-5,900-6,400 R, Db-7,500-7,900 R; Aug-Sept: Sb-4,600-5,000 R, Db-5,800-6,200 R; prices drop Oct-April, extra bed-1,700-2,000 R, visa invitation-600 R, half-pension deals at attached restaurant, air-con, elevator, guest computer, Wi-Fi, Stremyannaya Ulitsa 18, tel. 406-0450, www.cronwell.ru, booking@stremyannaya-hotel.com).

$$ M Hotel has 61 very central rooms tucked away in a quiet courtyard off Pereulok Krylova, a narrow street south of Nevsky Prospekt and the Gostiny Dvor Metro stop (May and July-Sept: Sb-4,400 R, Db-5,100-6,200 R; prices rise in June and drop Oct-April, extra bed-1,200 R, visa invitation-800 R, air-con, elevator, pay guest computer, Wi-Fi; at Sadovaya Ulitsa 22/2, but enter through archway at Pereulok Krylova 2; tel. 448-8383, www.mhotelspb.ru, sales@mhotelspb-ru).

$$ Hotel Kristoff is very close to the Vladimirskaya Metro station in an authentic, respectable residential neighborhood. It has no elevator, but all 31 rooms are either one or two floors above street level (mid-May-July: Sb-5,300 R, Db-6,200 R; mid-April-mid-May and Aug-mid-Sept: Sb-4,300 R, Db-5,200 R; prices drop in winter, extra bed-900 R, visa invitation-500 R, air-con, guest computer, Wi-Fi, Zagorodny Prospekt 9, tel. 571-6643, www.kristoff.ru/en, info@kristoff.ru).

HOSTELS

$ Soul Kitchen Hostel is one of the most all-around pleasant hostels I've seen, anywhere. Creatively run, it offers a rare combination of casual hostel fun and sane comfort—it's the kind of hostel you'd like to just hang out in. They have about 60 beds in 19 rooms, including three large dorms. Most rooms have eclectic flea-market decor and face the Moyka River. With ample private rooms, it's a good choice even for non-hostelers, especially families (flexible rates, but roughly 1,000 R for a dorm bed, Db-3,000-4,000 R, family room sleeps up to 5, visa invitation-1,000 R, no breakfast but there's a kitchen, guest computers, Wi-Fi, pay laundry, free landline calls to the US, Naberezhnaya reki Moyki 62, tel. 314-0400, www.soulkitchenhostel.com, soulkitchenjunior@gmail.com).

$ Hostel Life, with 81 beds in 22 rooms (including two private "VIP" rooms), is competently run, affiliated with Hostelling International, and has a super location just off Nevsky. To enter, ring the bell and take the elevator to the fourth floor (flexible rates, but generally 1,000-1,200 R for a dorm bed, D-3,200 R, "VIP" Db-4,200 R, visa invitation-800 R, visa registration-300 R extra, includes sheets and breakfast, elevator, guest computers, Wi-Fi, kitchen, laundry facilities, lockers; at Nevsky Prospekt 47, but enter just around corner on Vladimirsky Prospekt; tel. 318-1808, www.hostel-life.ru, booking@hostel-life.ru).

Eating in St. Petersburg

St. Petersburg has a huge selection of eating options. It's easy to find attractive cafés and restaurants, but hard to find value-priced ones. While Nevsky Prospekt is lined with inviting eateries, you'll eat better for less if you explore even a block off the main touristy drag. The listings below are all well-located or good values, and all have English-language menus.

Many cafés offer speedy, convenient light meals (sandwiches, light meals, salads, and crêpes—*bliny*). Столовая (Stolovaya, "diner") is a good word to look for if you're in need of a quick and easy meal. Russians are big on soups and appetizers, and it's perfectly reasonable to order two or three of these at a meal and skip the main dishes. Some restaurants have "business lunch" specials, served until 15:30 or 16:00.

ST. PETERSBURG

St. Petersburg Restaurants & Nightlife

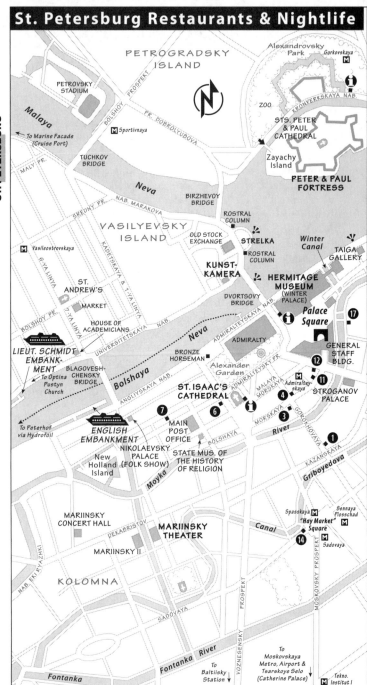

PETROGRADSKY ISLAND

Alexandrovsky Park

Gorkovskaya M

PETROVSKY STADIUM

BOLSHOY PROSPEKT

PR. DOBROLYUBOVA

ZOO

KRONVERKSKAYA NAB.

STS. PETER & PAUL CATHEDRAL

Malaya

← To Marine Facade (Cruise Port)

M Sportivnaya

TUCHKOV BRIDGE

MALY PR.

Neva

Zayachy Island

PETER & PAUL FORTRESS

SKEDNY PR.

NAB. MARAKOVA

BIRZHEVOY BRIDGE

VASILYEVSKY ISLAND

OLD STOCK EXCHANGE

ROSTRAL COLUMN

STRELKA

Winter Canal

TAIGA GALLERY

M Vasileostrovskaya

KADETSKAYA & 1 YA LINYA

ROSTRAL COLUMN

KUNST-KAMERA

HERMITAGE MUSEUM (WINTER PALACE)

6 YA LINYA

ST. ANDREW'S

MARKET

DVORTSOVY BRIDGE

Palace Square

❼

BOLSHOY PR.

3 YA LINYA

HOUSE OF ACADEMICIANS

UNIVERSITETSKAYA NAB.

Neva

ADMIRALTEYSKAYA NAB.

❶ i

GENERAL STAFF BLDG.

LIEUT. SCHMIDT EMBANK-MENT

ADMIRALTY

ADMIRALTEYSKY PR

❶❷

← To Optina Pustyn Church

BLAGOVESH-CHENSKY BRIDGE

Bolshaya

ANGLIYSKAYA NAB.

BRONZE HORSEMAN

Alexander Garden

MALAYA MORSKAYA

M Admiralteyskaya

STROGANOV PALACE

❶❶

← To Peterhof via Hydrofoil

ENGLISH EMBANKMENT

ST. ISAAC'S CATHEDRAL

❹

MORSKAYA

GOROKHOVAYA

❼

MAIN POST OFFICE

❻

i

❸

NIKOLAEVSKY PALACE (FOLK SHOW)

New Holland Island

STATE MUS. OF THE HISTORY OF RELIGION

BOLSHAYA

River

❶

Moyka

KAZANSKAYA

MARIINSKY CONCERT HALL

DEKABRISTOV

MARIINSKY THEATER

Canal

Spasskaya M

Sennaya Plosschad

"Hay Market" Square

M

MARIINSKY II

❶❹

Sadovaya M

NAB. EKI RYAZHKI

KOLOMNA

MOSKOVSKY PROSPEKT

SADOVAYA

VOZNESENSKY PROSPEKT

Fontanka River

Fontanka

To Baltiisky Station

To Moskovskaya Metro, Airport & Tsarskoye Selo (Catherine Palace)

Tekno. Institut I M

ST. PETERSBURG

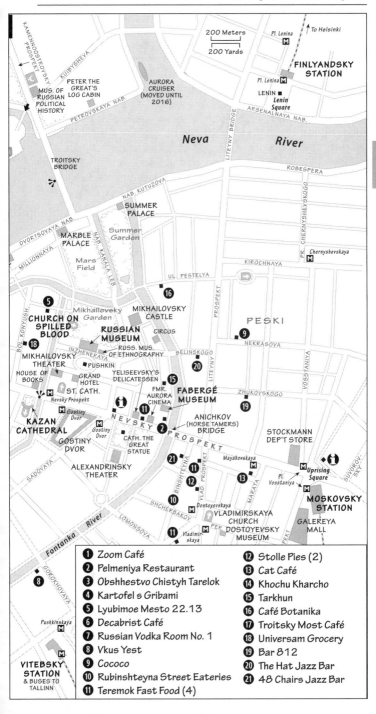

200 Meters
200 Yards

Pl. Lenina → To Helsinki

FINLYANDSKY STATION

Pl. Lenina

LENIN ■
Lenin Square

KAMENNOOSTROVSKY PROSPEKT

KUYBYSHEVA

PETER THE GREAT'S LOG CABIN

MUS. OF RUSSIAN POLITICAL HISTORY

AURORA CRUISER (MOVED UNTIL 2016)

PETROVSKAYA NAB.

ARSENALNAYA NAB.

Neva   River

TROITSKY BRIDGE

ROBESPERA

NAB. KUTUZOVA

LITEYNY BRIDGE

DVORTSOVAYA NAB.

SUMMER PALACE

Summer Garden

MARBLE PALACE

MILLIONNAYA

NAB. KANALA LEB

Mars Field

KIROCHNAYA

PR. CHERNYSHEVSKOGO

Chernyshevskaya

UL. PESTELYA

5

Mikhailoveky Garden

16

MIKHAILOVSKY CASTLE

CHURCH ON SPILLED BLOOD

RUSSIAN MUSEUM

CIRCUS

PESKI

9

NEKRASOVA

18

MIKHAILOVSKY THEATER

INZHENERNAYA

RUSS. MUS. OF ETHNOGRAPHY

BELINSKOGO

HOUSE OF BOOKS

■ PUSHKIN

YELISEEVSKY'S DELICATESSEN

20

15

PROSPEKT

VOSSTANIYA

GRAND HOTEL

ST. CATH.

Nevsky Prospekt

1

FMR. AURORA CINEMA

FABERGÉ MUSEUM

ZHUKOVSKOGO

19

KAZAN CATHEDRAL

Gostiny Dvor

NEVSKY

11

2

ANICHKOV (HORSE TAMERS) BRIDGE

LITEYNY

GOSTINY DVOR

Gostiny Dvor

CATH. THE GREAT STATUE

PROSPEKT

STOCKMANN DEP'T STORE

SUVOROV-SKY

ALEXANDRINSKY THEATER

21

Mayakovskaya

ii Uprising Square

MOSKOVSKY STATION

BINSHTEYNA

11

VLAD PROSPEKT

12

13

MARATA

Pl. Vosstaniya

10

SHCHERBAKOV

Dostoyevskaya

GALEREYA MALL

RUBINSHTEYNA

LOMONOSOVA

Fontanka   River

11

VLADIMIRSKAYA CHURCH

DOSTOYEVSKY MUSEUM

PER.

PEKT

Vladimirskaya

8

GOROKHOVAYA

Pushkinskaya

VITEBSKY STATION

& BUSES TO TALLINN

1 Zoom Café
2 Pelmeniya Restaurant
3 Obshhestvo Chistyh Tarelok
4 Kartofel s Gribami
5 Lyubimoe Mesto 22.13
6 Decabrist Café
7 Russian Vodka Room No. 1
8 Vkus Yest
9 Cococo
10 Rubinshteyna Street Eateries
11 Teremok Fast Food (4)

12 Stolle Pies (2)
13 Cat Café
14 Khochu Kharcho
15 Tarkhun
16 Café Botanika
17 Troitsky Most Café
18 Universam Grocery
19 Bar 812
20 The Hat Jazz Bar
21 48 Chairs Jazz Bar

RUSSIAN FOOD

Cosmopolitan St. Petersburg has international tastes, so truly "traditional" Russian restaurants are scarce (and mostly aimed at either at tourists or a fine-dining crowd). More commonly, you'll see restaurants with eclectic international menus (Mediterranean, Thai, burgers, etc.) and a few, token Russian classics.

Russians love soup—popular kinds are beet borscht, fish *ukha*, cabbage *shchi*, and meat *solyanka*. Russian cuisine is heavy on small dishes that we might think of as appetizers or sides, such as *pelmeni* and *vareniki* (types of dumplings), *kasha* (buckwheat groats) prepared in various ways, *bliny*, and high-calorie salads. As in Italy, the main dishes tend to be the least exciting part of the meal. You'll see beef stroganoff and chicken Kiev on menus at touristy restaurants, but these dishes are rarely served in Russian homes—they were both introduced to Russia in the late 19th century and are really more European than Russian. Berries, mushrooms, sour cream and yogurt, fresh garden vegetables, and herbs like dill and cilantro are common in home cooking. Bread is often served as an automatic side order in restaurants.

In recent years, both local and Western franchise restaurants have sprouted up all over Russia. You'll see Subway, Pizza Hut, KFC, McDonald's, and more. Popular Russian chains such as Teremok and Chainaya Lozhka serve authentic food and can be convenient time-savers during a day of sightseeing.

Russian beer is good. It goes without saying that there are many vodkas to choose from. Russians like to drink inexpensive sparkling wine that's still called *Sovyetskoye shampanskoye* (Soviet champagne). Try *kvas*, a fizzy, fairly sweet, grain-based beverage that is marketed as non-alcoholic (but often has a negligible alcohol content) and *mors* (berry juice). In Russia, always drink bottled water, which is available widely in shops.

SIT-DOWN RESTAURANTS

All of these youthful places (except the last one) offer a peek at Russian hipster culture and diverse menus with international and Russian dishes.

Zoom Café (Zoom Кафе) has a lively atmosphere and fresh menu. Popular and a good value, it's in a pleasant basement-level dining room just off Griboyedov Canal, a bit south of Nevsky Prospekt (160-240-R soups, 240-480-R main courses, by the corner of Gorokhovaya and Kazanskaya at Gorokhovaya Ulitsa 22, Mon-Fri 9:00-24:00, Sat 11:00-24:00, Sun 13:00-24:00, food served until 22:30, tel. 612-1329). A block beyond Zoom, across the canal, Gorokhovaya street is lined with more enticing options that skew toward the young and creative end of the culinary spectrum.

Pelmeniya (Пельмения) is a great place to sample the food for which it's named: delicious filled dumplings. Besides Russian *pelmeni,* choices include *khinkali* (from Georgia, with a thick dough "handle"), *varenyky* (from Ukraine, like Polish pierogi), *manti* (from Turkey and the Caucasus), *gyoza* (from Asia), and even ravioli. The modern interior overlooks the Fontanka River next to the Anichkov Bridge (140-240-R small portion, 250-400-R large portion, well-described English menu, daily 11:00-23:00, Fontanka 25, tel. 571-8082). Farther along the Fontanka embankment, past the nearby Fabergé Museum, you'll find several fun and funky little cellar bars and cafés.

Obshhestvo Chistyh Tarelok (Общество Чистых Тарелок/ "Clean Plates Society") has a great energy, powered by loud music and a lively thirtysomething clientele. The mismatched-lumber bar and oversized Ikea chandeliers hint at the varied international fare, from burgers to curry to some Russian standbys (200-270-R soups, 300-500-R meals, daily 12:00-late, Gorokhovaya 13, tel. 934-9764, www.cleanplates.ru).

Kartofel s Gribami (Картофель с Грибами/"Potatoes with Mushrooms") is a fun, jazzy, and central hangout serving unpretentious but thoughtfully crafted Russian "street food"—such as *kapsalon* (a traditional casserole, available with various fillings) and the stuffed-pita sandwich called *shaverma* (300-400-R dishes, daily 12:00-24:00, Gorokhovaya 12, tel. 994-0983).

Lyubimoe Mesto 22.13 (Любимое Место/"Favorite Place 22.13"), is a bombastic, multilevel, colorful restaurant just around the corner from the Church on Spilled Blood. Its trendy interior is crammed under old vaults, and the pricey but crowd-pleasing menu offers something for everyone (300-500-R starters, soups, and pizzas, 400-600-R main courses and big salads, Konyushennaya Ploshchad 2, tel. 647-8050).

Decabrist Café (Декабрист Кафе), casual and lively, has a rustic but modern interior in a handy location near St. Isaac's Cathedral. They have light meals and soups (200-350 R), burgers and traditional Russian dishes (300-400 R), and a 250-R three-course weekday lunch deal (daily 8:00-22:00, Yakubovicha 2, tel. 912-1891, www.decabrist.net).

***Stuffy, Traditional Russian Cuisine:* Russian Vodka Room No. 1,** connected with St. Petersburg's vodka museum, is a fancier, more expensive restaurant with classy food and service (and yes, 200 types of vodka) that caters to tourists. You can choose between the elegant, old-time interior or the sidewalk seating, facing the busy boulevard. It's a little beyond St. Isaac's Cathedral—trolleybuses #5 and #22 stop conveniently on the same street. The huge building has multiple restaurants—look for the Vodka Room between entrances (подъезд) 5 and 6 (500-1,000-R main courses, daily 12:00-24:00, Konnogvardeisky Bulvar 4, tel. 570-6420).

"New Russian" Farm-to-Table Eateries

In recent years, some "New Nordic" culinary influence—with an emphasis on locally grown or foraged ingredients, traditional flavors, and modern techniques—has crept into Russia from its Scandinavian neighbors. And a handful of spunky young restaurants are reinventing the Russian classics, cleverly deconstructing them with a contemporary flair. For something a notch above the places listed earlier, foodies dig into these two.

Vkus Yest (Вкус Есть, "Taste Eat"), with a spare, bare-brick-walls dining room, faces the Bolshoi Drama Theater across the Fontanka River, and there's jazz on the soundtrack. Brief, constantly changing, and adventurous, the menu is fun to explore. The name is a pun: Есть means both "to eat" and "there is" (200-350-R soups and pastas, 350-600-R main courses, daily 12:00-23:00, Fontanka 23, tel. 983-3376, www.ofwgroup.ru).

Cococo (Кококо) fills its laid-back, mellow cellar with rustic tables and decor that's a mix of old and new. The fun-to-read placemat menu includes old dishes done a new way, as well as some more innovative alternatives. Compared to Vkus Yest, it's pricier, the portions are smaller, and it's a bit hit-or-miss—but it's still well worth trying (350-450-R soups, 450-800-R main courses, open daily 12:00-late, Nekrasova 8, tel. 579-0016, www.kokoko.spb.ru)

Rubinshteyna Street

This street offers the best (relatively) untouristy restaurant comparison-shopping in town. Begin where it meets Nevsky Prospekt (near the end of my self-guided walk, just a block east of the Fontanka), and stroll the street all the way to Zagorodnyi Prospekt, surveying your options en route. The variety is staggering: English pub, Sardinian wine bar, competing tea rooms, tapas bar (sound it out: БАРСЛОНА is "Barslona," a pun on Barcelona and "elephant bar"), Middle Eastern, Cuban, Irish, Italian, Georgian, Mexican, French, and more. You can simply follow your instincts here, but be sure to check out these two.

Fartuk (Фартук, at #15/17) has Russian-international fusion cuisine—from pastas to wok dishes—in an interior that's trendy, but not too trendy, plus sidewalk tables (160-260-R soups, 300-500-R main courses, tel. 764-5256).

Café Mitte, at #27, serves breakfast all day, plus 220-R sandwiches, in a bright, hip setting with a chill vibe (daily 10:00-23:00, tel. 416-1416).

SPEEDY CHAIN RESTAURANTS

Teremok (Теремок) is a chain with branches literally all over town. It's quick and convenient for those who don't speak Russian, handy for families, and lets you share and try lots of different dishes. Though sometimes derided as "Russian fast food," it actually serves a perfectly healthy array of Russian standards at very affordable prices. Choose borscht, *ukha* (fish soup), *pelmeni* (dumplings), sweet or savory *bliny* (crepes), or *kasha* (buckwheat groats) prepared in various ways. *Kvas* and *mors*

(berry juice) are on the drinks menu. It's the setting which is fast-foody, complete with orange uniforms for the staff, plastic trays filled at the sales counter, and trash bins for your paper plates and napkins. Expect somewhat brisk service, and if you don't see the English menu brochure, ask for it—or just point to the photos on the posted menu (100-200-R main courses; Bolshaya Morskaya Ulitsa 11, Nevsky Prospekt 60, and Vladimirsky Prospekt 3 are three of many locations; all open daily at least 10:00-23:00).

Stolle (Штолле), another chain, specializes in crispy pies, both savory and sweet. Their handiest location, near the start of Nevsky Prospekt (at #11), combines order-at-the-counter, point-to-what-you-want efficiency with a refined drawing-room atmosphere. This makes it popular with local tour guides...and with pickpockets. Ask for their English menu. They tend to sell out of many flavors later in the day (pies sold by size—figure about 200 R for a large portion, daily 9:00-22:00).

GEORGIAN FOOD

Although any Georgian will tell you it is not "Russian," Georgian cuisine is a much appreciated, flavorful alternative that's popular with Russians and visitors alike. If you've never tried Georgian food before, grab your chance. (Why Georgian restaurants aren't sweeping the States, I'll never know.) As with Russian food, the secret is to order appetizers. Some of the classic Georgian dishes are *khachapuri* (хачапури)—hot bread filled with cheese, somewhat like a calzone; *khinkali* (хинкали)—a hearty filled dumpling gathered into a thick, doughy "handle" and dipped into sauces; *pkhali* (пхали)—chopped greens; chicken *satsivi* (сациви)—diced chicken in a spicy yellow sauce; *baklazhan* (баклажан)—eggplant, *lobio* (лобио)—beans, served hot or cold; and plenty of *lavash* (лаваш)—bread. If you want soup, try *kharcho* (харчо), a spicy broth with lots of meat and onions. Main dishes are less special (often grilled meat). Georgian cuisine fills the same niche in Russian life as Italian cuisine does in Germany and northern Europe—raven-haired immigrants from the south run neighborhood restaurants serving hot cheese-bread.

Cat Café (КЭт Кафе)—an institution for expats in St. Petersburg since the end of communism—has a cozy, traditional interior with only eight tables and a friendly vibe (300-500-R *khachapuri*, 250-375-R soups, 300-500-R main courses, reservations recommended, Stremyannaya Ulitsa 22, daily 12:00-23:00, tel. 571-3377, www.cafe-cat.ru).

Khochu Kharcho (Хочу Харчо, literally "I want Georgian soup") is a big, boisterous, industrial-strength restaurant facing the busy Sennaya square (where three Metro lines converge). This sprawling mash-up of modern and traditional comes with several seating areas, a busy open kitchen with a wood-fired grill and tandoor oven, and an enticing photo menu that makes ordering easy. While aimed squarely at Russian tourists (think of it as the local answer to the Hard Rock Café), it offers a lively and accessible—if pricey—sample of Georgian fare (350-500-R soups, 400-550-R *khachapuri,* 450-800-R main dishes, open daily 24 hours, Sadovaya 39—next to the small footbridge at the southwest corner of the square, tel. 640-1616).

Tarkhun (Таркун, "Tarragon"), a block off the Fontanka River between the Fabergé Museum and the circus, is a more upscale place to try Georgian fare (300-400-R soups, 350-600-R main dishes, daily 12:00-23:30, Karavannaya 14, tel. 377-6525).

VEGETARIAN FARE

Café Botanika (Кафе Ботаника) is a few blocks beyond the Russian Museum, past the Summer Garden and just over the Fontanka River. It's fresh and attractive, with seating both indoors and streetside. The menu includes Russian, Indian, Italian, and Japanese dishes (200-250-R soups, 300-500-R main courses, daily 11:00-24:00, Ulitsa Pestelya 7, tel. 272-7091).

Troitsky Most (Троицкий Мост) is a tiny, inexpensive vegetarian café just north of Nevsky along the Moyka River. Order at the counter and then find a seat—a board, partly translated into English, lists the day's specials (130-150-R main courses, daily 9:00-23:00, Naberezhnaya Reki Moyki 30).

St. Petersburg Connections

BY TRAIN

St. Petersburg has four main train stations: Trains to **Helsinki** leave from Finlyandsky Vokzal (Финляндский Вокзал, Finland Station, Metro: Ploshchad Lenina); trains to **Moscow** leave from Moskovsky Vokzal (Московский Вокзал, Moscow Station, Metro: Ploshchad Vosstaniya); suburban trains to Pushkin (for the Catherine Palace at **Tsarskoye Selo**), as well as trains to the Baltic states, leave from Vitebsky Vokzal (Витебский Вокзал, Vitebsk Station, Metro: Pushkinskaya); and suburban trains to Peterhof leave from Baltiisky Vokzal (Балтийский Вокзал, Baltic Station, Metro: Baltiiskaya)—but it's better to go to Peterhof by bus or hydrofoil.

Day-trippers can buy tickets for suburban trains at the station before departure, either from ticket windows or Russian-only automatic machines.

To Helsinki: The four daily trains to Finland rarely sell out. You can buy tickets online at www.vr.fi. If you prefer to buy them in person, the best place is at the station (Finlyandsky Vokzal). Face the station facade, then go around the left side of the building and all the way to the end, where you'll find a modern hall and ticket office, open 24 hours (little English spoken).

To Moscow: St. Petersburg is connected to the capital by speedy Sapsan trains (4-5/day, 4 hours at 125 miles per hour, pricey, tend to sell out several days in advance) and a slower night train (8 hours). To get tickets, the most user-friendly option is probably to go through a travel agency—either in St. Petersburg or abroad—which will purchase tickets for you for a service fee. Look for ticket help from Real Russia (www.realrussia.co.uk), which can arrange etickets for you, or Sindbad Travel, Russia's youth travel agency (email them at trains@sindbad.ru). Tickets are also available online from the Russian railways site (www.rzd.ru), but it's only in Russian; even if you get a Russian speaker to help, the system may not accept your non-Russian credit card. The ticket machines in stations are also an option—but these, too, are in Russian only and formidable to use. Finally, right in the center, there's the Soviet-era Central Railway Booking Office (Железнодорожные Кассы) at Kanal Griboyedova 24, but prepare for a long wait and little or no English spoken. It's across the canal from the Kazan Cathedral and just a few doors from Nevsky Prospekt—look for the green-and-yellow Кассы sign with a train (Mon-Sat 8:00-20:00, Sun 8:00-18:00).

BY BUS

Bus is the best way to reach **Tallinn,** with almost a dozen daily departures on Lux Express (7-hour trip) and easy online ticket purchases (www.luxexpress.eu). Buses leave from Baltiisky Vokzal (Балтийский Вокзал, Baltic Station, at Naberezhnaya Obvodnogo Kanala 120, Metro: Baltiiskaya). Note that these buses don't use the "official" St. Petersburg bus station (at Naberezhnaya Obvodnogo Kanala 36, near the Obvodny Kanal Metro station).

There are also buses to **Helsinki** (some listed at www.matkahuolto.fi), but the train is much quicker and more user-friendly (though more expensive).

BY PLANE

St. Petersburg's Pulkovo Airport (airport code: LED, www.matkahuolto.fi) handles both domestic and international flights. To reach the airport from downtown St. Petersburg, first take the Metro to the Moskovskaya station, exit on the outbound end of the station, and go all the way through the underground tunnel. You'll emerge by the stops for bus #39 or express bus #39A, which go to the airport (run every 15-20 minutes, 15-35 minutes to reach the airport). Minibus #K39, departing from the same place, runs a similar route. You can also ask your hotel to order a taxi (about 600-900 R; from the airport, look for the official taxi booth in the arrivals hall). Allow extra time for traffic and to pass through airport security.

BY CRUISE SHIP

Most cruises arriving in St. Petersburg dock at the enormous **Marine (Morskoy) Facade,** built at the western tip of Vasilyevsky Island (www.ppspbmf.ru). Each of the four Marine Facade terminals has roughly the same services, including ATMs, basic TI kiosks, and extensive gift shops (a good place to burn off leftover rubles before boarding your ship out). **Taxis** line up out front, charging 600-800 R for a ride downtown (figure 1,400 R one-way to Peterhof, or 1,200 R to Tsarskoye Selo; if no taxis are standing by, look for someone with a TAXI clipboard). But it's easy, cheap, and very local to ride **public transportation** from the Marine Facade into downtown: At the curb in front of the terminal, look for the stop for bus #158 (25 R, pay conductor, 2/hour, stops at all Marine Facade terminals); after leaving the port and driving past apartment blocks, the bus turns left onto a big boulevard with tram tracks, with several shops on the right—get off here, at the Primorskaya Metro station. Exiting the bus, walk straight ahead and look for the Metro sign (it looks like an "M" that's bulging on the sides). Head into the Metro station, turn right to find the ticket window, buy a token (31 R), insert the token in the turnstile, ride down the escalator, and ride the train two stops to Gostiny Dvor. You'll pop out right downtown, in the middle of Nevsky Prospekt.

A lucky few ships—generally smaller, luxury vessels—dock along the **Neva River embankment.** There are two cruise terminals here: the Lieutenant Schmidt (Leytenanta Shmidta) embankment, on the north bank; and the English (Angliyskaya) embankment, on the south bank. From either one, you can walk along the riverfront into town.

For more in-depth cruising information, pick up my *Rick Steves Northern European Cruise Ports* guidebook.

BY PASSENGER FERRY

St. Peter Line ferries arrive at St. Petersburg's **Sea Station (Morskoy Vokzal)** terminal building, which sits at the far end of Vasilyevsky Island. From in front of the terminal, trolley buses #10 and #11 head downtown, stopping first near the Strelka viewpoint on the Neva before crossing over to stop near the Hermitage, then heading all the way up Nevsky Prospekt (with more stops) to Uprising Square and beyond.

FINLAND

FINLAND

Suomi

Finland is a fun, fascinating, sadly overlooked corner of Europe. Its small population fills a sprawling, rocky, forested land that shares a long border with Russia. The Finns have often been overshadowed by their powerful neighbors, the Swedes and the Russians. And yet, they've persevered magnificently, with good humor, a zest for architecture and design, a deep love of saunas, and an understandable pride in things that are uniquely Finnish.

For much of their history, the Finns embraced a simple agrarian and fishing lifestyle. They built not cities, but villages—easy pickings for their more ambitious neighbors. From medieval times to 1809, Finland was part of Sweden. Destructive city fires left little standing from this period, but Finland still has a sizeable Swedish-speaking minority, bilingual street signs, and close cultural ties to Sweden.

In 1809, Sweden lost Finland to Russia. Under the next century of relatively benign Russian rule, the "Grand Duchy of Finland" began to industrialize, and Helsinki grew into a fine and elegant city. Still, at the beginning of the 1900s, the rest of Finland was mostly dirt-poor and agricultural, and its people were eagerly emigrating to northern Minnesota. (Read Toivo Pekkanen's *My Childhood* to learn about the life of a Finnish peasant in the early 1900s.)

In 1917, Finland and the Baltic States won their independence from Russia, fought brief but vicious civil wars against their pro-Russian domestic factions, and then enjoyed two decades of prosperity... until the secret Nazi-Soviet pact of August 1939 assigned them to the Soviet sphere of influence. When Russia invaded, only Finland resisted successfully. White-camouflaged Finnish ski troops won the Winter War against the Soviet Union in  1939-1940 and held off the Russians in what's called the Continuation War from 1941 to 1944.

After World War II, Finland was made to suffer for having

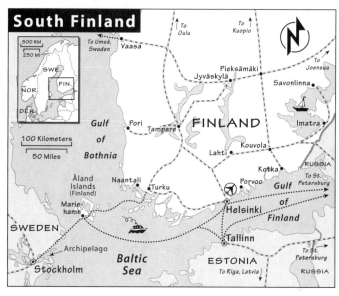

allied itself for a time with Nazi Germany and for having fought against one of the Allied Powers. The Finns were forced to cede Karelia (eastern Finland) and part of Lapland to the USSR, to accept a Soviet naval base on Finnish territory, and to pay huge reparations to the Soviet government. Still, Finland's bold, trend-setting modern design and architecture blossomed, and it built up successful timber, paper, and electronics industries. All through the Cold War, Finland teetered between the West and the Soviet Union, trying to be part of Western Europe's strong economy while treading lightly and making nice with her giant neighbor to the east.

The collapse of the Soviet Union has done to Finland what a good long sauna might do to you. When Moscow's menace vanished, so did about 20 percent of Finland's trade. After a few years of adjustment, Finland bounced back quickly, joining the European Union and adopting the euro currency. In the past, Finns would move to Sweden (where they are still the biggest immigrant group), looking for better jobs in Stockholm. Some still nurse an inferiority complex, thinking of themselves as poor cousins to the Swedes. But now Finland is the most technologically advanced country in Europe, and its talented young people are more likely to seek their fortunes here. Home to the giant mobile-phone company Nokia, Finland has more mobile-phone numbers than fixed ones, and ranks fourth among European nations (15th globally) in the number of Internet users per capita.

We think of Finland as Scandinavian, but it's better to call it

FINLAND

Finland Almanac

Official Name: Republic of Finland.

Population: Finland is home to 5.3 million people (40 per square mile). The majority are Finnish in descent (93.4 percent). Other ethnicities include Swedish (5.6 percent), Russian, Estonian, Roma, and Sami (less than 1 percent each). The official languages are Finnish, spoken by 91 percent, and Swedish, spoken by 5.5 percent. Small minorities speak Sami and Russian. Finland is about 79 percent Lutheran, 1 percent Orthodox, 1 percent other Christian, and 19 percent unaffiliated.

Latitude and Longitude: 64°N and 26°E, similar latitude to Nome, Alaska.

Area: 130,500 square miles (about the size of Washington state and Oregon combined).

Geography: Finland is bordered by Russia to the east, Sweden and Norway to the north, the Baltic Sea to the west, and Estonia (across the Gulf of Finland) to the south. Much of Finland is flat and covered with forests, with the Lapland region extending north of the Arctic Circle. Finland is home to thousands of lakes and encompasses nearly as many islands: It has 187,800 lakes and 179,500 islands (the last time I counted).

Biggest City: Helsinki is the capital of Finland and has a population of 604,000; 1.3 million people—about one in four Finns—live in the Helsinki urban area.

Economy: Finland's Gross Domestic Product is $195 billion and its per-capita GDP is $35,900. Manufacturing, timber, engineering, electronics, and telecommunications are its chief industries, with mobile phones among its top exports.

Currency: €1 (euro) = about $1.40.

Government: Finland has both a president, responsible for foreign policy, and a prime minister, who—along with the 200-member Parliament (Eduskunta)—is responsible for domestic legislation. President Sauli Niinistö began his six-year term in March of 2012. Alexander Stubb was appointed prime minister in June of 2014.

Flag: The Finnish flag is white with a blue Scandinavian cross. The blue represents the lakes of Finland, and the white its winter snow.

The Average Finn: He or she is 43 years old, has 1.73 children, will live to be 80, and is tech savvy; the United Nations' Technology Achievement Index ranks Finland first in the world (the US ranks second).

"Nordic." Technically, the Scandinavian countries are Denmark, Sweden, and Norway—all constitutional monarchies with closely related languages. Add Iceland, Finland, and maybe Estonia—former Danish or Swedish colonies that speak separate languages—and you have the "Nordic countries." Iceland, Finland, and Estonia are also republics, not monarchies. In 1906, Finnish women were the first in Europe to vote. The country's president from 2000 to 2012 was a woman, and today, 40 percent of the Finnish parliament is female.

Finnish is a difficult-to-learn Uralic language whose only relatives in Europe are Estonian (closely) and Hungarian (distantly). Finland is officially bilingual, and about 1 in 20 residents speaks Swedish as a first language. You'll notice that Helsinki is called *Helsingfors* in Swedish. Helsinki's street signs list places in both Finnish and Swedish. Nearly every educated young person speaks effortless English—the language barrier is just a speed bump. But to get you started, I've included a selection of Finnish survival phrases on the following page.

The only essential word needed for a quick visit is *kiitos* (KEE-tohs)—that's "thank you," and locals love to hear it. *Hei* (hey) means "hi" and *hei hei* (hey hey) means "goodbye." *Kippis* (KIHP-pihs) is what you say before you down a shot of Finnish vodka or cloudberry liqueur *(lakka)*.

Finnish Survival Phrases

In Finnish, the emphasis always goes on the first syllable. Double vowels (e.g., *ää* or *ii*) sound similar to single vowels, but are held a bit longer. The letter *y* sounds like the German *ü* (purse your lips and say "oh"). In the phonetics, ī sounds like the long *i* in "light," and bolded syllables are stressed.

English	Finnish	Pronunciation
Good morning. (formal)	Hyvää huomenta.	hew-vaah **hwoh**-mehn-tah
Good day. (formal)	Hyvää päivää.	hew-vaah **pī**-vaah
Good evening. (formal)	Hyvää iltaa.	hew-vaah **eel**-taah
Hi. / Bye. (informal)	Hei. / Hei-hei.	hey / hey-hey
Do you speak English?	Puhutko englantia?	**poo**-hoot-koh **ehn**-glahn-tee-yah
Yes. / No.	Kyllä. / Ei.	**kewl**-lah / ay
Please.	Ole hyvä.	**oh**-leh **hew**-vah
Thank you (very much).	Kiitos (paljon).	**kee**-tohs (**pahl**-yohn)
You're welcome.	Kiitos. / Ei kestä.	**kee**-tohs / ay **kehs**-tah
Can I help you?	Voinko auttaa?	**voin**-koh **owt**-taah
Excuse me.	Anteeksi.	**ahn**-teek-see
(Very) good.	(Oikein) hyvä.	(**oy**-kayn) **hew**-vah
Goodbye.	Näkemiin.	**nah**-keh-meen
one / two	yksi / kaksi	**ewk**-see / **kahk**-see
three / four	kolme / neljä	**kohl**-meh / **nehl**-yah
five / six	viisi / kuusi	**vee**-see / **koo**-see
seven / eight	seitsemän / kahdeksan	**sayt**-seh-mahn / **kah**-dehk-sahn
nine / ten	yhdeksän / kymmenen	**ew**-dehk-sahn / **kewm**-meh-nehn
hundred	sata	**sah**-tah
thousand	tuhat	**too**-haht
How much?	Paljonko?	**pahl**-yohn-koh
local currency: euro	euro	**ay**-oo-roh
Where is...?	Missä on...?	**mee**-sah ohn
...the toilet	...WC	**vay**-say
men	miehet	**mee**-ay-heht
women	naiset	**nī**-seht
water / coffee	vesi / kahvi	**veh**-see / **kah**-vee
beer / wine	olut / viini	**oh**-luht / **vee**-nee
Cheers!	Kippis!	**kip**-pis
The bill, please.	Saisinko laskun, kiitos.	**sī**-seen-koh **lahs**-kuhn **kee**-tohs

HELSINKI

The Finnish capital (Europe's youngest) feels like an outpost of both the Nordic and European worlds—it's the northernmost capital of the EU, and a short train ride from Russia. Yet against all odds, this quirky metropolis thrives, pleasing locals and tickling tourists. While it lacks the cutesy cobbles of Copenhagen, the dramatic setting of Stockholm, or the futuristic vibe of Oslo, Helsinki holds its own among Nordic capitals with its endearing Finnish personality. It's a spruce-and-stone wonderland of stunning 19th- to 21st-century architecture, with a bustling harborfront market, a lively main boulevard, fine museums, a scintillating design culture, dueling cathedrals (Lutheran and Orthodox), a quirky east-meets-west mélange of cultures...and a welcoming Finnish spirit to tie it all together.

Gusting winds swirl crying seagulls against a perfectly azure sky scattered with cotton-ball clouds. Rock bands and folk-dancing troupes enliven the Esplanade from the stage in front of Café Kappeli, sunny days lure coffee sippers out onto the sidewalks, and joyous festivals fill the summer (when the sky is still bright after midnight). And in this capital of a country renowned for design, window-

shopping the Design District—with unique home decor, clever kitchen gadgets, eye-grabbing prints, delicately handmade jewelry, and unique clothes that make a fashion statement with a Finnish accent—has a funny way of turning browsers into buyers.

While budget flights affordably connect Helsinki to the other Scandinavian capitals (and beyond), for many travelers, the next best thing to being in Helsinki is getting there on Europe's most enjoyable overnight boat. The trip from Stockholm starts with dramatic archipelago scenery, a setting sun, and a royal *smörgåsbord* dinner. Dance until you drop and sauna until you drip. Budget travel rarely feels this hedonistic. Sixteen hours after you depart, it's "Hello Helsinki." You can also cross—much more quickly—by boat to or from Tallinn, Estonia. For details on these options, see "Helsinki Connections," near the end of this chapter.

PLANNING YOUR TIME

On a three-week trip through Scandinavia, Helsinki is worth at least the time between two successive nights on the overnight boat—about seven hours. To do the city justice, two days is ideal. (Wear layers; Helsinki can be windy and cold.)

For a quick one-day visit, start with the 1.75-hour orientation bus tour that meets the boat at the dock. Then take my self-guided walking tour through the compact city center from the harbor—enjoying Helsinki's ruddy harborfront market and getting goose bumps in the churches—ending at the underground Temppeliaukio Church.

With more time, explore the Design District, dive into Finnish culture in the open-air folk museum, or take a walk in Kaivopuisto Park. If the weather's good, head for Suomenlinna, the island fortress where Helsinki was born. If it's bad, go for a sauna. Enjoy a cup of coffee at the landmark Café Kappeli before sailing away.

Orientation to Helsinki

Helsinki (pop. 604,000) has a compact core. The city's natural gateway is its main harbor, where ships from Stockholm and Tallinn dock. At the top of the harbor is Market Square (Kauppatori), an outdoor food and souvenir bazaar. Nearby are two towering, can't-miss-them landmarks: the white Lutheran Cathedral and the red-brick Orthodox Cathedral.

Helsinki's grand pedestrian boulevard, the Esplanade, begins right at Market Square, heads up past the TI, and ends after a few blocks in the central shopping district. At the top end of the Esplanade, the broad, traffic-filled Mannerheimintie avenue veers north through town past the train and bus stations on its way to many of

Helsinki History

Helsinki is the only European capital with no medieval past. Although it was founded in the 16th century by the Swedes in hopes of countering Tallinn as a strategic Baltic port, it stayed a village until the 18th century. Then, in 1746, Sweden built a huge fortress on an island outside its harbor, and Helsinki boomed as it supplied the fortress. After taking over Finland in 1809, the Russians decided to move Finland's capital and university closer to St. Petersburg—from Turku to Helsinki. They hired a young German architect, Carl Ludvig Engel, to design new public buildings for Helsinki and told him to use St. Petersburg as a model. This is why the oldest parts of Helsinki (around Market Square and Senate Square) feel so Russian—stone buildings in yellow and blue pastels with white trim and columns. Hollywood used Helsinki for the films *Gorky Park* and *Dr. Zhivago*, because filming in Russia was not possible during the Cold War.

Though the city was part of the Russian Empire in the 19th century, most of its residents still spoke Swedish, which was the language of business and culture. In the mid-1800s, Finland began to industrialize. The Swedish upper class in Helsinki expanded the city, bringing in the railroad and surrounding the old Russian-inspired core with neighborhoods of four- and five-story apartment buildings, including some Art Nouveau masterpieces. Meanwhile, Finns moved from the countryside to Helsinki to take jobs as industrial laborers. The Finnish language slowly acquired equal status with Swedish, and eventually Finnish speakers became the majority in Helsinki (though Swedish remains a co-official language).

Since downtown Helsinki didn't exist until the 1800s, it was more conscientiously designed and laid out than other European capitals. With its many architectural overleafs and fine Neoclassical and Art Nouveau buildings, Helsinki often turns guests into students of urban design and planning. Good neighborhoods for architecture buffs to explore are Katajanokka, Kruununhaka, and Eira.

All of this makes Helsinki sound like a very dry place. It's not. Despite its sometimes severe cityscape and chilly northern latitude, splashes of creativity and color hide around every corner. With a shorter (and, admittedly, less riveting) history than this book's other big cities, it helps to approach Helsinki as a city of today. Ogle its fine architecture, and delve into the boutiques of the Design District for some of Scandinavia's most eye-pleasing fashion and home decor. As you browse, remember that for the past several decades, global trends—from Marimekko's patterned fabrics to Nokia's sleek cell phones to the Angry Birds gaming empire—have been born right here in Helsinki.

HELSINKI

Helsinki's museums and architectural landmarks. The "Helsinki Tram #2/#3 Tour" also provides a good drive-by introduction to the main sights, and takes you into outlying neighborhoods that most tourists miss.

Linguistic Orientation: Finnish is completely different from the Scandinavian languages of Norwegian, Danish, and Swedish. That can make navigating a bit tricky. Place names ending in *-katu* are streets, *-tie* is "road" or "way," and *-tori* or *-aukio* means "square." Complicating matters, Finland's bilingual status means that most street names, tram stops, and map labels appear in both Finnish and Swedish. The two names often look completely different (for example, the South Harbor—where many overnight boats arrive— is called Eteläsatama in Finnish and Södra Hamnen in Swedish; the train station is Rautatieasema in Finnish, Järnvägsstationen in Swedish). The Swedish names can be a little easier to interpret than the Finnish ones. In any event, I've rarely met a Finn who doesn't speak excellent English.

TOURIST INFORMATION

The friendly, energetic **main TI,** just off the harbor, offers great service, and its brochure racks are fun to graze through. It's located a half-block inland from Market Square, on the right just past the fountain, at the corner of the Esplanade and Unioninkatu (May-Sept Mon-Fri 9:00-20:00, Sat-Sun 9:00-18:00, Oct-April closes two hours earlier, free Wi-Fi, guest computer, tel. 09/3101-3300, www.visithelsinki.fi). Pick up a city map, a public-transit map, and the free *Helsinki This Week* magazine (nicely illustrated, with articles on what to do in town as well as lists of sights, hours, concerts, and events). Ask about the scenic #2/#3 tram route/map. If interested in design, ask for publications about the local design culture; if music's your thing, ask about concerts—popular venues are Kallio Church and the Lutheran Cathedral.

The tiny **train station TI,** which consists of a one-person desk inside the Helsinki Expert office, provides many of the same services and publications.

Helsinki Expert: This private service, owned by Strömma/ Sightseeing Helsinki, sells the Helsinki Card (described next), ferry tickets (€8 booking fee), and sightseeing tours by bus and boat. They have one branch in the train station hall, another occupying the front desks in the main TI on Market Square, and small, summer-only sightseeing kiosks on the Esplanade and by the harbor (all branches open Mon-Fri 9:00-15:00, Sat 10:00-14:00, closed Sun, tel. 09/2288-1600, www.stromma.fi).

Helsinki Card: If you're planning to visit a lot of museums in Helsinki, this card can be a good deal. The card includes free

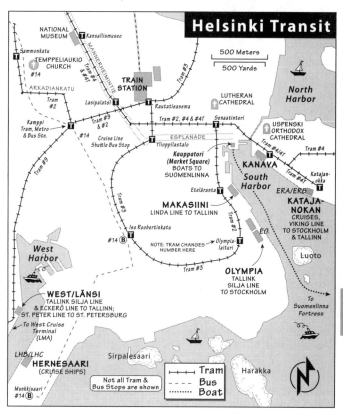

Helsinki Transit

NATIONAL MUSEUM — Kansallismuseo

Sammonkatu

TEMPPELIAUKIO CHURCH #14

ARKADIANKATU

Tram #2

Kamppi Tram, Metro & Bus Stn.

Lasipalatsi

Tram #9 & #2

#14

Cruise Line Shuttle Bus Stop

Tram #3

West Harbor

Iso Roobertinkatu

#14 B

NOTE: TRAM CHANGES NUMBER HERE

Tram #3

WEST/LÄNSI
TALLINK SILJA LINE & ECKERÖ LINE TO TALLINN; ST. PETER LINE TO ST. PETERSBURG

To West Cruise Terminal (LMA)

LHB/LHC
HERNESAARI
(CRUISE SHIPS)

Munkkisaari #14 B

500 Meters
500 Yards

TRAIN STATION

Rautatieasema

Tram #2, #4 & #4T

Senaatintori

ESPLANADE

Ylioppilastalo

Kauppatori (Market Square) BOATS TO SUOMENLINNA

Eteläranta

MAKASIINI
LINDA LINE TO TALLINN

LUTHERAN CATHEDRAL

North Harbor

USPENSKI ORTHODOX CATHEDRAL

Tram #4/4T

KANAVA

South Harbor

Tram #4

Katajan-okka

ERA/ERB

KATAJA-NOKAN
CRUISES, VIKING LINE TO STOCKHOLM & TALLINN

Luoto

Olympia-laituri

EO

OLYMPIA
TALLINK SILJA LINE TO STOCKHOLM

To Suomenlinna Fortress

Sirpalesaari

Harakka

Not all Tram & Bus Stops are shown

Tram
Bus
Boat

HELSINKI

entry to over 50 museums, fortresses, and other major sights; free use of buses, trams, and the ferry to Suomenlinna; a free city bus tour or harbor cruise (your choice—plus a discount on the other, plus a discount on the hop-on, hop-off bus); and a 72-page booklet (€44/24 hours, €54/48 hours, €64/72 hours, €3 less if bought online and picked up on arrival at the main TI's Helsinki Expert desk; sold at all Helsinki Expert locations, most hotels, and both Viking Line and Tallink Silja ferry terminals, www.helsinkicard.com).

For a cheaper alternative, you could buy a public-transit day ticket (see "Getting Around Helsinki," later), take my self-guided walk or tram tour, visit the free churches (Temppeliaukio Church, Lutheran Cathedral, Uspenski Orthodox Cathedral, and Kamppi Chapel of Silence), and stop by the free Helsinki City Museum.

ARRIVAL IN HELSINKI

By Boat: For details on taking the overnight boat from Stockholm to Helsinki, or the boat across the Gulf of Finland from Tallinn to

Helsinki, see "Helsinki Connections" near the end of this chapter. Helsinki's main South Harbor (Eteläsatama) has four terminals (terminaali); for locations, see the previous map and the color map in the front of this book. The Olympia and Makasiini terminals are on the south side (to the left as you face inland) of the main harbor. The Katajanokan terminal is on the north side (right) of the main harbor. Most Viking Line boats use the Katajanokan terminal; most Tallink Silja boats use the Olympia terminal. The Makasiini terminal is mostly for fast boats to Tallinn. Trams stop near all the main-harbor terminals (tram #4T near Katajanokan, tram #2/#3 near Olympia).

The Länsi terminal, in Helsinki's West Harbor (Länsistama), is for large car ferries to/from Tallinn and St. Peter Line boats to St. Petersburg. You can get to downtown Helsinki on tram #9 (leaves from right outside the door, zips you to the train station downtown) or by taxi (about €15).

By Cruise Ship: Cruises arrive at four different terminals in Helsinki; for all the details, see the end of this chapter.

By Train and Bus: The train station, an architectural landmark, is near the top of the Esplanade, a 15-minute walk from Market Square. Local buses leave from both sides of the building, trams stop out front, and the Metro runs underneath. The long-distance bus station is two blocks (or one tram stop) away, on the other side of Mannerheimintie, at the Kamppi shopping mall; the ticket office and machines are on the ground floor, with bus platforms below.

By Plane: Helsinki Airport is about 10 miles north of the city (airport code: HEL, www.helsinki-vantaa.fi). To get between the airport and downtown Helsinki, take the Finnair bus (€6.30, 3/hour, 35-minute trip, www.finnair.com; stops at some downtown hotels on request; return buses leave for airport from platform 30 at Elielinaukio on west side of train station) or public bus #615 (€5, pay driver, not covered by transit tickets or Helsinki Card, 3-6/hour, 45-minute trip, also stops at Hakaniemi; return buses leave for airport from platform 3 at Rautatientori on east side of train station). Or take the Yellow Line door-to-door shared van service (€20 for 1-2 people, €30 for 3-4 people, €40 for 5-6 people, tel. 010-00700 or toll tel. 0600-555-555, www.yellowline.fi). An ordinary taxi from the airport runs about €35-40.

HELPFUL HINTS

Time: Finland and Estonia are one hour ahead of Sweden and the rest of Scandinavia.

Money: Finland's currency is the euro. ATM machines are labeled *Otto.*

Telephones: Finland's phone system generally uses area codes, but has some national or mobile numbers (starting with 010 or 020) that must be dialed in full when you're calling from anywhere in the country.

Internet Access: For the tourist, Helsinki is one of Europe's handiest cities for free Wi-Fi; along the Esplanade and throughout the city center, look for the "Helsinki City Open" network. Most hotels, cafés, and museums also have hot spots. The **City Hall,** facing Market Square and the harbor, has six free, fast terminals and speedy Wi-Fi in its inviting lobby (get code for terminal from desk, Mon-Fri 9:00-19:00, Sat-Sun 10:00-16:00).

Pharmacy: A **24-hour pharmacy**—*apteekki*—is located at Mannerheimintie 96 (at Kansaneläkelaitos stop for tram #2, #4/4T, or #10, tel. 020-320-200).

Laundry: PesuNet, primarily a dry-cleaning shop, welcomes travelers to use its half-dozen self-service machines. It's within a few blocks of recommended hotels, and the Iso Roobertinkatu stop for tram #3 is around the corner. Multitaskers can browse the nearby Design District to pass waiting time (€10/load, not coin-op—pay staff who will help, Mon-Thu 8:00-19:00, Fri 8:00-18:00, Sat 10:00-15:00, closed Sun, Punavuorenkatu 3, tel. 09/622-1146).

Bike Rental: Try **Greenbike** (one-speed bike-€5/hour or €20/all day; three-speed bike-€30/all day; May-Aug daily 10:00-18:00, shorter hours and closed Sun-Mon off-season, Bulevardi 32—but entrance is just around the corner on Albertinkatu, mobile 050-550-1020, www.greenbike.fi). Another option is at the locksmith shop just inside the Metro station facing the **Kamppi plaza**—but they have higher prices and less helpful service (€24/4 hours, €30/all day, €35/24 hours, Mon-Fri 7:00-21:00, Sat 9:00-18:00, Sun 12:00-18:00, tel. 09/739-010); Greenbike sometimes has a temporary location set up on this plaza, as well.

Best View: The **Torni Tower's Ateljee Bar** offers a free panorama view. Ride the elevator from the lobby of the venerable Torni Hotel (built in 1931) to the 12th floor, where you can browse around the perch or sit down for a pricey drink (€5 coffee, €8-10 alcohol, Sun-Thu 14:00-24:00, Fri-Sat 12:00-24:00, Yrjönkatu 26, tel. 020-123-4604).

Meet the Finns: With **Cozy Finland's** "Meet the Finns" program, you can match your hobbies with a local—and suddenly, you're searching out classic comics at the flea market with a new Finnish friend. Their most popular service involves arranging dinner at a local host's home (around €60); contact Cozy Finland for exact prices (www.cosyfinland.com).

What's With the Slot Machines? Finns just have a love affair with lotteries and petty gambling. You'll see coin-operated games of chance everywhere, including restaurants, supermarkets, and the train station.

Updates to This Book: For updates to this book, check www.ricksteves.com/update.

GETTING AROUND HELSINKI

In compact Helsinki, you won't need to use public transportation as much as in Stockholm.

By Bus and Tram: With the public-transit route map (available at the TI, also viewable on the Helsinki Region Transport website—www.hsl.fi) and a little mental elbow grease, the buses and trams are easy, giving you Helsinki by the tail. The single Metro line is also part of the system, but is not useful unless you're traveling to my recommended sauna.

Single tickets are good for an hour of travel (€3 from driver, €2.50 at ticket machines at a few larger bus and tram stops). A day ticket (€8/24 hours of unlimited travel, issued on a plastic card you'll touch against the card reader when entering the bus or tram) pays for itself if you take four or more rides; longer versions are also available (€4 per extra 24 hours, 7-day maximum). Day tickets can be bought at the ubiquitous yellow-and-blue R-Kiosks (convenience stores), as well as at TIs, the train station, Metro stations, ticket machines at a handful of stops, and on some ferries, but not from drivers. The Helsinki Card also covers public transportation. All of these tickets and cards are only valid within the city of Helsinki, not the suburbs; for example, you pay extra for the public bus to the airport.

Tours in Helsinki

As in Stockholm, the big company Strömma (also called Sightseeing Helsinki and Helsinki Expert) has a near monopoly on city tours, whether by bus, boat, or foot. For a fun, cheap tour, take public tram #2/#3—it makes the rounds of most of the town's major sights in an hour. Use my self-guided "Helsinki Tram #2/#3

HELSINKI

Tour" (described later and rated ▲▲) to follow along with what you see, and also pick up the helpful tram #2/#3 explanatory brochure—free at TIs and often on board.

▲▲▲Orientation Bus Tours

These 1.75-hour "Helsinki Panorama" bus tours give an ideal city overview with a look at all of the important buildings, from the remodeled Olympic Stadium to Embassy Row. You stay on the bus the entire time, except for a 10-minute stop or two (when possible, they try to stop at the Sibelius Monument and/or Temppeliaukio Church). You'll learn strange facts, such as how Finns took down the highest steeple in town during World War II so that Soviet bombers flying in from Estonia couldn't see their target. Tours get booked up, so it's wise to reserve in advance online or ask your hotelier to help (€31, free with Helsinki Card, tel. 09/2288-1600, www.stromma.fi, sales@stromma.fi).

Bus Tours Departing from Boat Dock: Conveniently, tours depart from the Viking Line and Tallink Silja boat docks at 10:30, soon after the boats arrive from Stockholm. Tours end back at the dock they started from, though you can get off downtown near the end of the tour. If you want to take the bus tour and end up downtown for an overnight stay, stow your bag on the bus, and get off in the city center before the end of the tour (cost-effectively using the tour for transportation as well as for information). Viking Line tours usually have recorded commentary, while Tallink Silja tours typically have a live guide in the summer (June-Aug).

Bus Tour Departing from the Center: The same 1.75-hour bus tour (usually with recorded commentary) leaves later in the day from the corner of Fabianinkatu and the Esplanade. The 11:00 tour goes daily year-round (additional departures possible April-Aug).

Hop-On, Hop-Off Bus Tours

If you'd enjoy the tour described above, but want the chance to hop on and off at will, consider **Open Top Tours** (owned by Strömma/Helsinki Sightseeing, green buses), with a 1.5-hour loop that connects downtown Helsinki, several outlying sights—including the Sibelius Monument and Olympic Stadium—as well as the Hernesaari cruise terminal. Buses run every 30-45 minutes and make 13 stops (€27, €39 combo-ticket also includes harbor tour—see next, all tickets good for 24 hours, mid-May-late Sept daily 10:00-16:00, www.stromma.fi). A different company, **Sightseeing City Tour** (red buses), offers a similar route for similar prices, but has fewer departures (www.citytour.fi).

Harbor Tours

Three boat companies compete for your attention along Market Square, offering snoozy cruises around the harbor and its islands

Helsinki at a Glance

▲▲▲**Temppeliaukio Church** Awe-inspiring, copper-topped 1969 "Church in the Rock." **Hours:** June-Sept Mon-Sat 10:00-17:45, Sun 11:45-17:45; closes one hour earlier off-season. See page 158.

▲▲**Uspenski Orthodox Cathedral** Orthodoxy's most prodigious display outside of Eastern Europe. **Hours:** Tue-Fri 9:30-20:00, Sat 10:00-15:00, Sun 12:00-15:00, closed Mon. See page 152.

▲▲**Lutheran Cathedral** Green-domed, 19th-century Neoclassical masterpiece. **Hours:** June-Aug Mon-Sat 9:00-24:00, Sun 12:00-24:00; Sept-May Mon-Sat 9:00-18:00, Sun 12:00-18:00. See page 153.

▲▲**Suomenlinna Fortress** Helsinki's harbor island, sprinkled with picnic spots, museums, and military history. **Hours:** Museum daily May-Sept 10:00-18:00, Oct-April 10:30-16:30. See page 161.

▲▲**Seurasaari Open-Air Folk Museum** Island museum with 100 historic buildings from Finland's farthest corners. **Hours:** June-Aug daily 11:00-17:00; late May and early Sept Mon-Fri 9:00-15:00, Sat-Sun 11:00-17:00, buildings closed mid-Sept-mid-May. See page 164.

▲**Senate Square** Consummate Neoclassical square, with Lutheran Cathedral. **Hours:** Always open. See page 139.

roughly hourly from 10:00 to 18:00 in summer (typically 1.5 hours for €17-24; www.royalline.net, www.ihalines.fi, www.stromma.fi). The narration is slow-moving—often recorded and in as many as four languages. I'd call it an expensive nap. Taking the ferry out to Suomenlinna and back gets you onto the water for much less money (€5 round-trip, covered by day ticket or Helsinki Card). If you do take a harbor cruise, here's how the competing companies differ: **Helsinki Sightseeing/Strömma** (yellow-and-white boats) offers the best and priciest route, going through a narrow channel in the east to reach sights that the other cruises miss. The other companies focus on the harbor itself and Suomenlinna fortress; of these, **Royal Line** (green-and-white boats) has the best food service on board, while **IHA** (blue-and-white boats) is more likely to have a live guide (half their boats have live guides, the others have recorded commentary).

▲**Helsinki City Museum** Tells the city's history well and in English. **Hours:** Mon-Fri 9:00-17:00, Thu until 19:00, Sat-Sun 11:00-17:00. See page 154.

▲**Ateneum, The National Gallery of Finland** Largest collection of art in Finland, including local favorites plus works by Cézanne, Chagall, Gauguin, and Van Gogh. **Hours:** Tue and Fri 10:00-18:00, Wed-Thu 9:00-20:00, Sat-Sun 10:00-17:00, closed Mon. See page 154.

▲**National Museum of Finland** The scoop on Finland, featuring folk costumes, an armory, czars, and thrones; the prehistory and 20th-century exhibits are best. **Hours:** Tue-Sun 11:00-18:00, closed Mon. See page 157.

▲**Sibelius Monument** Stainless-steel sculptural tribute to Finland's greatest composer. **Hours:** Always open. See page 159.

▲**Design Museum** A chronological look at Finland's impressive design pedigree, plus cutting-edge temporary exhibits. **Hours:** June-Aug daily 11:00-18:00; Sept-May Tue 11:00-20:00, Wed-Sun 11:00-18:00, closed Mon. See page 159.

HELSINKI

Pub Tram

In summer, this antique red tram makes a 50-minute loop through the city while its passengers get looped on the beer for sale on board (€9 to ride, €6 beer, mid-May-Aug Tue-Sat 14:00-20:00, no trams Sun-Mon, leaves at the top of each hour from in front of the Fennia building, Mikonkatu 17, across from train-station tower, www.koff.net).

Local Guides

Helsinki Expert can arrange a private guide (book at least three days in advance, €204/2 hours, tel. 09/2288-1222, sales@stromma.fi). **Christina Snellman** is a good, licensed guide (mobile 050-527-4741, chrisder@pp.inet.fi). **Archtour** offers local guides who specialize in Helsinki's architecture (tel. 09/477-7300, www.archtours.com).

Helsinki Walk

This self-guided walk—worth ▲▲▲—offers a convenient spine for your Helsinki sightseeing. I've divided the walk into two parts: On a quick visit, focus on Part 1 (which takes about an hour). To dig deeper into the city's architectural landmarks—and reach some of its museums—continue with Part 2 (which adds about another 45 minutes). Note that several points of interest on this walk are described in more detail later, under "Sights in Helsinki."

PART 1: THE HARBORFRONT, SENATE SQUARE, AND ESPLANADE

• *Start at the obelisk in the center of the harborfront market.*

❶ Market Square

At the square's heart is the **Czarina's Stone,** with its double-headed eagle of imperial Russia. It was the first public monument in Helsinki, designed by Carl Ludvig Engel and erected in 1835 to celebrate the visit by Czar Nicholas I and Czarina Alexandra. Step over the chain and climb to the top step for a clockwise spin-tour:

Begin by facing the **harbor.** The big, red Viking ship and white Silja ship are each floating hotels for those making the 40-hour Stockholm-Helsinki round-trip. Now pan to the right. The brick-and-tan building along the harborfront is the Old Market Hall, with some enticing, more upscale options than the basic grub at the outdoor market (for a rundown on both options, see "Eating in Helsinki," later). Between here and there, a number of harbor cruise boats vie for your business. Farther to the right, the trees mark the beginning of Helsinki's grand promenade, the Esplanade (where we're heading). Hiding in the leaves is the venerable iron-and-glass Café Kappeli. The yellow building across from the trees is the TI. From there, a string of Neoclassical buildings face the harbor. The blue-and-white City Hall building was designed by Engel in 1833 as the town's first hotel, built to house the czar and czarina. The Lutheran Cathedral is hidden from view behind this building (we'll go there soon). Next, after the short peach-colored building, is the Swedish Embassy (flying the blue-and-yellow Swedish flag and designed to look like Stockholm's Royal Palace). Then comes the Supreme Court and, tucked back in the far corner, Finland's Presidential Palace. Finally, standing proud, and reminding Helsinki of the Russian behemoth to its east, is the Uspenski Orthodox Cathedral.

Explore the colorful **outdoor market**—part souvenirs and crafts, part fruit and veggies, part fish and snacks. Sniff the stacks of trivets, made from cross-sections of juniper twigs—an ideal, fragrant, easy-to-pack gift for the folks back home (they smell even nicer when you set something hot on them).

Done exploring? With your back to the water, walk left to the end of Market Square and cross the street (tiptoeing over tram tracks) to reach the fountain, *Havis*

Amanda. Designed by Ville Vallgren and unveiled here in 1908, the fountain has become the symbol of Helsinki, the city known as the "Daughter of the Baltic"—graduating students decorate her with a school cap. The voluptuous figure, modeled after the artist's Parisian mistress, was a bit too racy for the conservative town, and Vallgren had trouble getting paid. But as artists often do, Vallgren had the last laugh: For more than a hundred years now, the city budget office (next to the Sasso restaurant across the street) has seen only her backside.

• *Follow Havis Amanda's right cheek across the street, go right one block (toward the harborfront), then turn left up Sofiankatu street (passing, on your right, the City Hall—with free Wi-Fi, Internet terminals, huge public WCs in the basement, and free exhibits on Helsinki history—often photography). Near the end of the block, on the left, you may see the free **Helsinki City Museum** (unless it's 2016 or later, in which case it will have moved one block east). You'll pop out right in the middle of...*

❷ Senate Square

This was once a simple town square with a church and City Hall—but its original buildings were burned when Russians invaded in 1808. Later, after Finland became a grand duchy of the Russian Empire, the czar sent in architect Carl Ludvig Engel (a German who had lived and worked in St. Petersburg) to give the place some Neo-class. The result: the finest Neoclassical square in Europe. Engel represents the paradox of Helsinki: The city as we know it was built by Russia, but with an imported European architect, in a very intentionally "European" style. So Helsinki is, in a sense, both entirely Russian...and not Russian in the slightest.

The statue in the center of the square honors **Russian Czar Alexander II.** While he wasn't popular in Russia (he was assassinated), he was well-liked by the Finns. That's because he gave Finland more autonomy in 1863 and never pushed the "Russification" of Finland. The statue shows him holding the Finnish constitution,

HELSINKI

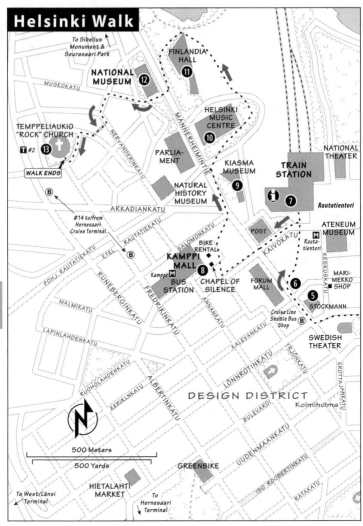

Helsinki Walk

To Sibelius
Monument &
Seurasaari Park

FINLANDIA
HALL **11**

NATIONAL
MUSEUM **12**

MUSEOKATU

HELSINKI
MUSIC
CENTRE **10**

TEMPPELIAUKIO
"ROCK" CHURCH

T #2 **13**

WALK ENDS

MANNERHEIMINTIE

NERVANDERINKATU

PARLIA-
MENT

KIASMA
MUSEUM **9**

NATURAL
HISTORY
MUSEUM

NATIONAL
THEATER

TRAIN
STATION

i **7**

Rautatientori

B

ARKADIANKATU

ATENEUM
MUSEUM

Rauta-
tientori

#14 to/from
Hernesaari
Cruise Terminal

RAUTATIEKATU

POST

KAIVOKATU

KESKUSKATU

B

ETEL.

SALOMONKATU

BIKE
RENTAL

KAMPPI
MALL **8**

M

POHJ. RAUTATIEKATU

RUNEBERGINKATU

FREDRIKINKATU

Kampit **M**

BUS
STATION

CHAPEL OF
SILENCE

FORUM
MALL **6**

MARI-
MEKKO
SHOP

5

STOCKMANN

MALMIKATU

LAPINLAHDENKATU

ANNANKATU

KALEVANKATU

Cruise Line
Shuttle Bus
Stop **B**

SWEDISH
THEATER

RUOHOLAHDENKATU

EERIKINKATU

ALBERTINKATU

LÖNNROTINKATU

YRJÖNKATU

DESIGN DISTRICT

BULEVARDI

Kolmihulma

EROTTAJANKATU

N

500 Meters

500 Yards

UUDENMAANKATU

GREENBIKE

ISO ROOBERTINKATU

RATAKATU

HIETALAHTI
MARKET

To West/Länsi
Terminal

To
Hernesaari
Terminal

HELSINKI

which he supported. It defined internal independence and affirmed autonomy.

The huge **staircase** leading up to the **Lutheran Cathedral** is a popular meeting (and tanning) spot in Helsinki. This is where students from the nearby university gather...and romances are born.

Head up those stairs and survey Senate Square from the top. Scan the square from left to right. First, 90 degrees to your left is the **Senate building** (now the prime minister's office). The small, blue, stone building with the slanted mansard roof in the far-left corner, from 1757, is one of just two pre-Russian-conquest build-

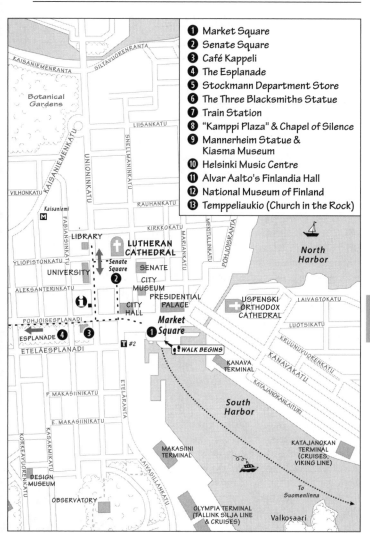

1. Market Square
2. Senate Square
3. Café Kappeli
4. The Esplanade
5. Stockmann Department Store
6. The Three Blacksmiths Statue
7. Train Station
8. "Kamppi Plaza" & Chapel of Silence
9. Mannerheim Statue & Kiasma Museum
10. Helsinki Music Centre
11. Alvar Aalto's Finlandia Hall
12. National Museum of Finland
13. Temppeliaukio (Church in the Rock)

ings remaining in Helsinki. **Café Engel** (opposite the cathedral at Aleksanterinkatu 26) is a fine place for a light lunch or cake and coffee. The café's winter lighting seems especially designed to boost the spirits of glum, daylight-deprived Northerners.

Continue looking right. Facing the Senate directly across the square is its twin, the **University of Helsinki's** main building (36,000 students, 60 percent female). Symbolically (and physically), the university and government buildings are connected via the cathedral, and both use it as a starting point for grand ceremonies.

Farther to the right, and tucked alongside the cathedral, the line of once-grand Russian administration buildings now house the **National Library.** In czarist times, the National Library received a copy of every book printed in the Russian Empire. With all the chaos Russia suffered throughout the 20th century, a good percentage of its Slavic texts were destroyed. But Helsinki, which enjoyed relative stability, claims to have the finest collection of Slavic books in the world. This fine, purpose-built Neoclassical building is generally open to the public and worth a look (though it may be closed for renovation through late 2015).

If you'd like to visit the **cathedral interior,** now's your chance; the entrance is tucked around the left side as you face the towering dome.

• *When you're ready, head back down the stairs and angle right through the square, continuing straight down Unioninkatu.*

Along **Unioninkatu,** do a little window-shopping; this is the first of many streets we'll see lined with made-in-Finland shops (though these are more touristy than the norm). In addition to the jewelry shops and clothes boutiques, look for the Schröder sporting goods store (on the left, at #23), which shows off its famous selection of popular Finnish-made Rapala fishing lures—ideal for the fisher folk on your gift list. At the end of this street (on the right), you'll spot the TI, with a Helsinki Expert desk inside (handy for booking bus tours and other activities).

• *Facing Havis Amanda's backside once more, turn right and head into the grassy median, with the delightful...*

❸ Café Kappeli

If you've got some time, dip into this old-fashioned, gazebo-like oasis of coffee, pastry, and relaxation (get what you like at the bar inside and sit anywhere). In the 19th century, this was a popular hangout for local intellectuals and artists. Today the café offers romantic tourists waiting for their ship a great €3-cup-of-coffee memory (daily 9:00-24:00). The bandstand in front hosts nearly daily music and dance performances in summer.

• *Beyond Café Kappeli stretches...*

❹ The Esplanade

Helsinki's top shopping boulevard sandwiches a park in the middle (another Engel design from the 1830s). The grandiose street names Esplanadi and Bulevardi, while fitting today, must have been bombastic and almost comical in rustic little 1830s Helsinki. To help you imagine this elegant promenade in the 19th century, informative signs (in English) explain Esplanade Park's background and its many statues.

The north side (on the right, with the TI) is interesting for window-shopping, people-watching, and sun-worshipping. In fact, after the first block, browsers may want to leave the park and cross over to that side of the street. In just a few steps, you'll pass flagship stores for several household-name Finnish designers.

First up, at #25B, **Iittala** displays dishes and other glassware, both decorative and functional. Popping into the shop, you'll see Alvar Aalto's signature wavy-mouthed vases, which haven't gone out of fashion since 1936; Oiva Toikka's iconic "dew drop"-patterned chalices and pedestal bowls, from 1964, as well as his bird sculptures; and a mini-museum of glass art in the back (Art & Design Studio).

Back on the Esplanade, a few doors down at #27C, **Kalevala Jewelry** sells quality made-in-Finland jewelry. Some pieces look modern, while others are inspired by old Scandinavian, Finnish, and Sami themes. Next door (also at #27C), **Aarikka** is more affordable and casual, with costume jewelry, accessories, and home decor made mostly from big, colorful spheres of wood.

In the next block, the hulking, ornately decorated **Hotel Kämp** (#29) is a city landmark. **Galleria Esplanad** (entrance at #31) is a super-exclusive mall with big-name Finnish and international fashion stores. Then, after the recommended **Strindberg Café** (one of many fine spots along the Esplanade to nurse a drink), at the corner, is perhaps Finland's most famous export: **Marimekko,** whose mostly floral patterns adorn everything from purses to shower curtains to iPhone cases (two more Marimekko branches—specializing in clothes and kids' stuff—are within a block of here).

Directly across the Esplanade's park median from Marimekko is another landmark of world design, **Artek.** Founded by designers Alvar and Elissa Aalto, this shop showcases expensive, high-end housewares in the modern, practical style that Ikea commercialized successfully for the mass market.

In the block after Marimekko, at #39, is the huge **Academic Bookstore** (Akateeminen Kirjakauppa), designed by Alvar Aalto, with an extensive map and travel section, periodicals, English books, and Café Aalto.

At the very top of the Esplanade, the park dead-ends at the **Swedish Theater.** Built under Russian rule to cater to Swedish residents of a Finnish city, this building encapsulates Helsinki's complex cultural mix. (The theater's recommended Teatterin Grilli is handy for a drink or meal out in the park.) The Finnish National Theater—catering to the other segment of the city's bilingual population—is nearby, close to the train station.

• At the end of the Esplanade, on the right, you'll reach...

❺ Stockmann Department Store

This prestigious local institution is Finland's answer to Harrods or Macy's. Stockmann is the biggest, best, and oldest department store in town, with a great gourmet supermarket in the basement. Just beyond is Helsinki's main intersection, where Esplanade and Mannerheimintie meet.

• Turn right on Mannerheimintie. At the far side of Stockmann, you'll see a landmark statue, the...

❻ Three Blacksmiths

While there's no universally accepted meaning for this statue (from 1932), most say it celebrates human labor and cooperation

and shows the solid character of the Finnish people. On the base, note the rare, surviving bullet damage from World War II. The Soviet Union used that war as an opportunity to invade Finland—which it had lost just 20 years prior—to try to reclaim their buffer zone. In a two-part war (the "Winter War," then the "Continuation War"), Finland held fast and emerged with its freedom—and relatively little damage.

Stockmann's entrance on Aleksanterinkatu, facing the *Three Blacksmiths,* is one of the city's most popular meeting points. Everyone in Finland knows exactly what it means when you say: "Let's meet under the Stockmann's clock." Tram #2/#3 makes a stop around the corner from the clock, on Mannerheimintie. Across the street from the clock, the Old Student Hall is decorated with mythic Finnish heroes.

• For a shortcut to our next stop, duck through the passage (marked City-Käytävä) directly across the street from Stockmann's clock. This will take you through a bustling commercial zone. You'll enter—and continue straight through—the City Center shopping mall. Emerging on the far side, you're face-to-face with the harsh (but serene) architecture of the...

❼ Train Station

This Helsinki landmark was designed by Eliel Saarinen (see sidebar). The four people on the facade symbolize peasant farmers with lamps coming into the Finnish capital. Duck into the main hall and the Eliel Restaurant inside to catch the building's ambience.

Exiting, with your back to the train station, look to the left; diagonally across the square is Finland's National Gallery, the

HELSINKI

Ateneum (with works by obscure but talented Finns, as well as better-known international artists). Directly across the square (and not visible from here), it faces the **Finnish National Theater**—the counterpoint to the Swedish Theater we saw earlier.

• *We've worked our way through the central part of town. Now, if you're ready to explore some interesting buildings and monuments, continue with...*

PART 2: MANNERHEIMINTIE AND HELSINKI'S ICONIC ARCHITECTURE

The rest of this walk follows the boulevard called Mannerheimintie, which serves as a showcase for much of Helsinki's iconic architecture; this walk also helps you reach some of the city's farther-flung sights. (Details on many of these appear later, under "Sights in Helsinki.")

• *With your back to the station, turn right and follow the tram tracks (along Kaivokatu street) back out to the busy boulevard called Mannerheimintie. Cross the street and the tram tracks, and continue straight ahead, toward what looks like a giant wood block. You'll pop out the bustling plaza in front of the Kamppi shopping mall, called...*

❽ "Kamppi Plaza" (Narinkkatori) and the Chapel of Silence

This is a hub of Helsinki—both for transportation (with a Metro stop and bus station nearby) and for shopping (with the towering Kamppi Center shopping mall). Turn your attention to the round, wooden structure at the corner of the plaza nearest the Esplanade. This is one of Helsinki's newest and most surprising bits of architecture: the Kamppi **Chapel of Silence.** Enter through the doorway in the black building just to the right, and enjoy a moment or three of total serenity.

• *Leaving the chapel, cut through the middle of the big plaza, with the shopping mall on your left and the low-lying yellow building on your right. Through the gap at the end of the square, you'll see an equestrian statue. Go meet him.*

❾ Carl Gustaf Mannerheim and the Kiasma Museum

The busy street's namesake was a Finnish war hero who frustrated the Soviets both in Finland's "Civil War" for independence, and again later, in World War II. Mannerheim and his fellow Finns put up a fierce resistance, and the Soviets finally gave up and redirected their efforts to the race to Berlin. While the Baltic States—across the Gulf of Finland—were "liberated" by the Red Army, dooming them to decades under the Soviet system, the Finns managed to refuse this assistance. Mannerheim became Finland's first postwar

HELSINKI

Two Men Who Remade Helsinki

Eliel Saarinen (1873-1950)

At the turn of the 20th century, architect Eliel Saarinen burst on the scene by pioneering the Finnish National Romantic style. Inspired by peasant and medieval architectural traditions, his work was fundamental in creating a distinct—and modern—Finnish identity. The château-esque National Museum of Finland, designed by Saarinen and his two partners after winning a 1902 architectural competition, was his first major success (see page 157). Two years later, Saarinen won the contract to construct the Helsinki train station (completed in 1919). Its design marks a transition into the Art Nouveau style of the early 1900s. The landmark station—characterized by massive male sculptures flanking its entrance, ornate glass and metalwork, and a soaring clock tower—presently welcomes over 300,000 travelers each day.

In the early 1920s, Saarinen and his family emigrated to the US where his son, Eero, would become the architect of such iconic projects as the Gateway Arch in St. Louis and the main terminal at Dulles International Airport near Washington, DC.

Alvar Aalto (1898-1976)

Alvar Aalto was a celebrated Finnish architect and designer working in the Modernist tradition; his buildings used abstract

forms and innovative materials without sacrificing functionality. Finlandia Hall in Helsinki is undoubtedly Aalto's most famous structure, but that's just the beginning. A Finnish Frank Lloyd Wright, Aalto concerned himself with nearly every aspect of design, from furniture to light fixtures. Perhaps most notable of these creations was his sinuous Savoy Vase, a masterpiece of simplicity and sophistication that is emblematic of the Aalto style. His designs became so popular that in 1935 he and his wife opened Artek, a company that manufactures and sells his furniture, lamps, and textiles to this day (see page 166).

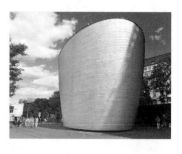

president, and thanks to his efforts (and those of countless others), Finland was allowed to chart its own democratic, capitalist course after the war. (Even so, Finland remained officially neutral through the Cold War, providing both East and West a political buffer zone.)

Mannerheim is standing in front of the glassy home of the **Kiasma Museum,** with changing exhibits of contemporary art. A bit farther along and across the street from Kiasma, with its stoic row of Neoclassical columns, stands the Finnish **Parliament.**

From Mannerheim and Kiasma, head down into the grassy, sloping park. At the lowest point, watch out—you're crossing a busy **bicycle highway** that cuts right through the middle of the city center. Look left under the tunnel to see how they turned a disused old rail line into a subterranean pedalers' paradise.

• *The glassy building dominating the end of the park is the...*

⑩ Helsinki Music Centre (Musiikkitalo)

Completed in 2011, this structure is even bigger than it looks: two-thirds of it is underground, and the entire complex houses seven

separate venues. It's decorated, inside and out, with bold art (such as the gigantic pike on tiptoes that stands in the middle of the park). As you approach the bottom of the building, step into the atrium (Mon-Fri 8:00-22:00, Sat 10:00-22:00, Sun 10:00-20:00) and look up to ogle the shimmering silver sculpture. While you're there, consider stopping by the ticket desk (on the lower floor) to ask about performances while you're in town; unfortunately, the season is September through April—low time for tourists. Upstairs is a music store. The interior features a lot of pine and birch accents, which warm up the space and improve the (Japanese-designed) acoustics. It didn't take long for the Music Centre to become an integral part of the city's cultural life; in the first season of performances alone, some 400,000 people attended events here. They also offer English tours of the facility (see "Sights in Helsinki," later).

Back outside, circle around the back side of the Music Centre. Follow the straight, flat promenade that runs alongside a grassy park used for special events, and a former industrial zone that's slated for further redevelopment; the train tracks are just beyond.

• Crossing the street, you'll see (on the left) perhaps the most important work of Finnish architecture...

⓫ Alvar Aalto's Finlandia Hall

While famous, this big, white building can be a bit difficult for nonarchitects to appreciate. Walk through the long parking lot

all the way to the far end, and look back for a more dramatic view. The building—entirely designed by Aalto, inside and out—opened in 1971 and immediately became a national icon. Notice how Aalto employs geometric shapes and sweeping lines to create a striking concert hall, seating up to 1,700 guests. Aalto designed the inclined roof to try to maximize the hall's acoustics—imitating the echo chamber of an old-fashioned church tower—with marginal success.

Turn to face shimmering **Töölönlahti Bay** (not a lake, but an inlet of the Baltic Sea)—ringed by a popular walking and jogging track. From here, you can see more Helsinki landmarks: across the lake and a bit to the left, the white tower marks the Olympic Stadium that hosted the world in 1952. And to the right are the rides of Helsinki's old-time amusement park, Lenininpuisto.

• If you'd like to extend this walk with a leisurely stroll, join the natives on the waterfront path (which offers even better views of Finlandia Hall). Otherwise, consider...

More Helsinki Sights

To reach two more major sights, go up the stairs immediately to the right of Finlandia Hall, then continue all the way up to the main road. Directly across the street stands what looks like a château with a steeple. This building houses the fine ⓬ **National Museum of Finland,** which tells this country's story with lots of artifacts.

There's one more great architectural treasure in Helsinki, about a 10-minute walk behind the National Museum: the sit-and-wipe-a-tear beautiful "Church in the Rock," ⓭ **Temppeliaukio.** Once inside, sit. Enjoy the music. It's a wonderful place to end this walk.

To continue on to the **Sibelius Monument,** located in a lovely park setting, take bus #24 (direction: Seurasaari) from nearby Arkadiankatu street. The same ticket is good for your return trip (within one hour), or ride it to the end of the line for the bridge to Seurasaari Island and Finland's open-air folk museum. From there, bus #24 returns to the top of the Esplanade.

All three of these sights are explained in more detail later, under "Sights in Helsinki."

Helsinki Tram Tour

Of Helsinki's many tram routes, #2/#3 seems made-to-order for a tourist's joyride, and is worth ▲▲. In fact, the TI hands out a free little map with the described route, making this self-guided tour easier to follow.

If you buy a single ticket, just stay on the tram for the entire circuit (€3 from driver, €2.50 from ticket machines at a few major stops, good for one hour). Using a day ticket (see "Getting Around Helsinki," earlier) or a Helsinki Card allows you to hop off to tour a sight, then catch a later tram (runs every 10 minutes).

You can't get lost because the route makes a figure-eight, and an hour after you start, you end up back at the beginning. The only confusing thing is that the tram has different names during different parts of the figure-eight; the top-left and bottom-right lobes are #2, the other lobes are #3, and the letter on the tram's sign changes at the north and south ends of the route. A few departures circle only the top or bottom loop, so confirm with the driver before boarding that your tram will make the entire figure-eight.

❶ Market Square: While you can hop on anywhere, it's most convenient to start—and end—at Market Square by the TI. Stand at the tram stop that is between the fountain and the market, and wait for one of the frequent #2 trams. Since the tracks split here briefly, it's hard to get on in the wrong direction; still, confirm that the destination listed on the front of the tram is *Eläintarha*, not *Kaivopuisto*. From Market Square, you'll first pass **Senate Square** (with the gleaming white Lutheran Cathedral, a statue of Alexander II—Finland's favorite czar, and many of the oldest buildings in town) and then head up Aleksanterinkatu street. It's Helsinki's Fifth Avenue-type main shopping drag (tram stop: Aleksanterinkatu).

❷ Finnish National Theater/Train Station: After the Mikonkatu stop, you'll pass a big square. Fronting it is Finland's granite National Theater, in Art Nouveau style. The statue in the square honors Aleksis Kivi, the father of Finnish literature, who in 1870 wrote *The Seven Brothers*, the first great novel in Finnish. The mid-19th century was a period of national awakening. By elevating the language to high culture, Kivi helped inspire his countrymen to stand strong and proud during a period of attempted "Russification." On the left is the **Ateneum,** Finland's national art gallery. From there (on the right), you'll pass the striking train station—with its iconic countrymen stoically holding their lamps—designed by the great Finnish architect, Eliel Saarinen.

Helsinki Tram Tour

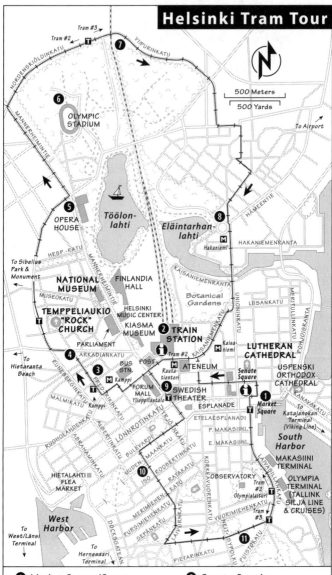

N

500 Meters
500 Yards

To Airport

Tram #3
Tram #2

VIIPURINKATU

NORDENSKIÖLDINKATU

7

6 OLYMPIC STADIUM

MANNERHEIMINTIE

Töölön-lahti

5 OPERA HOUSE

Eläintarhan-lahti

8

HÄMEENTIE

HAKANIEMENRANTA

Hakaniemi

MERITULLINKATU

To Sibelius Park & Monument

HESP.-KATU

KAISANIEMENRANTA

NATIONAL MUSEUM

FINLANDIA HALL

Botanical Gardens

LIISANKATU

UNIONINKATU

MUSEOKATU

HELSINKI MUSIC CENTER

TEMPPELIAUKIO "ROCK" CHURCH

KIASMA MUSEUM

2 TRAIN STATION

Kaisa-niemi

LUTHERAN CATHEDRAL

KAISANIEMENK.

PARLIAMENT

To Hietaranta Beach

4 ARKADIANKATU

RUNEBERGINKATU

FREDRIKINKATU

BUS STN.

Kamppi

POST

Tram #2

ATENEUM

Rauta-tientori

Senate Square

USPENSKI ORTHODOX CATHEDRAL

MALMIKATU

Kamppi

FORUM MALL

9 Ylioppilastalo

SWEDISH THEATER

KANAVAKATU

RUOHOLAHDENKATU

ALBERTINKATU

ABRAHAMINKATU

LÖNNROTINKATU

BULEVARDI

UUDEN MAANKATU

ISO ROOBERTINKATU

YRJÖNKATU

KORKEAVUORENKATU

ESPLANADE

1 Market Square

ETELÄESPLANADI

P. MAKASIINI.

E. MAKASIINI.

To Katajanokan Terminal (Viking Line)

South Harbor

MAKASIINI TERMINAL

OLYMPIA TERMINAL (TALLINK SILJA LINE & CRUISES)

10 HIETALAHTI FLEA MARKET

RATAKATU

MERIMIEHENKATU

PURSIMIEHENKATU

SEPÄNKATU

UUDENMAANKATU

OBSERVATORY

Tram #2

Olympialaituri

VUORIMIEHENKATU

Tram #3

11

West Harbor

To West/Länsi Terminal

To Hernesaari Terminal

DOCKSGATEAN

LAIVURINKATU

NEITSYTPOLKU

VUORIMIEHENKATU

PIETARINKATU

PUISTOKATU

LAIVASILLANKATU

1 Market Square/Senate Square/Shopping Street

2 Finnish National Theater/Train Station

3 Shopping & Entertainment District

4 School of Economics & Trendy Apartments

5 Finnish National Opera House

6 Sports Complex

7 Classic Amusement Park (Linnanmäki)

8 Working-Class District

9 Three Blacksmiths Statue

10 Design District: Funky & Artsy Shops

11 Embassy Row

HELSINKI

❸ **Shopping and Entertainment District:** Crossing the busy Mannerheimintie boulevard, you'll pass the Kamppi mall, with the bus station in its basement and the wood-cylinder Kamppi Chapel of Silence in front (tram and Metro stop: Kamppi). The adjacent Tennis Palace is a cultural zone with galleries and movie theaters.

❹ **School of Economics and Trendy Apartments:** After passing the yellow brick buildings of the School of Economics (on your left, note facade—Kauppakorkeakoulut stop), you'll enter a neighborhood with lots of desirable 1920s-era apartments. Young couples start out here, move to the suburbs when they have their kids, and return as empty-nesters. The Temppeliaukio Church (a.k.a. "Church in the Rock"), while out of sight, is just a block uphill from the next stop (Sammonkatu).

❺ **Finnish National Opera House:** Built in 1993, the National Opera House is the white, sterile, shower-tile building on the right (tram stop: Ooppera). The next stop (Töölön halli) is a short walk from the Sibelius Monument and its pretty park (detour along a street called Sibeliuksenkatu).

❻ **Sports Complex:** A statue honors long-distance runner Paavo Nurmi (early 20th-century Finn who won a slew of Olympic gold medals, on left). The white building with the skinny tower (in the distance on the right) marks the Olympic Stadium, used for the summer games in 1952. After the Auroran sairaala stop, you'll see skateboarders enjoying a park of their own (on the right). At the next stop, Eläintarha, the tram may pause as it changes to become #3 (stay seated).

❼ **Classic Amusement Park:** Linnanmäki, Helsinki's low-end, Tivoli-like amusement park is by far the most-visited sight in town (on the right, free admission to park, rides cost €4-6, open daily until late, tram stop: Alppila, www.linnanmaki.fi). Roller-coaster nuts enjoy its classics from the 1950s.

❽ **Working-Class District:** Next you'll enter an old working-class neighborhood. Its soccer fields (on your left) are frozen into ice rinks for hockey in the winter. You'll pass the striking granite **Kallio Church** (Art Nouveau, on your right) and **Hakaniemi** square, with a big indoor/outdoor market (on your left). Crossing a saltwater inlet, you'll pass Helsinki's **Botanical Gardens** (on the right), and then head back toward the town center. As you return to the train station with its buff lamp-holders, you've completed the larger, top loop of the figure-eight.

❾ **The *Three Blacksmiths* Statue:** After turning left on big, busy Mannerheimintie, you'll pass the most famous statue in town, the *Three Blacksmiths* (on your left), which honors hard work and cooperation. Towering above the smiths is the Stockmann department store. Then (at the Ylioppilastalo stop), the round, white Swedish Theater marks the top of the town's graceful park—the

HELSINKI

Esplanade—which leads back down to the harbor (where you began this tour). From here, you'll loop through the colorful and artsy Design District.

❿ **Design District—Funky and Artsy Shops:** The cemetery of the church (which dates from 1827) on the right was cleaned out to make a park. It's called the "Plague Park," recalling a circa-1700 plague that killed more than half the population. Coming up, funky small boutiques, cafés, and fun shops line the streets (stops: Fredrikinkatu, Iso Roobertinkatu, and Viiskulma). After the Art Deco brick church (on your right), the tram makes a hard left (at the Eiran sairaala stop, for a hospital) and enters a district with Art Nouveau buildings. Look down streets on the right for facades and decorative turrets leading to the Baltic Sea.

⓫ **Embassy Row and Back to Market Square:** After the Neitsytpolku stop, spy the Russian Embassy (on left), still sporting its hammer and sickle; it was built to look like London's Buckingham Palace. Across the street is the Roman Catholic church, and beyond that (on the right), a street marked "no entry" leads to a fortified US Embassy. Returning to the harbor, you'll likely see the huge Tallink Silja ship that leaves at 17:00 each evening for Stockholm. Its terminal (the appropriately named Olympiaterminaali) was built for the 1952 Olympics, which inundated Helsinki with visitors. Across the harbor stands the Uspenski Orthodox Cathedral. Then, after passing the cute brick Old Market Hall (with several great little eateries), you'll arrive back at Market Square, where you started.

Sights in Helsinki

NEAR THE SOUTH HARBOR
▲▲Uspenski Orthodox Cathedral
This house of worship was built for the Russian military in 1868 (at a time when Finland belonged to Russia). *Uspenski* is Russian for the Assumption of Mary. It hovers above Market Square and faces the Lutheran Cathedral, just as Russian culture faces Europe.

Cost and Hours: Free; Tue-Fri 9:30-20:00, Sat 10:00-15:00, Sun 12:00-15:00, closed Mon, Kanavakatu 1 (about a 5-minute walk beyond the harborfront market).

Visiting the Cathedral: Before heading inside, view the exterior. The uppermost "onion dome" represents the "sacred heart of Jesus," while the smaller ones represent the hearts of the 12 apostles.

The cathedral's interior is a potentially emotional icon experience. Its rich images are a stark contrast to the sober Lutheran Cathedral. While commonly called the "Russian church," the cathedral is actually Finnish Orthodox, answering to the patriarch in Constantinople (Istanbul). Much of eastern Finland (parts of the Karelia region) is Finnish Orthodox.

The cathedral's Orthodox Mass is beautiful, with a standing congregation, candles, incense, icons in action, priests behind the iconostasis (screen), and timeless music (human voices only—no instruments). In the front left corner, find the icon featuring the Madonna and child, surrounded by rings and jewelry (under glass), given in thanks for prayers answered. Across from the icon is a white marble table with candle holes and a dish of wheat seeds, representing recent deaths. Wheat seeds symbolize that death is not the end, it's simply a change.

Though the cathedral is worthwhile, the one in Tallinn is more richly decorated; skip this one if you're visiting both cities and are short on time.

▲▲Lutheran Cathedral

HELSINKI

With its prominent green dome, gleaming white facade, and the 12 apostles overlooking the city and harbor, this church is Carl Ludvig Engel's masterpiece.

Cost and Hours: Free; June-Aug Mon-Sat 9:00-24:00, Sun 12:00-24:00; Sept-May Mon-Sat 9:00-18:00, Sun 12:00-18:00; sometimes closes for events; on Senate Square, www.helsinginseurakunnat.fi. In summer, free organ concerts are held on Sundays at 20:00.

Visiting the Cathedral: Enter the building around the left side. Finished in 1852, the interior is pure architectural truth.

Open a pew gate and sit, surrounded by the saints of Protestantism, to savor Neoclassical nirvana. Physically, this church is perfectly Protestant—austere and unadorned—with the emphasis on preaching (prominent pulpit) and music (huge organ). Statuary is limited to the local Reformation big shots: Martin Luther, Philipp Melanchthon (Luther's Reformation sidekick), and the leading Finnish reformer, Mikael Agricola. A follower of Luther at Wittenberg, Agricola brought the Reformation to Finland. He also translated the Bible into Finnish and is considered the father of the modern Finnish language. Agricola's Bible is to Finland what the Luther Bible is to Germany and the King James Bible is to the English-speaking world.

▲Helsinki City Museum

This interesting museum, a few steps off of Senate Square, gives an excellent, accessible overview of the city's history in English. At the beginning of 2016, they are scheduled to move one block east, to Katariinankatu. But until then, they'll be showing off the enjoyable "Mad About Helsinki" exhibit. The ground floor is a sentimental look at some of the people of Helsinki's favorite places: seafront gardens, the cathedral steps, amusement park attractions, and home sweet home (with a mock-up of a typical Helsinki kitchen). The upstairs exhibit traces the history of the city from the 1550s, taking the novel approach of zooming in on individual, everyday people—from different historical periods and social classes—to better understand why each of them chose to call Helsinki home. While this specific exhibit may not make the move to the new location, it's an indication of the clever, intimate, and affectionate approach the museum brings to its subject.

Cost and Hours: Free, Mon-Fri 9:00-17:00, Thu until 19:00, Sat-Sun 11:00-17:00, Sofiankatu 4—or one block east on Katariinankatu beginning in 2016, www.helsinkicitymuseum.fi.

BEYOND THE ESPLANADE

These sights are scattered in the zone west of the Esplanade, listed roughly in the order you'll reach them from the city center (and in the order they appear on my self-guided walk, earlier).

▲Ateneum, The National Gallery of Finland

This museum showcases Finnish artists (mid-18th to 20th century) and has a fine international collection, including works by Cézanne, Chagall, Gauguin, and Van Gogh. They also have good temporary exhibits. However, as the building is being renovated through late 2015, many of their star canvases are out on loan, and the "greatest hits" of their Finnish collection has been condensed on the ground floor. Before buying your ticket, be clear on what's on view today. Either way, the collection is hard to appreciate without the €3 audioguide (though the laminated English information sheets in a few rooms are helpful).

Cost and Hours: €12, Tue and Fri 10:00-18:00, Wed-Thu 9:00-20:00, Sat-Sun 10:00-17:00, closed Mon, near train station at Kaivokatu 2, tel. 0294-500-401, www.ateneum.fi.

Visiting the Museum: The Finnish section provides the opportunity to be introduced to talented artists who aren't well known outside their homeland. Get swept up in the lyrical, romantic canvases of Akseli Gallen-Kallela (1865-1931), who illustrated scenes from the Finnish national epic, *Kalevala*. (In 1835, Elias Lünnrot collected folkloric tales from humble, rural Finnish peasants and assembled them into this romantic poem, which was designed to be

Sauna

Finland's vaporized fountain of youth is the sauna—Scandinavia's answer to support hose and facelifts. A traditional sauna

is a wood-paneled room with wooden benches and a blistering-hot wood-fired stove topped with rocks. Undress entirely before going in. Lay your towel on the bench, and sit or lie on it (for hygienic reasons). Ladle water from the bucket onto the rocks to make steam. Choose a higher bench for hotter temperatures. Let yourself work up a sweat, then, just before bursting, go outside to the shower for a Niagara of liquid ice. Suddenly your shower stall becomes a Cape Canaveral launch pad, as your body scatters to every corner of the universe. A moment later you're back together and can re-enter the steam room. Repeat as necessary. The famous birch branches are always available for slapping your skin. Finns claim this enhances circulation while emitting a refreshing birch aroma that opens your sinuses. For more on the history of saunas, see www.sauna.fi.

Your hostel, hotel, or cruise ship may have a sauna, which may be heated only at specific times. Some saunas are semi-public (separate men's and women's hours), while others are for private use (book a 45- to 60-minute time slot; to save money, split the cost with a group of friends, either mixed or same-sex). Public saunas are a dying breed these days, because most Finns have private saunas in their homes or cabins. But some public saunas survive in rougher, poorer neighborhoods.

For a good, traditional sauna with a coarse and local crowd, try the **Kotiharjun Sauna.** Pay €12 plus €3 for a towel (cash only), find a locker, strip (keep the key on your wrist), and head for the steam. Cooling off is nothing fancy—just a bank of cold showers. A woman in a fish-cleaner's apron will give you a wonderful scrub with Brillo pad-like mitts (€9, only on Tue and Fri-Sat 16:00-19:00). Regulars relax with beers on the sidewalk just outside (open Tue-Sun 14:00-21:30, closed Mon, last entry 1.5 hours before closing; men—ground floor, women—upstairs; 200 yards from Sörnäinen Metro stop, Harjutorinkatu 1, tel. 09/753-1535, www.kotiharjunsauna.fi).

The **Kulttuurisauna** sits in a little park along the Baltic—to cool off, take a dip in the sea. Designed and operated by a husband-and-wife, Finnish-Japanese, artist-and-architect team, it's both modern and traditional. This is a *savusauna* (smoke sauna, without a chimney)—and, while the room is ventilated before bathers arrive, the smoky atmosphere lingers (€15, towel rental-€4, all nude and gender-segregated, Wed-Sun 16:00-21:00, closed Mon-Tue, last entry at 20:00, just north of downtown at Hakaniemenranta 17, nearest tram/bus stop is Hakaniemi—about a 10-minute walk away, www.kulttuurisauna.fi).

HELSINKI

sung—a very important cultural touchstone for the Finnish people, during a time when their culture and language were subordinated by Sweden and Russia.) Gallen-Kallela's scenes tapped into the spirit of the burgeoning Finnish National Revival. Also appreciate the stylized, gauzy, Impressionistic portraits by Helene Schjerf-beck.

▲Kamppi Chapel of Silence (Kampin Kappeli)

Sitting unassumingly on the busy, commercialism-crazy plaza in front of the Kamppi shopping mall/bus-station complex, this restful space was opened by the city of Helsinki in 2012 to give residents and visitors a place to escape the modern world. The teacup-shaped wooden structure, clad in spruce and with an oval footprint, encloses a 38-foot-tall cylinder of silence. Indirect light seeps in around the edges of the ceiling, bathing the clean, curved, alder-wood paneling in warmth and tranquility. Does it resemble Noah's Ark? The inside of an egg? The architects left it intention-ally vague—up to each visitor's interpretation. Although it's a church, there are no services; the goal is to keep it open for anyone needing a reflective pause. Locals drop by between their shopping chores to sit in a pew and ponder their deity, wrestle with tough issues...or just get a break from the chaos of urban life. Along with the Church in the Rock, it's one more example of a poignant and peaceful spot where secular modern architecture and spiritual sen-timent converge beautifully.

Cost and Hours: Free, Mon-Fri 7:00-20:00, Sat-Sun 10:00-18:00, Simonkatu 7, enter through adjacent low-profile black building.

Kiasma Museum

Finland's museum of contemporary art, designed by American ar-chitect Steven Holl, hosts temporary exhibitions and doesn't have a permanent collection. Ask at the TI or check online to find out what's showing.

Cost and Hours: €10, Tue 10:00-17:00, Wed-Fri 10:00-20:30, Sat 10:00-18:00, Sun 10:00-17:00, closed Mon, Mannerhe-iminaukio 2, near train station, tel. 0294-500-501, www.kiasma.fi.

Natural History Museum

Run by the University of Helsinki, this museum has about eight million animal specimens, the largest collection of its kind in Fin-land. Displays range from spiders to dinosaurs, all with English descriptions.

Cost and Hours: €10; June-Aug Tue-Sun 10:00-17:00, closed Mon; Sept-May Tue-Fri 9:00-16:00 except Thu until 18:00, Sat-Sun 10:00-16:00, closed Mon; up the street behind the Parliament at Pohjoinen Rautatiekatu 13, www.luomus.fi.

Helsinki Music Centre (Musiikkitalo)

This modern facility, open since 2011, provides a home for the arts in Helsinki. Containing seven different venues, its biggest draw may be the park that surrounds it, decorated with wildly creative contemporary art. While you can stop in anytime it's open to look around, music lovers can also consider taking in a performance (season runs Sept-April), and architecture fans may want to take an English tour.

Cost and Hours: Building open Mon-Fri 8:00-22:00, Sat 10:00-22:00, Sun 10:00-20:00; English tours offered most days in summer for €12, check website for schedule; Mannerheimintie 13A, tel. 020-707-0400, www.musiikkitalo.fi.

Finlandia Hall (Finlandia-Talo)

Alvar Aalto's most famous building in his native Finland means little to the nonarchitect without a tour. To see the building from

its best angle, view it from the seaside parking lot, not the street—where nearly everyone who looks at the building thinks, "So what?"

Cost and Hours: €12.50 for a tour, call ahead or visit website to check times; hall information shop open Mon-Fri 9:00-19:00, closed Sat-Sun; Mannerheimintie 13e, tel. 09/40241, www.finlandiatalo.fi.

▲National Museum of Finland (Kansallismuseo)

This pleasant, easy-to-handle collection is in a grand building designed by three of this country's greatest architects—including Eliel Saarinen—in the early 1900s. Divided into four sections, the exhibit chronologically traces the land of the Finns from prehistory to the 20th century. The Neoclassical furniture, folk costumes, armory, and other artifacts are interesting, but the highlights are Finland's largest permanent archaeological collection (covering the prehistory of the country) and the 20th-century exhibit,

which brings Finland's story up to the modern day. While the collection is impressive and well-described in English, those descriptions are quite dry, and the museum is a bit hard to appreciate. The interactive top-floor workshop is worth a look for its creative teaching.

Cost and Hours: €8, free on Fri 16:00-18:00; open Tue-Sun

11:00-18:00, closed Mon; Mannerheimintie 34, tel. 09/4050-9552, www.nba.fi. The museum café, with a tranquil outdoor courtyard, has light meals and Finnish treats such as lingonberry juice and reindeer quiche (open until 17:00). It's just a five-minute walk from Temppeliaukio Church.

Visiting the Museum: Following the clear English-language descriptions, visit each of the museum's four parts, in chronological order. First, straight ahead from the ticket desk is the **Prehistory of Finland,** where you'll learn how Stone, Bronze, and Iron Age tribes in this area lived. You'll see lots of early stone tools (ax and arrow heads), pottery, human remains, and—at the end of the exhibit—Iron Age weapons and jewelry.

You'll proceed into **The Realm,** which picks up the story with the Middle Ages (represented by the 14th-century St. Birgitta, Sweden's top saint). You'll pass through dimly lit halls of mostly wood-carved church art—from roughly hewn Catholic altarpieces to brightly painted, post-Reformation, Lutheran pulpits—then learn about Finland's time as part of Sweden (the introduction ∿f the Renaissance). Continuing upstairs, you'll find out about the different social classes in historical Finland—the nobility, the peasants, the clergy, the rulers and monarchs, and the burghers (craftsmen and guild members). You'll see a Rococo-period drawing room and—transitioning from Swedish to Russian rule—portraits of Russia's last czars around an impressive throne.

From there, temporary exhibits lead back to the main hall, where you can continue into **A Land and Its People.** In this display of Finnish peasant traditions, you'll see farming and fishing tools, a thought-provoking exhibit about the indigenous Sami people (distributed across the northern reaches of Finland, Sweden, Norway, and Russia), and a particularly fine collection of beautifully decorated tools used for spinning—folk art used to make folk art.

From the folk furniture, find the stairs back down to the ground floor and the **SF-1900** exhibit (that's Suomi/Finland from 1900), starting with the birth of modern Finland in 1917 and its 1918 civil war. A six-minute loop of archival footage shows you early-20th-century Finland. Touchscreen tables help tell the story of the fledgling nation, as do plenty of well-presented artifacts (including clothing, household items, vehicles, and a traditional outhouse).

▲▲▲Temppeliaukio Church

A more modern example of great church architecture (from 1969), this "Church in the Rock" was blasted

HELSINKI

out of solid granite. It was designed by architect brothers Timo and Tuomo Suomalainen, and built within a year's time. Barren of decor except for a couple of simple crosses, the church is capped with a copper-and-skylight dome; it's normally filled with live or recorded music and awestruck visitors. Grab a pew. Gawk upward at a 13-mile-long coil of copper ribbon. Look at the bull's-eye and ponder God. Forget your camera. Just sit in the middle, ignore the crowds, and be thankful for peace...under your feet is an air-raid shelter that can accommodate 6,000 people.

Cost and Hours: Free, June-Sept Mon-Sat 10:00-17:45, Sun 11:45-17:45, closes one hour earlier off-season and for special events and concerts, Lutherinkatu 3, tel. 09/2340-6320, www.helsinginseurakunnat.fi.

Getting There: The church is at the top of a gentle hill in a residential neighborhood, about a 15-minute walk north of the bus station or a 10-minute walk behind the National Museum (or take tram #2 to Sammonkatu stop).

▲Sibelius Monument

Six hundred stainless-steel pipes called "Love of Music"—built on solid rock, as is so much of Finland—shimmer in a park to honor Finland's greatest composer, Jean Sibelius. It's a forest of pipe-organ pipes in a forest of trees. The artist, Eila Hiltunen, was forced to add a bust of the composer's face to silence critics of her otherwise abstract work. City orientation bus tours stop here for 10 min-

utes—long enough. Bus #24 stops here (30 minutes until the next bus, or catch a quick glimpse on the left from the bus) on its way to the Seurasaari Open-Air Folk Museum. The #2 tram, which runs more frequently, stops a few blocks away.

THE DESIGN DISTRICT, SOUTHWEST OF THE ESPLANADE

Exploring Helsinki's Design District—described in detail under "Shopping in Helsinki," later—can be a sightseeing highlight for many visitors. A good starting point is the Design Museum, which sits just a few blocks south of the Esplanade.

▲Design Museum

Design is integral to contemporary Finnish culture, and this fine museum—with a small but insightful permanent collection and well-presented temporary exhibits—offers a good overview. Worth

▲▲▲ to those who came to Finland just for the design, it's interesting to anybody.

Cost and Hours: €10; June-Aug daily 11:00-18:00; Sept-May Tue 11:00-20:00, Wed-Sun 11:00-18:00, closed Mon; Korkeavuorenkatu 23, www.designmuseum.fi.

Visiting the Museum: From the ticket desk on the ground floor, turn left and enter the permanent exhibit, called **Finnish Form.** Several actual items and good English descriptions trace the evolution of domestic design from the 1870s, when "applied arts"—merging artistic aesthetics and function—first caught on throughout Europe. You'll see how a fine line separated design and industrial production in those early days, and learn how the Finland pavilion at the 1900 World's Fair in Paris first thrust this nation onto the world design map.

In the post-WWI era (peaking in the 1930s), Functionalism focused on stripping away needless and cumbersome decoration—the goal was to boil an item down to its structural parts, and to celebrate those parts in a way that maximized both usefulness and beauty. You'll see early works by the first and last name in Finnish design, Alvar Aalto, who designed elegantly streamlined furnishings for a tuberculosis sanatorium (1929-1933). In 1935, Aalto founded the home decor company Artek—sort of a proto-Ikea—which still stands on the Esplanade.

After World War II, Finland entered a Golden Age of design. The 1950s and 1960s saw a population boom, and the majority of Finns shifted from rural to urban lifestyles, resulting in lots of new homes that needed to be furnished. You'll see some recognizable objects here, from the characteristic "dew drop" dishes to items you may have in a drawer at your house (such as Olof Bäckströms's orange-handled scissors).

Design hit some challenges with the environmentalism and the oil crisis of the 1960s and 1970s, when the mass-production of plastics became both economically and ethically more challenging. Finnish designers recalibrated their focus to over-the-top ergonomics rather than mass production. Some of these innovations wound up as little more than quirky footnotes (such as Eero Aarnio's egg-shaped "Pallo" chair, from 1966) while others eventually went mainstream: Esko Pajamies' "Koivutaru" chair, from 1974, suspiciously resembles the Ikea "Poäng" chair that furnishes every college dorm room in America.

The present-day exhibits more or less match what you'll see in shop windows around Helsinki today, and remind us that many fixtures of contemporary American life—such as Nokia cell phones (see them evolve from huge to tiny)—were born in this tiny, obscure, chilly little European country.

Upstairs and downstairs, you'll find typically excellent **temporary exhibits** that allow individual Finnish designers to take center stage.

OUTER HELSINKI

A weeklong car trip up through the Finnish lakes and forests to Mikkeli and Savonlinna would be relaxing, but you can actually enjoy Finland's green-trees-and-blue-water scenery without leaving Helsinki. Here are three great ways to get out and go for a walk on a sunny summer day. If you have time, do at least one of them during your stay.

▲▲Suomenlinna Fortress

The island guarding Helsinki's harbor served as a strategic fortress for three countries: Finland, Sweden, and Russia. It's now a popular park, with delightful paths, fine views, and a visitors center. On a sunny day, it's a delightful place to stroll among hulking buildings with recreating Finns. The free Suomenlinna guidebooklet (stocked at the Helsinki TI, ferry terminal, and the visitors center) cov-

ers the island thoroughly. The island has one good museum (the Suomenlinna Museum, at Suomenlinna Centre—described later) and several skippable smaller museums, including a toy museum and several military museums (€3-4 each, open summer only).

Getting There: Catch a ferry to Suomenlinna from Market Square. Walk past the high-priced excursion boats to the public HKL ferry (€5 round-trip, covered by day ticket and Helsinki Card, 15-minute trip, May-Aug 2-3/hour—generally at :00, :20, and :40 past the hour, but pick up schedule to confirm; Sept-April every 40-60 minutes). If you'll be taking at least two tram rides within 24 hours of visiting Suomenlinna, it pays to get a day ticket instead of a round-trip ticket. A private ferry, JT Line, also runs a "water bus" to Suomenlinna from Market Square in summer (€7 round-trip, May-Sept 2/hour, tel. 09/534-806, www.jt-line.fi). As it costs a bit more and runs less frequently, the JT Line is only worthwhile if you're in a rush to get to the Suomenlinna Centre and museum (since the water bus uses a dock here instead of the northern port used by the public ferry).

Tours: The one-hour English-language island tour departs

HELSINKI

Suomenlinna Timeline

1748—Construction began on Sveaborg ("Sweden Fortress").

1788—The fort was used as a base for a Swedish war against Russia.

1808—It was surrendered by Sweden to Russia.

1809—Finland became part of the Russian Empire, and the fort was used as a Russian garrison for 108 years.

1855—French and British navies bombarded the fort during the Crimean War, inflicting heavy damage.

1917—Finland declared independence.

1918—The fort was annexed by Finland and renamed Suomenlinna ("Finland Fortress").

1939—The fort served as a base for the Finnish navy.

1973—The Finnish garrison moved out, the fort's administration was transferred to the Ministry of Education, and the fort was opened to the public.

HELSINKI

from the Suomenlinna Centre (€10, free with Helsinki Card; June-Aug daily at 11:00, 12:30, and 14:30; Sept-May 1/day Sat-Sun only). The tour is fine if you're a military history buff, but it kind of misses the point of what's now essentially a giant playground for all ages.

Background: The fortress was built by the Swedes with French financial support in the mid-1700s to counter Russia's rise to power. (Russian Czar Peter the Great had built his new capital, St. Petersburg, on the Baltic and was eyeing the West.) Named Sveaborg ("Fortress of Sweden"), the fortress was Sweden's military pride and joy. With five miles of walls and hundreds of cannons, it was the second strongest fort of its kind in Europe after Gibraltar. Helsinki, a small community of 1,500 people before 1750, soon became a boomtown supporting this grand "Gibraltar of the North."

The fort, built by more than 10,000 workers, was a huge investment and stimulated lots of innovation. In the 1760s, it had the world's biggest and most modern dry dock. It served as a key naval base during a brief Russo-Swedish war in 1788-1790. But in 1808, the Russians took the "invincible" fort without a fight—by siege—as a huge and cheap military gift.

Today, Suomenlinna has 1,000 permanent residents, is home to Finland's Naval Academy, and is most appreciated by locals for its fine scenic strolls. The island is large—actually, it's six islands connected by bridges—and you and your imagination get free run of the fortifications and dungeon-like chambers. When it's time to eat, you'll find a half-dozen cafés and plenty of picnic opportunities.

Visiting Suomenlinna: Across from the public ferry landing are the Jetty Barracks, housing a small information desk (a good place to pick up the free island map/booklet, if you haven't already), convenient WC, free modern art exhibit, and the pricey Panimo brewpub/restaurant. From here, start your stroll of the island. You'll wander on cobbles past dilapidated shiplap cottages that evoke a more robust time for this once-strategic, now-leisurely island. The garrison church on your left, which was Orthodox until its 20th-century conversion to Lutheranism, doubled as a lighthouse.

A five-minute walk from the ferry brings you to the **Suomenlinna Centre,** which houses the worthwhile Suomenlinna Museum. Inside the (free) lobby, you'll find an information desk, gift shop, café, and giant model of all six islands that make up Suomenlinna—handy for orientation. The exhibits themselves are well-presented but dryly explained: fragments of old walls, cannons, period clothing, model ships, and so on; the upstairs focuses on the site's transition from a fortress to a park. The main attraction is the fascinating 25-minute "multivision" show, presenting the island's complete history, which runs twice hourly and has a headphone soundtrack in English (€6.50 for museum and film, daily May-Sept 10:00-18:00, Oct-April 10:30-16:30, tel. 09/684-1850, www.suomenlinna.fi).

From the Suomenlinna Centre, cross the bridge—noticing the giant, rusted seaplane hall on the right, housing the Regatta Club, with a fun sailboat photo exhibition and shop. On the far side of the hall, peer into the gigantic dry dock.

Back on the main trail, climb five minutes uphill to the right into **Piper Park** (Piperin Puisto). Hike up past its elegant 19th-century café (with rocky view tables), and continue up and over the ramparts to a surreal swimming area. From here, follow the waterline—and the ramparts—to the south. You'll walk above bunkers burrowed underground, like gigantic molehills (or maybe Hobbit  houses). Periodic ladders let you scramble down onto the rocks. Imposing cannons, now used as playsets and photo-op props for kids, are still aimed ominously at the Gulf of Finland—in case, I imagine, of Russian invasion...or if they just get fed up with all of those cruise ships. Reaching the southern tip of the island, called King's Gate, peek out through the cannon holes. Then make your walk a loop by circling back to the Suomenlinna Centre and, beyond that, the ferry dock for the ride home.

Peninsula Promenade

For a breezy, salty seaside walk, consider this promenade around the Kaivopuisto Park peninsula. Allow 1.5 hours at a leisurely pace. From Market Square, wander past the brick Old Market Hall and Tallink Silja terminal (with its huge ship likely at the dock) and follow the shoreline pedestrian path. The first island you come to, Valkosaari, hosts the local yacht club—NJK—the oldest in Scandinavia, with a classy restaurant (daily 17:00-24:00). The next island, Luoto, is home to the posh Palace Kämp by the Sea restaurant (with shuttle boat service). During a typical winter, the bay freezes (18 inches of ice is strong enough to allow cars to drive to the islands—in the past there was even a public bus route that extended to an island during the winter). The fortress island of Suomenlinna is in the distance. The hill you're circling (on the right) is home to several embassies; ahead, Ursula Café, with its fine harbor views, is good for a coffee break.

Around the corner, the next island, Uunisaari, belonged to the military until the 1980s. Its unique plant life (much studied by local students) is believed to have hitched a ride all the way to Finland from Siberia on the boots of Russian soldiers. The odd-looking pier nearby is a station for washing rugs (those are not picnic tables). Saltwater brightens the rag rugs traditionally made by local grandmas. While American men put on aprons and do the barbecue, Finnish men wash the carpets. After the scrub, the rugs are sent through big mechanical wringers and hung on nearby racks to dry in the wind. The posted map shows 11 such stations scattered around Helsinki. Buy an ice cream at the nearby stand and watch the action (best in the morning).

In the distance looms Helsinki's big new West Harbor port, hosting 300 cruise ships a year. From here you can follow Neitsytpolku street back to the town center, keeping an eye out for fun Art Nouveau buildings.

▲▲Seurasaari Open-Air Folk Museum

Inspired by Stockholm's Skansen, also on a lovely island on the edge of town, this is a collection of 100 historic buildings from every corner of Finland. It's wonderfully furnished and gives rushed visitors an opportunity to sample the far reaches of Finland without leaving the capital city. If you're not taking a tour, get the €1.20 map or the helpful €6 guidebook. You're welcome to bring a picnic, or you can have a light lunch (snacks and cakes) in the Antti farmstead at the center of the park.

Off-season, when the buildings are closed, the place is empty and not worth the trouble.

Cost and Hours: Free park entry, €8 to enter buildings; June-Aug daily 11:00-17:00; late May and early Sept Mon-Fri 9:00-15:00, Sat-Sun 11:00-17:00; buildings closed mid-Sept-mid-May; tel. 09/4050-9660, www.seurasaari.fi.

Tours: English tours are free with €8 entry ticket, offered mid-June-mid-Aug generally at 15:00, and take one hour (confirm times on their website).

Getting There: To reach the museum, ride bus #24 (from the top of the Esplanade, 2/hour) to the end (note departure times for your return) and walk across the quaint footbridge.

NEAR HELSINKI

Porvoo, the second-oldest town in Finland, has wooden architecture that dates from the Swedish colonial period. This coastal town can be reached from Helsinki by bus (one hour) or by excursion boat from Market Square.

Turku, the historic capital of Finland, is a two-hour bus or train ride from Helsinki. Overall, Turku is a pale shadow of Helsinki, and there is little reason to make a special trip. It does have a handicraft museum in a cluster of wooden houses (the only part of town to survive a devastating fire in the early 1800s), an old castle, a fine Gothic cathedral (this was the first part of Finland to be Christianized, in the 12th century), and a market square. Viking and Tallink Silja boats sail from Turku to Stockholm every morning and evening, passing through the especially scenic Turku archipelago.

Naantali, a cute, commercial, well-preserved medieval town with a quaint harbor, is an easy 20-minute bus ride from Turku.

Shopping in Helsinki

Helsinki may be the top shopping town in the Nordic countries. Even in this region that prides itself on its creative design culture, Helsinki is a trendsetter; many Finnish designers are household names worldwide. Plus, the city's rather chilly architecture and weather often force people inside, making browsing in the shops a productive thing to do while escaping from a passing squall. The easiest place to get a taste of Finnish design is along the Esplanade, but with even a little more time, it's worth delving into the nearby Design District.

Opening Times: Most shops are open all day long Mondays through Fridays (generally 10:00 until 17:00 or 18:00), and often have shorter hours on Saturday (likely opening at 10:00 or 12:00 and closing around 16:00), and most are closed on Sundays. Larger shops have longer hours, including brief opening hours on Sundays. While specific hours are not listed for each shop below, I have noted those that seriously buck these trends (and you can find complete hours for any shop online).

ALONG THE ESPLANADE

Helsinki's elegant main drag, the Esplanade, is a coffee-sipper's and window-shopper's delight. Practically every big name in Finn-

ish design (and there are lots of them) has a flagship store along this people-pleasing strip. These tend to be open a bit longer than the hours noted above; most are open until 19:00 (or even 20:00) on weekdays, until 17:00 on Saturdays, and even on Sundays (typically 12:00-16:00 or 17:00).

On my self-guided walk, earlier, I pointed out several Esplanade shops worth dipping into: Consider the purses, scarves, clothes, and fabrics from **Marimekko,** the well-known Finnish fashion company famous for striped designs (at #33A, www.marimekko. com). Two more Marimekko branches are a short walk away: one specializing in children's items halfway up the cross-street, Mikonkatu, at #2D; and another specializing in clothing one block farther up the Esplanade, then right up Keskuskatu to the intersection with Aleksanterinkatu. **Aarikka** (#27C, www.aarikka.com) and **Iittala** (#25B, www.iittala.com) have Finnish housewares and ceramics, while **Kalevala** (at #27C, along with Aarikka) sells finely crafted, handmade jewelry (www.kalevalakoru.com).

Across the street, on the south side of the Esplanade, are more shops: **Artek,** Alvar and Elissa Aalto's flagship store (#18, www. artek.fi); **Finlayson** is a more affordable option for Finnish home decor and design (one block closer to the harbor at #14, www. finlayson.fi).

The Esplanade is capped by the enormous, eight-floor **Stockmann** department store, arguably Scandinavia's most impressive (Mon-Fri 9:00-21:00, Sat 9:00-18:00, Sun 12:00-18:00, great basement supermarket, Aleksanterinkatu 52B, www.stockmann. fi). Bookworms enjoy the impressive **Academic Bookstore** just downhill from Stockmann (#39, same hours as Stockmann).

Fans of Tove Jansson's Moomin children's stories will enjoy the **Moomin Shop,** on the second floor of the Forum shopping mall at Mannerheimintie 20, across the busy tram-lined street from Stockmann (Mon-Fri 9:00-21:00, Sat 9:00-18:00, Sun 12:00-18:00, www.moomin.fi).

THE DESIGN DISTRICT

Helsinki's Design District is a several-block cluster of streets that are lined with a dizzying array of one-off boutiques, galleries, and other shops highlighting local designers. From high fashion to comfy everyday clothes, and from lovingly handcrafted jewelry to clever kitchen doodads, this is an engaging zone to explore. For a handy orientation to the options in this ever-changing area, visit www.designdistrict.fi, and get tips at the TI—they often hand out maps or brochures illustrating your options.

While the Design District sprawls—roughly southwest of the Esplanade nearly all the way to the waterfront—the following sub-areas are most worthy of exploration.

Kolmikulma Park and Nearby

Just a block south of the Esplanade's top end (down Erottajanka-tu), the park called Kolmikulma (literally "Triangular," also called Diana Park for its spear-throwing statue centerpiece) is a handy epicenter of Design District liveliness. From here, streets fan out to the west. A few choices ring the park itself, while several more line the streets that stretch southwest.

Uudenmaankatu has the highest concentration of shops, especially fashion boutiques of local designers. **Nounou** (on the left, at #2) has very colorful glass pieces (open only Tue, Thu, and Sat); the recommended **Café Bar No. 9,** across the street, is a popular place to grab a filling meal. Farther along, **Astra Taivas** (on the right, at #13) is a hole-in-the-wall crammed with precarious shelves of secondhand glassware—causing even the most cautious visitor to feel like the proverbial bull in a china shop. At the end of the block, **Ivana Helsinki** (at #15, on the right) has pattered casual dresses. A detour to the right up the next street (Annankatu) takes you to **Momono,** a tight and endearing shop highlighting Finnish design (on the left at Annankatu 12).

Back on Uudenmaankatu, it's just one more (less interesting) block to Fredrikinkatu, with a lot more choices (described next).

Meanwhile, a block south, pedestrianized **Iso Roobertinkatu** has a few more less interesting choices, and also has lots of cheap eateries. **Formverk,** at the corner with Annankatu, has fun home decor and kitchenware (Annankatu 5).

Fredrikinkatu

This street, which crosses Uudenmaankatu two blocks west of the park, is one of the most engaging streets in town. (For a sneak peek of the many shops lining this street—only a few of which are noted here—see www.fredashops.fi.)

At the corner with Uudenmaankatu, **C. Hagelstam** is an antiquariat with cool vintage prints and antique books, while across the street, **Peroba** (at Uudenmaankatu 33) displays bold Scan design. From here, head north along Fredrikinkatu, which is lined with mostly fashion designers, plus **Kauniste** (on the left at #24, uniquely patterned fabrics and prints) and, at the end of the block on the left, **Chez Marius** (#26, a world of fun kitchen gadgets and cooking gear). This shop also marks the pleasant intersection with the tree- and tram-lined Bulevardi. **Day,** kitty-corner from the Chez Marius, has funky, quirky home decor and gifts (Bulevardi 11).

Continuing north across Bulevardi and along Fredrikinkatu, the next block has several home decor shops, including **Casuarina** (on the left at #30, with a spare, rustic, reclaimed aesthetic), and **Primavera Interiors** (across the street at #41, with a more artistic and funky style).

Browse your way two more blocks up Fredrikinkatu to the cross-street, **Eerikinkatu,** which also has lots of inviting little galleries and boutiques; two are at the same address, just around the corner to the left (at Eerikinkatu 18): **DesiPeli,** with a variety of home decor, including some very cool, Marimekko-type fabrics (closed Sun-Mon); and **Napa & Paja,** a collective gallery of three jewelry designers, showcasing their beautiful, unique, delicate designs. They also stock casual handbags and books about Finland.

Near the Design Museum

The Design Museum—a worthwhile stop in its own right (see "Sights in Helsinki," earlier), three long blocks south of the middle of the Esplanade on Korkeavuorenkatu—anchors an appealing area of boutiques. Continuing south of the museum about one block on **Korkeavuorenkatu,** you'll find vintage shops, kitchenware, antiques, pop-up stores, fashion boutiques, hair salons, and cafés. In particular, keep an eye out for **Pore Helsinki** (at #3), with casual fashion and accessories; and **Fasaani** (at #5). Fasaani (a.k.a. Helsinki Secondhand) is particularly worth a detour for bargain-hunters. It's a sprawling warren of an antique shop, with more than 10,000 square feet crammed with affordable pre-owned versions of many of the same home-decor items you'll see in galleries around town—furniture, dishes, glassware, and more. This place would be equally perfect for furnishing a Helsinki hipster flat or a remote cottage in the Finnish wilds (Mon-Fri 10:00-18:00, Sat 10:00-16:00, closed Sun, Korkeavuorenkatu 5, www.fasaani.fi).

OTHER SHOPPING OPTIONS

Market Square: This harborfront square is packed not only with fishmongers and producers, but also with stands selling Finnish souvenirs and more refined crafts (roughly Mon-Fri 6:30-17:00—or until 18:00 in summer, Sat 6:30-16:00, only tourist stalls open on Sun 10:00-16:00).

Modern Shopping Mall: For less glamorous shopping needs, the **Kamppi** mall above and around the bus station is good.

Flea Market: If you brake for garage sales, Finland's biggest flea market, the outdoor **Hietalahti Market,** is worth the 15-minute walk from the harbor or a short ride on tram #6 from Mannerheimintie to the Hietalahdentori stop (June-Aug Mon-Fri 9:00-19:00, Sat 8:00-16:00, Sun 10:00-16:00; less action, shorter hours, and closed Sun

off-season). The adjacent red-brick indoor Hietalahti Market Hall houses food stands (described later, under "Eating in Helsinki").

Sleeping in Helsinki

I've listed a wide range of accommodations in Helsinki, from fancy, well-located big hotels, to modest but cozy smaller hotels, to some unusually comfortable hostels that rent plenty of twin-bedded rooms. Also remember that some of the cheapest beds in Helsinki are on the overnight boats to Stockholm.

Every hotel in Helsinki employs "dynamic pricing," which means that rates for a room can fluctuate wildly from day to day. Peak-season months (with lots of business travel, as well as lots of tourism) are May, June, August, and September. July tends to be a bit slower (little to no domestic business travel), but it can still be busy with the tourist trade. The once-predictable patterns of deeply discounted rooms on weekends and in July and August no longer hold true.

This makes it tricky to give specific rates here. I've tried to list what you can expect, on average, for a standard double room in high season—but prices can range dramatically above and below what I list. Check hotel websites for exact rates. Better yet, plug your dates into a room-finding website (like Booking.com) to see what a variety of hotels are offering for the specific date(s) you're in town, then use my listings to decide which suits your style the best. Once you've determined the best deal, book directly with the hotel (which cuts out the middleman and could snare you an even better price).

HOTELS

On Friday and Saturday nights and from late June to early August, Helsinki's more expensive hotels (the ones denoted with **$$$**) usu-

Sleep Code

Abbreviations   (€1 = about $1.40, country code: 358)
S = Single, **D** = Double/Twin, **T** = Triple, **Q** = Quad, **b** = bathroom
Price Rankings

  $$$ Higher Priced—Most rooms €150 or more.

   $$ Moderately Priced—Most rooms €80-150.

    $ Lower Priced—Most rooms €80 or less.

Unless otherwise noted, credit cards are accepted, English is spoken, breakfast is included, and Wi-Fi is generally free. Public areas of all hotels are non-smoking, though a few still have rooms designated for smokers—if you're not one, you can request a non-smoking room. Prices change; verify current rates online or by email. For the best prices, always book directly with the hotel.

ally have great deals. Checking the hotel's own website can save you a bundle; the best deals are for a nonrefundable reservation.

$$$ Hotel Haven, with 77 elegantly appointed, comfortable rooms and a lobby that artfully mingles class and rustic comfort, owns a convenient location near both the harbor and the Esplanade. "Standard" rooms face the back, with some street noise; quieter "style" rooms face the harbor (but with no views). It's worth a splurge, particularly if you can snare a deal (rates change constantly but typically Db-€219 on weekdays or €184 on weekends, €30 more for a non-view "style" room, €80 more for a "deluxe" seaview room, air-con, Wi-Fi, elevator, Unioninkatu 17, tel. 09/681-930, www.hotelhaven.fi).

$$$ Hotel Rivoli Jardin is a cozy place with a handy location, tucked away just off the middle of the Esplanade and above the harbor. Warm and personal, it has an inviting lounge and 55 rooms with classic Finnish comfort and a few classy flourishes (Db-about €190, discounted to around €110 in summer and on weekends, bigger "superior" room for €20 extra also includes Wi-Fi—otherwise pay Wi-Fi, extra bed-€30, elevator, air-con, Kasarmikatu 40, tel. 09/681-500, www.rivoli.fi, rivoli.jardin@rivoli.fi). They also have 13 apartments (figure €150 for a 1-bedroom, €190 for a 2-bedroom).

$$$ Hotel Fabian, Hotel Haven's sister property a few blocks from the Esplanade, has 58 spacious and comfortable rooms with a black-and-white color scheme (standard "comfort" Db-€200 but can be as low as €130 in slow times, €30 more for bigger and sleeker "style" room, €60 more for "luxe" room with kitchenette, air-con, elevator, Wi-Fi, Fabianinkatu 7, tel. 09/6128-2000, www.hotelfabian.fi, sales@hotelfabian.fi).

$$$ Hotel Katajanokka is a former red-brick prison built in

1888. Its last prisoner checked out in 2002, and it was converted in 2007 into a four-star, business-class hotel. Its 106 rooms are very quiet—the walls are so thick that the hotel provides free Internet cables rather than Wi-Fi. While the windows no longer have bars (thanks to the local fire code) and walls have been removed so that two or three cells make a room, you can still imagine the guards strolling up and down the corridors. Check out the two original cells in the restaurant (Db-€170, around €110 in slow times, €10 more for a twin room, elevator, gym, bike rental, by Vyökatu stop of tram #4 near the Viking cruise ship terminal, Merikasarminkatu 1A, tel. 09/686-450, www.bwkatajanokka.fi, reception@ bwkatajanokka.fi).

$$$ **Scandic Grand Marina,** a huge 462-room, impersonal four-star hotel filling a big, brick warehouse building near the Viking cruise ship terminal, discounts its doubles from about €190 down to €105 (air-con, elevator, Wi-Fi, Katajanokanlaituri 7, tel. 09/16661, www.scandichotels.com/grandmarina, grandmarina@ scandichotels.com).

$$$ **GLO Hotel Art** has 171 modern rooms behind a striking Art Nouveau facade that makes it feel like a stony medieval château has landed in the middle of Helsinki (Db-€150, elevator, air-con, Wi-Fi, Lönnrotinkatu 29, tel. 010-344-4100, www. glohotels.fi, art@glohotels.fi).

$$$ **GLO Hotel Kluuvi,** which has 184 rooms and a well-designed spa-type quality, gives you an appreciation for how an extremely wealthy society manages to survive a long, dark winter. This temping splurge is quite trendy and a bit snobby. Perfectly situated just north of the Esplanade, it's worth considering if you prize elegance and location—especially if you can get a good discount (Db-€264, €10 less for a "small" room or €20 more for a "large" room, air-con, elevator, Wi-Fi, Kluuvikatu 4, tel. 010-3444-400, www.glohotels.fi).

$$ **Hotel Anna** is conscientiously run, reasonably priced, and feels like home. Its 64 well-worn rooms help raise funds for the Finnish Free Church (it's actually attached to a church—ask them to show you the shortcut to the choir loft). For more air in the rooms, ask at the desk for a key to open the larger windows (Sb-€110, Db-€145, extra bed-€15, reserve directly by email and mention this book for best prices—generally a 10 percent discount off prevailing rate, worth checking website for deals, 2-room Qb and family rooms available, elevator, guest computer, Wi-Fi, 4 blocks south of the top of the Esplanade—take tram #2/#3 to Iso Roobertinkatu, Annankatu 1, tel. 09/616-621, www.hotelanna.fi, info@ hotelanna.fi).

$$ **Hotelli Finn** is inexpensive and wonderfully central. Its 35 rooms are stowed quietly on the sixth floor of an office building

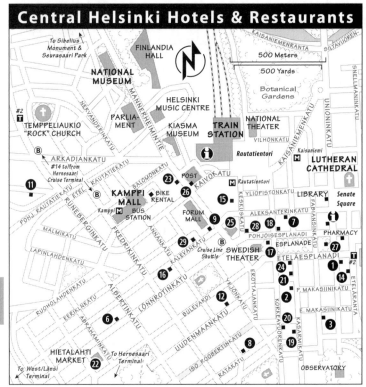

Central Helsinki Hotels & Restaurants

near the top of the Esplanade. It's also consciously short on amenities: no shower curtains in the tiny bathrooms, no desks or chairs in the rooms, no breakfast (though a nearby bakery offers a €7 buffet spread), and no real lobby or common space—just a dark, somewhat gloomy hallway. The price and location are right, though, and it's worth considering for a quick stay when other places aren't discounting (Sb-€69, Db-€79-99—up to €129 at busy times, third or fourth person-about €15, best to reserve on website, elevator, Wi-Fi, Kalevankatu 3B, tel. 09/684-4360, www.hotellifinn.fi, info@hotellifinn.fi).

$ Essex Home is a good budget alternative. Sweet Seija Lappalainen rents 13 apartments (all with kitchenettes) scattered around the residential streets of the Katajanokka peninsula (rates vary but generally studio Db-€69, 1-bedroom Db-€125, expect lots of stairs, Wi-Fi, Luotsikatu 9A, mobile 040-516-2714, www.essexhome.fi, info@essexhome.fi). The two "Essex Studio" rooms are a bit farther out.

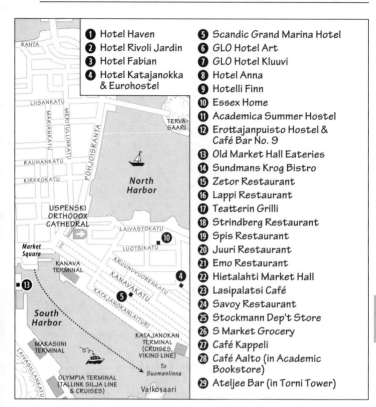

1. Hotel Haven
2. Hotel Rivoli Jardin
3. Hotel Fabian
4. Hotel Katajanokka & Eurohostel
5. Scandic Grand Marina Hotel
6. GLO Hotel Art
7. GLO Hotel Kluuvi
8. Hotel Anna
9. Hotelli Finn
10. Essex Home
11. Academica Summer Hostel
12. Erottajanpuisto Hostel & Café Bar No. 9
13. Old Market Hall Eateries
14. Sundmans Krog Bistro
15. Zetor Restaurant
16. Lappi Restaurant
17. Teatterin Grilli
18. Strindberg Restaurant
19. Spis Restaurant
20. Juuri Restaurant
21. Emo Restaurant
22. Hietalahti Market Hall
23. Lasipalatsi Café
24. Savoy Restaurant
25. Stockmann Dep't Store
26. S Market Grocery
27. Café Kappeli
28. Café Aalto (in Academic Bookstore)
29. Ateljee Bar (in Torni Tower)

HELSINKI

HOSTELS

Helsinki's hostels are unusually comfortable. While they offer €3 discounts for those with hostel cards, all ages are welcome with or without a hostel membership. Eurohostel and Academica are more like budget hotels than hostels.

$ Eurohostel, a modern hostel with 255 beds in 35 rooms, is 400 yards from the Viking ferry terminal and a 10-minute walk from Market Square. The more expensive rooms come with TVs. It's packed with facilities, including a laundry room, a members' kitchen with unique refrigerated safety-deposit boxes for your caviar and beer, a restaurant, and plenty of good budget-travel information. While generally fully booked in advance, they release no-show beds at 18:00. In the following rates, the lower price is for the older "backpacker" rooms, while the higher price is for the newer "Eurohostel" rooms (S-€47/€53, D-€56/€63, T-€75/€85, family room with up to 4 kids under age 15-€66/€74, shared twins available, includes sheets; breakfast-€9, free morning sauna, evening sauna-€7.50, private lockable closets, pay Wi-Fi, laundry-€3/

load, Vyökatu stop for tram #4 is around the corner, Linnankatu 9, tel. 09/622-0470, www.eurohostel.fi, eurohostel@eurohostel.fi).

$ Academica Summer Hostel is a university dorm that's professionally run as a hostel from June through August. Finnish university students have it good—the 326 rooms are hotel-quality with private baths and kitchenettes, though all doubles have twin beds. Guests can have a morning sauna and use the swimming pool for free (Sb-€49, Db-€62, Tb-€85, bed in shared 2-3-person room-€29, prices include sheets, breakfast-€7, safe deposit box, guest computer by reception, Wi-Fi, laundry-€5/load; tram #2 to the Kauppakorkeakoulut stop, then walk 5 minutes to Hietaniemenkatu 14, tel. 09/1311-4334, www.hostelacademica.fi, hostel.academica@hyy.fi).

$ Erottajanpuisto is a smaller, friendly, centrally located hostel on the third floor of a 19th-century apartment building in the heart of the happening Design District. This is a better place to stay than Eurohostel if you're looking to meet fellow travelers in the common room and don't mind lugging your bags up the stairs (15 rooms with 2-8 beds, dorm bed-€30, S-€60, D-€75, T-€99, cheaper off-season, includes sheets, breakfast-€7, lockers-€2, guest computer, Wi-Fi, kitchen, no elevator, Uudenmaankatu 9, tel. 09/642-169, www.erottajanpuisto.com, info@erottajanpuisto.com).

Eating in Helsinki

Helsinki's many restaurants are smoke-free and a good value for lunch on weekdays. Finnish companies get a tax break if they distribute lunch coupons (worth €9) to their employees. It's no surprise that most downtown Helsinki restaurants offer weekday lunch specials that cost exactly the value of the coupon. These low prices evaporate in the evenings and all day Saturday and Sunday, when picnics and Middle Eastern kebab restaurants are the only budget options. Dinner reservations are smart at nicer restaurants.

FUN HARBORFRONT EATERIES

Stalls on Market Square: Helsinki's delightful and vibrant square is magnetic any time of day...but especially at lunchtime. This really is the most memorable, casual, quick-and-cheap lunch place in town. A half-dozen orange tents (erected to shield diners from bird bombs) serve fun food on paper plates until 18:00. It's not unusual for the Finnish president to stop by here with visiting dignitaries. There's a crêpe place, and at the far end—my favorites—several salmon grills (€10-13 for a good meal). The only real harborside dining in this part of town is picnicking. While these places provide picnic tables, you can also have your food foil-wrapped to go and grab benches right on the water down near Uspenski Orthodox Cathedral.

Old Market Hall (Vanha Kauppahalli): Just beyond the harborside market is a cute, red-brick, indoor market hall. It's beautifully renovated with upscale-feeling woodwork, and quite tight inside (Mon-Sat 8:00-18:00, closed Sun). Today, along with produce stalls, it's a hit for its fun, inexpensive eateries. You'll find lots of enticing coffee shops with tempting pastries; various grilled, smoked, or pickled fish options (you'll smell it before you see it); mounds of bright-yellow paella; deli counters with delectable open-face sandwiches; a handy chance to sample reindeer meat; and an array of ethnic eats, from Middle Eastern and Lebanese meals to Vietnamese banh mi sandwiches. In the market hall, **Soppakeittiö** ("Soup Kitchen") serves big bowls of filling, tasty seafood soup for €9.50, including bread and water (Mon-Fri 11:00-16:00, Sat 11:00-15:00—except closed Sat in summer, closed Sun year-round).

Sundmans Krog Bistro is sedate and Old World but not folkloric, filling an old merchant's mansion facing the harbor. As it's the less fussy and more affordable (yet still super-romantic) little sister of an adjacent, posh, Michelin-rated restaurant, quality is assured. A rare and memorable extra is their Baltic fish buffet—featuring salmon, Baltic sprat, and herring with potatoes and all the toppings—€15 as a starter, €25 as a main course. The €19 lunch special (Mon-Fri 11:00-15:00) includes the buffet plus the main dish of the week—often more fish (€23-25 main courses, €40 three-course dinners, Mon-Fri 11:00-23:00, Sat 12:00-23:00, Sun 13:00-23:00, Eteläranta 16, tel. 09/6128-5450).

FINNISH-THEMED DINING: TRACTORS AND LAPP CUISINE

Zetor, the self-proclaimed *traktor* restaurant, mercilessly lampoons Finnish rural culture and cuisine (while celebrating it deep down). It's the kitschy Finnish answer to the Cracker Barrel. Sit next to a cow-crossing sign at a tractor-turned-into-a-table, in a "Finnish Western" atmosphere reminiscent of director Aki Kaurismäki's movies. For lunch or dinner, main courses run €17-23 and include reindeer, vendace (small freshwater fish), and less exotic fare. This place, while touristy and tacky, can be fun. It gets loud after 20:00 when the dance floor gets going (daily 12:00-24:00, 200 yards north of Stockmann department store, across street from McDonald's at Mannerheimintie 3, tel. 010-766-4450).

Lappi Restaurant is a fine place for Lapp cuisine, with an entertaining menu (they smoke their own fish) and creative decor that has you thinking you've traveled north and lashed your reindeer to the hitchin' post. The friendly staff serves tasty Sami dishes in a snug and very woody atmosphere. Dinner reservations are strongly recommended (€24-39 main courses, Mon-Fri 16:00-24:00, Sat 13:00-24:00, closed Sun, off Bulevardi at Annankatu 22, tel. 09/645-550, www.lappires.com).

VENERABLE ESPLANADE CAFÉS

Highly competitive restaurants line the sunny north side of the Esplanade—offering creative lunch salads and light meals in their cafés (with fine sidewalk seating), plush sofas for cocktails in their bars, and fancy restaurant dining upstairs.

Teatterin Grilli, attached to the landmark Swedish Theater, has several interconnected eateries inside and fine, park-side seating indoors and out. Order a salad from the café counter in the "Wine & Deli & Juice" bar, facing the Academic Bookstore (€10 with bread, choose two meats or extras to add to crispy base, Caesar salad option). The long cocktail bar is popular with office workers yet comfortable for baby-boomer tourists. Whether you order a meal or a drink, you're welcome to find a seat out on the leafy Esplanade terrace (café counter open Mon-Fri 9:00-20:30, Sat 11:00-20:30, Sun 12:00-20:30 except closed Sun in winter, at the top of the Esplanade, Pohjoisesplanadi 2, tel. 09/6128-5000). There's also a fancy restaurant.

Strindberg, near the corner of the Esplanade and Mikonkatu, has several parts—each one oozing atmosphere and class. Downstairs is an elegant café with outdoor and indoor tables great for people-watching (€8-15 sandwiches and salads). The upstairs cocktail lounge—with big sofas and bookshelves giving it a den-like coziness—attracts the after-work office crowd. Also upstairs, the inviting restaurant has huge main dishes for €20-30, with fish, meat, pasta, and vegetarian options; reserve in advance to try to get a window seat overlooking the Esplanade (restaurant open Mon 11:00-23:00, Tue-Sat 11:00-24:00, closed Sun; café open Mon 9:00-23:00, Tue-Sat 9:00-24:00, Sun 10:00-22:00, Pohjoisesplanadi 33, tel. 09/681-2030).

TRENDY EATERIES IN AND NEAR THE DESIGN DISTRICT

Predictably, several creative eateries cluster in the Design District, a short stroll south and west of the Esplanade. While these aren't for budget diners, they do offer a fresh and updated take on the cuisine of Finland. Many of these highlight the exciting "New Nordic" school of cooking, featuring fresh, seasonal, local ingredients—often foraged—with modern presentation.

Spis is your best Helsinki bet for splurging on Finnish New Nordic. Reserve ahead for one of the prized tables in its tiny, peeling-plaster, rustic-chic dining room (tasting menus only: €57/4 courses, €77/6 courses, Tue-Sat from 17:30, last seating at 20:30, closed Sun-Mon, Kasarmikatu 26, mobile 045-305-1211, www. spis.fi).

Juuri has a trendy, casual interior and serves a variety of "sapas" (Suomi tapas)—small plates highlighting Finland's culinary bounty. It's lunch-only on weekdays, but open for dinner on weekends (€5 small plates, €28 main courses, Mon-Fri 11:00-14:30 only, Sat 12:00-22:00, Sun 16:00-22:00, Korkeavuorenkatu 27, tel. 09/635-732).

Emo Restaurant is a pleasantly unpretentious, blue-jeans wine bar in a sleepy zone just a block off of the Esplanade. They serve up €10 small plates; most patrons share several (lunch Tue-Thu 11:30-14:30; dinner Mon-Sat 17:00-24:00, closed Sun; Kasarmikatu 44, mobile 010-505-0900, www.emo-ravintola.fi).

Pub Grub: **Café Bar No. 9** is a simpler, cheaper choice right in the heart of the Design District. Tucked between design shops, its borderline-divey bar vibe attracts a loyal local following, who enjoy digging into plates of unpretentious pub food (€10-16 meals, Uudenmaakatu 9, tel. 09-621-4059).

Market Hall: Hiding in a nondescript neighborhood at the edge of the Design District, the **Hietalahti Market Hall** is a fun place to browse for a meal. It's similar to the Old Market Hall along the South Harbor, but far less touristy. The elegantly renovated old food hall is filled with an enticing array of vendors, with delightful seating upstairs (Mon-Fri 8:00-18:00, Sat 8:00-17:00, closed Sun).

FUNCTIONAL EATING

Lasipalatsi, the renovated, rejuvenated 1930s Glass Palace, is on Mannerheimintie between the train and bus stations. The café (with a youthful terrace on the square out back) offers a self-service buffet (€10 weekday lunch before 15:00, €17 weekend brunch, €13 dinner after 15:00 any day); there are always €5 sandwiches and cakes (Mon-Fri 7:30-22:00, Sat 9:00-23:00, Sun 11:00-22:00, more expensive restaurant upstairs—closed Sun, across from post office at Mannerheimintie 22, tel. 09/612-6700).

DRESSY SPLURGE DINNERS

Savoy Restaurant, where locals go for special occasions, is expensive, formal, and drenched in Alvar Aalto design. Everything—from the chairs and lampshades to the doors—is 1937 original. The food is Continental with a Finnish touch. While the glassed-in terrace offers a great eighth-floor, rooftop view, the interior is where you'll experience a classic Finnish atmosphere. Reservations are advised (€42-47 main courses, €70 three-course lunch, €110-120 four- to five-course dinner, Mon-Fri 11:30-14:30 & 18:00-22:30,

Sat 18:00-22:30, closed Sun, Eteläesplanadi 14, tel. 09/6128-5300, www.ravintolasavoy.fi).

PICNICS

In supermarkets, buy the semi-flat bread (available dark or light) that Finns love—every slice is a heel. Finnish liquid yogurt is also a treat (sold in liter cartons). Karelian pasties, filled with rice or mashed potatoes, make a good snack. A beautiful, upscale supermarket is in the basement of the **Stockmann** department store—follow the *Delikatessen* signs downstairs (Mon-Fri 9:00-21:00, Sat 9:00-18:00, open most Sun 12:00-18:00, Aleksanterinkatu 52B). Two blocks north, a more workaday, inexpensive supermarket is **S Market,** under the Sokos department store next to the train station (Mon-Sat 7:00-22:00, Sun 10:00-22:00).

Helsinki Connections

BY BUS OR TRAIN

From Helsinki, it's easy to get to **Turku** (hourly, 2 hours by either bus or train) or **St. Petersburg, Russia** (see options later). For train info, visit www.vr.fi. For bus info in English, consult www.matkahuolto.fi.

BY OVERNIGHT BOAT BETWEEN STOCKHOLM AND HELSINKI

Two fine and fiercely competitive lines, Viking Line and Tallink Silja, connect the capitals of Sweden and Finland. Each line offers state-of-the-art, 2,700-bed ships with luxurious *smörgåsbord* meals, reasonable cabins, plenty of entertainment (discos, saunas, gambling), and enough duty-free shopping to sink a ship.

The fares are reasonable—when you consider that they include both international transportation and accommodations—because many locals sail to shop and drink tax-free. It's a huge operation.

The boats are filled with about 45 percent Finns, 45 percent Swedes, and 10 percent cruisers from other countries. The average passenger spends as much on booze and tax-free items as on the boat fare. To maintain their tax-free status, the boats make a midnight stop in the Åland Islands—a self-governing, Swedish-speaking province of Finland that's exempt from the European Union's value-added tax (VAT).

The Pepsi and Coke of the Scandinavian cruise industry vie to outdo each other with bigger and fancier boats. Of the two, Viking Line has the reputation as the party boat. Tallink Silja is considered more elegant. But both lines—used mostly by locals for a quick getaway and duty-free booze run—have their share of noisy, sometimes-irritating passengers. (See "Arrival in Helsinki" for terminal locations.)

Schedules and Tickets

Schedules: Both Viking Line (www.vikingline.fi) and Tallink Silja (www.tallinksilja.com) sail nightly between Stockholm and Helsinki year-round. In both directions, the boats leave between 16:30 and 17:30, and arrive the next morning around 10:00.

Cost: As with Scandinavian hotels, cruise fares vary by season, by day of the week, and by cabin class. Check both lines' websites to see the options for your itinerary. Mid-June to mid-August is most crowded and expensive. Off-season, Friday is the most expensive night to travel, while Sunday through Wednesday nights are the cheapest. In summer, a one-way ticket per person for the cheapest bed that has a private bath (in a tight, windowless, below-car-deck "C"-class stateroom shared with other travelers) costs €35-80; for a similar cabin, couples will pay a total of about €120-130 in peak times. Of course, the more you're willing to pay, the plusher your options. Travelers with rail passes that include Sweden or Finland get 20 to 40 percent discounts on both lines. There also may be discounts for early booking, seniors, and families (look for family-cabin rates). Note that the lines may not permit travel on some Stockholm-Finland routes by those ages 18-20 who are not accompanied by a parent or guardian; for details, check websites or contact the cruise lines.

Itinerary Options: "Round-trip" fares (across and back on **successive nights,** leaving you access to your bedroom throughout the day) generally cost less than two one-way trips. The drawback is that this itinerary leaves you with only a few hours on land. But you may be able to get the round-trip fare on **nonsuccessive nights** if you book a hotel through the cruise line for every intervening night. If it fits your schedule, this can be a good deal.

Reservations: *For summer or weekend sailings, reserve well in advance.* Book online with a credit card—you'll get a reservation number and pick up your boarding card at the port. You can also book by phone or in person, but you may be charged an extra fee (likely €5); however, they are typically happy to answer questions for no charge. **Viking Line's** Swedish number is tel. 08/452-4000, and its Finnish number is tel. 0600-41577 (a pricey toll line). For **Tallink Silja,** the customer service line is a German phone number: +49-40-547-541-222; their Swedish number is tel. 08/222-140, and their Finnish number is tel. 0600-15700 (a pricey toll line). Any travel agent in Scandinavia can also sell you a ticket (with a small booking fee).

Terminals in Stockholm and Helsinki

Terminal buildings are well-organized, with cafés, lockers, tourist information desks, lounges, and phones. Remember, 2,000-plus passengers come and go with each boat. Boats open 1.5 hours before departure, and you must be checked in 20 minutes before departure. Both lines offer safe and handy parking in Stockholm. Ask for details when you reserve your ticket.

In Stockholm: Viking Line has its own terminal (squeezed between cruise ships) along the Stadsgården embankment on Södermalm (facing the Old Town/Gamla Stan). To get there, it's easiest to ride Viking Line's shuttle bus from Stockholm's bus station right to the terminal (10 kr, departs according to boat schedule). You can also ride public bus #53 (from the train station or Gamla Stan) or #71 (from the Opera House or Gamla Stan) to the Londonviadukten stop, then hike five minutes down to the terminal. A taxi from the train station will cost you around 150 kr.

Tallink Silja's boats leave from the Frihamnen port, about three miles northeast of the city center. At Frihamnen, Tallink Silja boats use the terminal called Värtahamnen (at the northern end of the sprawling industrial port). To reach the terminal, it's simplest to catch the Tallink Silja shuttle bus from Stockholm's bus station (50 kr, departs according to boat schedule). By pub-lic transportation, you can either ride the T-bana to the Gärdet station, then walk about 10 minutes; or you can take public bus #76 all the way from downtown (Mon-Sat only, direction Rop-sten, get off at Färjeterminalen stop). Figure about 230-250 kr for a taxi from Gamla Stan, the train station, or other downtown areas.

For Stockholm public transport information, see www.sl.se.

In Helsinki: Both lines are perfectly central, on opposite sides of the main harbor, a 10-minute walk from the center.

Tips on Board

Meals: While ships have cheap, fast cafeterias as well as classy, romantic restaurants, they are famous for their *smörgåsbord* dinners. If you want the *smörgåsbord* experience, board the ship hungry. Dinner is self-serve in two sittings, one at about 17:30, the other around 20:00. You'll pay extra for both the dinner *smörgåsbord* (usually around €35-40) and for the breakfast buffet (€10); you can get discounts for prebooking both together. If you board without a reservation, go to the restaurant and make one. Make sure to re-serve your table, not just your meal; window seats are highly sought after. The key to eating a *smörgåsbord* is to take small portions and pace yourself. The price includes free beer, wine, soft drinks, and coffee. Of course, you can also bring a picnic and eat it on deck, or eat at one of the ship's other restaurants.

Scenery: During the first few hours out of Stockholm, your ship passes through the *Skärgården* (archipelago). The third hour features the most exotic island scenery—tiny islets with cute red huts and happy people. I'd have dinner at the first sitting (shortly after departure) and be on deck for sunset. But you can also take other factors into consideration: As the cruise progresses, it gets colder outside, and the ride can get choppier (as the ship leaves the protected archipelago and enters the open sea).

Time Change: Finland is one hour ahead of Sweden. Sailing from Stockholm to Helsinki, operate on Swedish time until you're ready to go to bed, then reset your watch. Morning schedules are Finnish time, and vice versa when you return. The cruise-schedule flier in English makes this clear—pick it up as you board.

Other Services: Many ships have saunas and massages (both for an extra charge, reserve as you board), and typically offer racks of *Stockholm* or *Helsinki This Week* magazines. For purchases, ships take credit cards, euros, and Swedish kronor. Ships have exchange desks, but not on-board ATMs; you'll find those in the terminals at each end.

HELSINKI

Adding Other Destinations

Tallinn: The Estonian capital can be spliced into your Helsinki itinerary in a number of ways: as a side-trip from Helsinki (or vice-versa), or as a triangle trip (Stockholm-Helsinki-Tallinn-Stockholm, must be booked as three one-ways).

Turku: Both Viking Line and Tallink Silja also sail from Stockholm to Turku in Finland, a shorter crossing (11 hours, departing daily at about 7:00-9:00 and 19:30-21:00). Turku, a "mini-Helsinki" with more medieval charm but less urban bustle, is two hours from Helsinki by bus or train. The cheaper fare saves you enough to pay for the train trip from Turku to Helsinki.

BY CRUISE SHIP

For more details on the following ports, and other cruise destinations, pick up my *Rick Steves Northern European Cruise Ports* guidebook.

Cruises arrive in Helsinki at various ports circling two large harbors—West Harbor (Länsistama) and South Harbor (Eteläsatama). Each individual cruise berth is designated by a three-letter code (noted in this section, along with each terminal's name in both Finnish and Swedish). For a map, see www.portofhelsinki.fi.

Getting Downtown: In addition to the public transit and/or walking options outlined later, many cruise lines offer a **shuttle bus** into downtown (likely €8 one-way, €12 round-trip; especially worth considering if you arrive at the farther-flung West Harbor). This bus usually drops you off across the street from Stockmann department store (near the corner of Mannerheimintie and Lönnrotinkatu). To reach the top of the Esplanade, cross the busy Mannerheimintie boulevard and proceed down the street between the huge, red-brick Stockmann and the white, round Swedish Theater (Svenska Teatern). Another option is to take a **hop-on, hop-off bus tour;** these meet arriving ships at Hernesaari terminal, and are easy to find around the South Harbor (for details, see "Tours in Helsinki," earlier).

West Harbor (Länsistama/Västra Hamnen)

This ugly industrial port is about two miles west of downtown. From either of the two cruise ports here, it's about a €15-20 taxi ride into town.

Hernesaari Terminal (Ärtholmen in Swedish): The primary cruise port for Helsinki sits on the eastern side of West Harbor. It has two berths (Quay B, code: LHB; and Quay C, code: LHC) and a tiny-but-handy TI kiosk where you can pick up free maps and brochures, buy a day ticket for public transit (€8, credit cards only), or use the free Wi-Fi. It's a five-minute walk to the stop for

bus #14, which takes you downtown: Head through the parking lot, turn left at the street, take the next right, and look for the bus stop marked *Pajamäki/Smedjebacka* (3-6/hour). From here, ride bus #14 to Kamppi (a 10-minute walk from the train station area and the Esplanade) or continue to Kauppakorkeakoulut (near Temppeliaukio, the Church in the Rock—get off the bus, walk straight ahead one block, then turn right up Luthernikatu to find the church). In summer, there's also a **ferry** that goes from Hernesaari to Market Square (€7 one-way, €10 all day, only 3/day starting at 9:30, late June-early Aug daily, early-late June and early-late Aug Sat-Sun only, 30 minutes, mobile 040-736-2329, www.seahelsinki.fi).

West Terminal (Länsiterminaali/Västra Terminalen): From the cruise berth at Melkki Quay (code: LMA), you'll walk 10 minutes through dull shipyards (follow the green line on the pavement) to the Länsiterminaali building, with ATMs and other services. From right in front of this terminal, tram #9 zips into town (6/hour, handiest downtown stop is Rautatieasema, at the train station).

South Harbor (Eteläsatama/Södra Hamnen)

This centrally located harbor, which fans out from Market Square, is an easy walk from downtown (taxis are unnecessary here, but if you take one, figure €10-15 to most points in the city center). Ringing this harbor are several terminals for both cruises and overnight boats; two are most commonly used by cruise ships.

Katajanokan Terminal (Skatudden in Swedish): The harbor's northern embankment has two cruise berths (codes: ERA and ERB). A third berth (code: EKL), used more by overnight boats than cruise ships, is closer to town. The Viking Line terminal in this area has ATMs, other services, and—across the street—the stop for **tram #4T,** which zips you right into town (stops at City Hall, Senate Square, Lasipalatsi near the train station, and National Museum). Or you can simply **walk** 15 minutes to Market Square (stroll between brick warehouses, with the harbor on your left, toward the white-and-green dome).

Olympia Terminal: Smaller cruise ships use this terminal (code: EO), along the southern embankment. Inside the terminal are ATMs and other services; out front is a stop for **tram #2,** which takes you to Senate Square, then the train station (Rautatieasema stop), then the Sammonkatu stop near Temppeliaukio (the Church in the Rock). It's also easy to **walk** into town from here—figure about 15 minutes (head around the harbor, with the water on your right, toward the white-and-green dome).

The South Harbor berths that are closest to downtown (**Kanava terminal** and **Makasiini terminal**) are used mostly by overnight boats, though occasionally overflow cruise ships may end up there. Either one is an easy five-minute walk to Market Square.

CONNECTING HELSINKI AND ST. PETERSBURG

Many visitors use Helsinki as a launch pad for a visit to St. Petersburg, Russia—just 240 miles east.

Visa Requirements: American and Canadian travelers to Russia need a visa, which must be arranged weeks in advance. You'll need to secure an official "invitation" in St. Petersburg and mail your passport to the Russian consulate (for details, US citizens should see www.russianembassy.org; Canadians can consult www.rusembassy.ca). Given the logistical headaches, it's smart to enlist an agency to help obtain an invitation and process your paperwork (I've had a good experience with www.passportvisasexpress.com). It's not cheap: Plan on $180 for the visa, around a $55 fee for the processing agency, plus around $55 to securely mail your passport to the embassy and back.

Visa Exceptions: If you arrive in St. Petersburg **on a cruise,** the visa requirement is waived provided you contract with a local tour operator (or join one of your cruise line's excursions) for a guided visit around the city—you'll have no free time. But there is an exception that gives you time on your own: If you go to St. Petersburg on a St. Peter Line ship (see below), then pay for a "shuttle service" from the dock into the city (typically €25 round-trip), you can technically stay up to 72 hours before returning with a St. Peter Line shuttle and boat. Although this is not a guided visit, it's treated as the "cruise exception" explained above—at least, it is as of this writing (in early 2015). **Important:** As this loophole may well be closed in the future—and all aspects of the Russian visa situation change frequently—carefully confirm these details before planning your trip.

By Land: You have two options. The **bus** is slower and cheaper (3-5/day, including overnight options; 8-9 hours, €35-40, less for students, www.matkahuolto.fi, arrives at Baltiisky Vokzal train station near the Baltiiskaya Metro stop); the Allegro **train,** operated by Finnish Railways, is much faster (4/day, 3.5 hours, €70-105 depending on demand, no student discount, www.vr.fi, book ahead online, arrives at Finlyandsky train station near Ploshchad Lenina Metro stop). There's also a daily overnight train to **Moscow.** Rail passes are not valid on the international trains to Russia.

By Sea: Many Baltic Sea **cruises** include a stop in St. Petersburg. But if you're on your own, **St. Peter Line** can take you there from Helsinki. Their *Princess Maria* sails every other day (3-4/week), departing from Helsinki's West Harbor (from the West/

Länsi terminal) at 18:00; 14.5 hours later, it reaches St. Petersburg (where it turns around and, at 19:00, heads back to Helsinki). In high season (July-late Aug), the cheapest bunk in a shared four-bed cabin costs €27 one-way; a round-trip "cruise" starts at €150. St. Peter Line's ship *Anastasia* connects St. Petersburg to Tallinn about once weekly, then continues on to Stockholm. For details, see www.stpeterline.com; Helsinki Expert also has information.

ESTONIA

ESTONIA

Eesti

The most accessible part of the former USSR, Estonia is shaped by its eclectic past and inspired by the prospect of an ever-brighter future. In the European Union, only three micro-states (Cyprus, Luxembourg, and Malta) have a smaller population than Estonia. But like its fellow Baltic countries (Latvia and Lithuania), Estonia has an endearing enthusiasm for the things that make it unique—proving that you don't have to be big to have a clear cultural identity.

Estonians are related to the Finns and have a similar history—first Swedish domination, then Russian (1710-1918), and finally independence after World War I. In 1940, Estonians were at least as affluent and as advanced as the Finns, but they could not preserve their independence from Soviet expansion during World War II. As a result, Estonia sank into a nearly 50-year period of communist stagnation. Since then, the country has made great strides in its recovery; it joined the EU and NATO in 2004, adopted the euro currency in 2011, and today feels pretty much as "Western" as its Nordic neighbors.

EU membership seemed like a natural step to many Estonians; they already thought of themselves as part of the Nordic world. Language, history, religion, and twice-hourly ferry departures connect Finns and Estonians. Only 50 miles separate Helsinki and Tallinn, and Stockholm is just an overnight boat ride away. Finns visit Tallinn to eat, drink, and shop more cheaply than at home. While some Estonians resent how Tallinn becomes a Finnish nightclub on summer weekends, most people on both sides are happy since the end of the Cold War to have friendly new neighbors.

You'd be wrong to think of this "former USSR" country as backward. Thanks to visionary and aggressive development policies implemented soon after independence—including the designation of Internet access as a basic human right—Estonia is now a global trendsetter in technology. By 1998, every school in Estonia was already online. The country has some of the fastest broadband speeds in the world, Estonians vote and file their taxes electronically, and

Estonia Almanac

Official Name: Eesti Vabariik—the Republic of Estonia—or simply Estonia.

Population: Estonia is home to 1.3 million people (77 per square mile). Nearly three in four are of Estonian heritage, and about one-quarter are of Russian descent, with smaller minorities of Ukrainians, Belarusians, and Finns. About 70 percent speak the official language—Estonian—and nearly 30 percent speak Russian. The majority of Estonians are unaffiliated with any religion. About 10 percent are Lutheran and 16 percent are Orthodox.

Latitude and Longitude: 59°N and 26°E, similar latitude to Juneau, Alaska.

Area: 17,500 square miles, about the size of New Hampshire and Vermont combined.

Geography: Between Latvia and Russia, Estonia borders the Baltic Sea and Gulf of Finland. It includes more than 1,500 islands and islets, and has the highest number of meteorite craters per land area in the world.

Biggest City: The capital of Estonia, Tallinn, has 400,000 people (500,000 in the metropolitan area).

Economy: Estonia's transition to a free-market system included joining the World Trade Organization and the European Union. In recent years, it's had one of the highest per capita income levels in Central Europe and boasts a per-capita GDP of $22,400. Its four major trading partners are Finland, Sweden, Russia, and Germany; the strengths of "E-stonia" are electronics and telecommunications.

Currency: €1 (euro) = about $1.40.

Government: Estonia is a parliamentary democracy, with a president elected by parliament and a prime minister. The 101-member parliament (Riigikogu) is elected by popular vote every four years.

Flag: The pre-1940 Estonian flag was restored in 1990. It has three equal horizontal bands with blue at the top, black in the middle, and white on the bottom. The blue represents Estonia's lakes and sea, and the loyalty and devotion of the  country to its people. The black symbolizes the homeland's rich soil and the hardships the people have suffered. The white represents hope and happiness.

The Average Estonian: He or she is 41 years old, has 1.4 children, and will live to be 74. About 58 percent of the population are women (they live longer), and when she sings the national anthem, she uses the same melody as Finland.

ESTONIA

Skype—used by travelers worldwide to keep in touch—was invented right here. The multibillion-dollar windfall from Skype's 2005 sale to eBay kickstarted a whole new venture-capital industry that is still paying dividends today.

And yet, despite its modernity, Estonian culture can be romantic—sometimes shaded with a tinge of darkness. This little

land has a long, jagged, hauntingly beautiful coastline, and over a thousand lakes. Fifty percent of the landscape is forest, while marshlands and bogs cover another twenty percent. Traditional folk music buoys the national spirit—especially at the Song Festival every five years, where a significant portion of the population convenes to pour out their souls in song. Some of Estonia's traditions may strike you as quirky. Estonians snack on nearly black rye bread slathered in garlic and bury their dead in evocative pine forests—where skinny trunks recede into the infinite heavens.

Even as Estonia will always face West, across the Baltic, it also faces East, into the Russian hinterlands. One difficult legacy of the Soviet experience is Estonia's huge Russian population. Most Estonian Russians' parents and grandparents were brought to Estonia in the 1950s and 1960s to work in now-defunct fac' and the northeastern cities. Twenty-five percent of lation is now ethnically Russian. Under Vladimir Putin, Ruṣ demanded better treatment of Estonia's Russian-speaking population. After Putin declared he would "protect" Russian speakers in Ukraine and fostered a separatist revolt there, some Estonians wondered if something similar could happen here. Making Russians feel at home in Estonia while building a distinctly Estonian culture and identity is one of independent Estonia's biggest challenges.

Most Estonians speak English—it's the first choice these days at school. About half can carry on a normal conversation in Eng-

lish. Estonian is similar to Finnish and equally difficult; only a million people speak it worldwide. Two useful phrases to know are *"Tänan"* (TAH-nahn; "Thank you") and *"Terviseks!"* (TEHR-vee-sehks; "Cheers!"). If you'd like to learn a few more phrases, see the Estonian survival phrases on the following page. The farther you go beyond the touristy zones, the more you see that Russian is still Estonia's second language. If you know some Russian, use it. It's the mother tongue of about 40 percent of Tallinners (many of whom have no intention of learning Estonian).

onian Survival Phrases

Estonian has a few unusual vowel sounds. The letter *ä* is pronounced "ah" as in "hat," but *a* without the umlaut sounds more like "aw" as in "hot." To make the sound *ö*, purse your lips and say "oh"; the letter *õ* is similar, but with the lips less pursed. Listen to locals and imitate.

In the phonetics, *ī* sounds like the long *i* in "light," and bolded syllables are stressed.

English	Estonian	Pronunciation
Hello. (formal)	*Tervist.*	**tehr**-veest
Hi. / Bye. (informal)	*Tere. / Nägemist.*	**teh**-reh / **nah**-geh-meest
Do you speak English?	*Kas te räägite inglise keelt?*	kahs teh **raah**-gee-teh **een**-glee-seh kehlt
Yes. / No.	*Jah. / Ei.*	yah / ay
Please. / You're welcome.	*Palun.*	**pah**-luhn
Thank you (very much).	*Tänan (väga).*	**tah**-nahn (**vah**-gaw)
Can I help you?	*Saan ma teid aidata?*	saahn mah tayd ī-dah-tah
Excuse me.	*Vabandust.*	**vaw**-bahn-doost
(Very) good.	*(Väga) hea.*	(**vah**-gaw) **hey**-ah
Goodbye.	*Hüvasti.*	**hew**-vaw-stee
one / two	*üks / kaks*	ewks / kawks
three / four	*kolm / neli*	kohlm / **nay**-lee
five / six	*viis / kuus*	vees / koos
seven / eight	*seitse / kaheksa*	**sayt**-seh / **kaw**-hehk-sah
nine / ten	*üheksa / kümme*	**ew**-hehk-sah / **kew**-meh
hundred	*sada*	**saw**-daw
thousand	*tuhat*	**too**-hawt
How much?	*Kui palju?*	kwee **pawl**-yoo
local currency: (Estonian) crown	*(Eesti) krooni*	(**eh**-stee) **kroo**-nee
Where is...?	*Kus asub...?*	koos ah-**soob**
...the toilet	*...tualett*	**too**-ah-leht
men	*mees*	mehs
women	*naine*	**nī**-neh
water / coffee	*vesi / kohvi*	**vay**-see / **koh**-vee
beer / wine	*õlu / vein*	**oh**-loo / vayn
Cheers!	*Terviseks!*	**tehr**-vee-sehks
The bill, please.	*Arve, palun.*	**ahr**-veh **pah**-luhn

ESTONIA

TALLINN

Tallinn is a rewarding detour for those who want to spice up their Scandinavian travels with a Baltic twist. Among Nordic medieval cities, there's none nearly as well-preserved as Tallinn. Its mostly intact city wall includes 26 watchtowers, each topped by a pointy red roof. Baroque and choral music ring out from its old Lutheran churches. I'd guess that Tallinn (with 400,000 people) has more restaurants, cafés, and surprises per capita and square inch than any city in this book—and the fun is comparatively cheap. Yes, Tallinn's Nordic Lutheran culture and language connect it with Scandinavia, but two centuries of czarist Russian rule and 45 years as part of the Soviet Union have blended in a distinctly Russian flavor. Overlying all of that, however, is the vibrancy of a free nation that's just a generation old. Estonian pride is in the air...and it's catching.

As a member of the Hanseatic League, the city of Tallinn was a medieval stronghold of the Baltic trading world. In the 19th and early 20th centuries, Tallinn industrialized and expanded beyond its walls. Architects encircled the Old Town, putting up

broad streets of public buildings, low Scandinavian-style apartment buildings, and single-family wooden houses. Estonia's brief period of independence ended in World War II, and after 1945, Soviet planners ringed the city with stands of now-crumbling concrete high-rises where many of Tallinn's Russian immi-

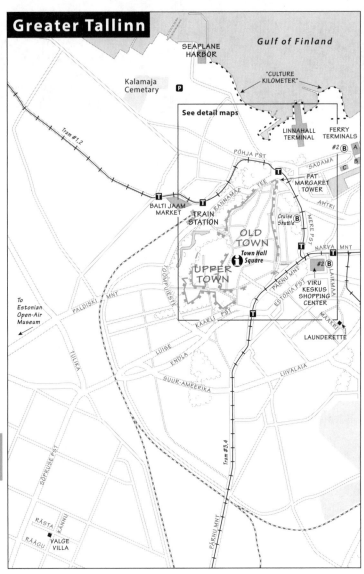

grants settled. The city still struggles to more effectively incorporate its large Russian minority.

The post-communist chapter has been a success story. Since independence in 1991, Tallinn has westernized at an astounding rate. The Old Town has been scrubbed into a pristine Old World theme park—a fascinating package of pleasing towers, ramparts, facades, *striptiis* bars, churches, shops, and people-watching. Meanwhile,

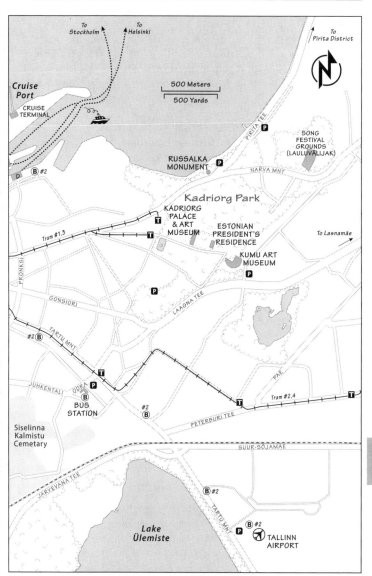

the outlying districts (such as the Rotermann Quarter) are a Petri dish of architectural experimentation. Cruise ships have discovered Tallinn, and cruisers mob its cobbles at midday. Given its compact scale, Tallinn can be easily appreciated as a side-trip (from Helsinki, or from a cruise ship). But the city rewards those who spend the night. More time gives you the chance to explore some of the more colorful slices of life outside the Old Town walls.

PLANNING YOUR TIME

On a three-week tour of Scandinavia, Tallinn is certainly worth a day. Most people find it works best as a full-day side-trip from Helsinki. Or take overnights in both Helsinki and Tallinn—either as a triangular detour from Stockholm, or on the way between Stockholm and St. Petersburg. And, of course, many come to Tallinn on a cruise ship.

Day-Trippers or Cruisers: Hit the ground running by following my self-guided walk right from the port. Enjoy a nice restaurant in the Old Town for lunch. Then spend the afternoon shopping and browsing (or choose one of the outlying sights: Seaplane Harbor for boats and planes, Rotermann Quarter for cutting-edge architecture, Estonian Open-Air Museum for folk culture, or Kumu Art Museum for Estonian art and a walk in nearby Kadriorg Park). Remember to bring a jacket—Tallinn can be chilly even on sunny summer days. And, given that locals call their cobbled streets "a free foot massage," sturdy shoes are smart, too.

With More Time: Start off with the self-guided walk, but slow things down a bit. Because Tallinn can be inundated midday with cruise passengers and day-trippers, it makes sense to tour the Old Town early or late, then get out of town when it's crowded to hit some outlying sights. Check concert schedules if you'll be around for the evening.

Orientation to Tallinn

Tallinn's walled Old Town is an easy 15-minute walk from the ferry and cruise terminals, where most visitors land (see "Arrival in Tallinn," later). The Old Town is divided into two parts (historically, two separate towns): the upper town (Toompea) and the lower town (with Town Hall Square). A remarkably intact medieval wall surrounds the two towns, which are themselves separated by another wall.

Town Hall Square (Raekoja Plats) marks the heart of the medieval lower town. The main TI is nearby, as are many sights and eateries. Pickpockets are a problem in the more touristy parts of the Old Town, so keep valuables carefully stowed. The area around the Viru Keskus mall and Hotel Viru, just east of the Old Town, is useful for everyday shopping (bookstores and supermarkets), practical services (laundry), and public transport.

TOURIST INFORMATION

The hardworking TI has maps, concert listings, and free brochures (May-Aug Mon-Fri 9:00-19:00—until 20:00 mid-June-Aug, Sat-Sun 9:00-17:00—until 18:00 mid-June-Aug; Sept-April Mon-Fri 9:00-18:00, Sat-Sun 9:00-15:00; a block off

Town Hall Square at Kullassepa 4, tel. 64 ___ ___ , tallinn.ee, visit@tallinn.ee). Look for the _Pocket_, a booklet with restaurant, hotel, an ___ at the TI and elsewhere around town, b ___ copies at your hotel, and you can downloa ___ inyourpocket.com).

Tallinn Card: This card—sold at the TIs, airport, train station, travel agencies, ferry ports, and big hotels—gives you free use of public transport and entry to more than 40 museums and major sights (€24/24 hours, €32/48 hours, €40/72 hours, comes with good info booklet, www.tallinncard.ee). It includes one tour of your choice (orientation walk or one of two hop-on, hop-off bus routes), plus a 50 percent discount on any others (see "Tours in Tallinn," later, for specifics). If you're planning to take one of these tours and to visit several sights, this card will likely save you money—do the math.

ARRIVAL IN TALLINN

For advice on taking taxis, and more details on the public transportation and ticket options mentioned below, see "Getting Around Tallinn," later.

By Boat or Cruise Ship: Tallinn has four terminals lettered A through D, a fifth one called Linnahall (used only by the fast Linda Line boat), and a dedicated cruise terminal. A-Terminal, B-Terminal, and C-Terminal are clustered together; the cruise terminal is just to the north; D-Terminal is a 10-minute walk to the east (and the farthest from Old Town); the Linnahall terminal is a 10-minute walk to the west (just over the large stairway). Each terminal offers baggage storage. Be sure to confirm which terminal your return boat will use. The main cruise pier can accommodate two large ships; when more are in town, they may use one of the other terminals.

If you have no luggage, you can **walk** 15 minutes to reach the center of town—just follow signs to the city center and set your sights on the tallest spire in the distance (or follow my self-guided walk, later). (If you'd rather first visit the Seaplane Harbor, look for a red-gravel path—straight ahead as you leave the cruise port, marked _Kultuurikilomeeter_—which takes you there on a long, scenic, mostly seaside stroll.)

If you have bags, it's best to grab a **taxi**—otherwise your rolling suitcase will take a pounding on the Old Town's cobbled streets and gutter-ridden sidewalks. While the legitimate taxi fare to anywhere in

Old Town should be less than €5, unscrupulous cabbies to charge double or triple.

To get into town by bus, you have several options: Public **bus** 2 goes from A-Terminal and D-Terminal directly to the A. Laikmaa stop—behind Hotel Viru and the Viru Keskus mall, just south of the Old Town—then continues to the airport (2/hour, buy Ühiskaart smartcard from R-Kiosk shops in terminals, or pay €1.60 for a ticket on board). Cruise lines sometimes offer a shuttle bus into town (to the Russian Cultural Center, near Hotel Viru), but—since it's so easy to just stroll from the port into town—this isn't worth paying for.

By Plane: The convenient Tallinn airport (Tallinna Lennujaam), just three miles southeast of downtown, has a small info desk (airport code: TLL, www.tallinn-airport.ee, tel. 605-8888). A **taxi** to the Old Town should cost €8-10. Public **bus #2** runs every 20-30 minutes from the lower entrance (floor 0) into town; the seventh stop, A. Laikmaa, is behind the Viru Keskus mall, a short walk from the Old Town (buy Ühiskaart smartcard from R-Kiosk store in terminal—or pay €1.60 for a single ticket on board; to reach the bus stop, follow bus signs down the escalator, go outside, and look left).

By Train and Bus: While Tallinn has a sleepy and cute little train station (called Balti Jaam), few tourists will need to use it. The station, a five-minute walk across a busy road from the Old Town (use the pedestrian underpass), is adjacent to the big, cheap Hotel Shnelli and the colorful Balti Jaam Market. Tallinn's long-distance bus station *(autobussijaam)* is midway between downtown and the airport, and served by bus #2 and trams #2 and #4.

HELPFUL HINTS

Money: Estonia uses the euro. You'll find ATMs (sometimes marked *Otto*) at locations around Tallinn.

Time: Estonia is one hour ahead of continental Europe, which means it's generally seven/ten hours ahead of the East/West Coasts of the US.

Telephones: In case of a medical emergency, dial 112. For police, dial 110. Most Estonian phone numbers are seven to eight digits with no area codes. Tallinn numbers begin with 6, and mobile phones (more expensive to call) begin with 5. (From outside Estonia, you'll first dial the country code: 372.)

Internet Access: Every hotel I list offers free Wi-Fi, and some have a computer for guests to use. Public Wi-Fi is easy to find around Tallinn; look for the free "Tallinn WiFi" network. The **main TI** has one terminal where you can briefly check your email for free.

Laundry: The Viru Keskus mall has a handy **Top Clean** laundry

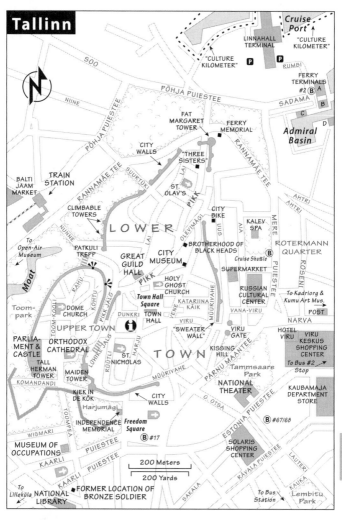

drop-off service downstairs (Mon-Fri 8:00-20:00, Sat 10:00-20:00, closed Sun; underground facing bus stalls 1 and 2, tel. 610-1405, www.puhastuskeskus.ee).

Otherwise, **Pesumaja Sol** is just beyond the Viru Keskus mall and Kaubamaja department store (just walkable from the Old Town, or take tram #2 or #4 to the Paberi stop, a few blocks away). Choose between self-serve (€6/load, ask staff to interpret Estonian-only instructions) or full-service (€16/load, Mon-Fri 7:00-20:00, Sat 8:00-16:00, closed Sun, Maakri 23, tel. 677-1551).

Travel Agency: Estravel, at the corner of Suur-Karja and

Müürivähe, is handy and sells boat tickets for no extra fee (Mon-Fri 9:00-18:00, closed Sat-Sun, Suur-Karja 15, tel. 626-6233).

Bike Rental: Head for **City Bike,** at the north end of the Old Town near the ferry terminals (€10/6 hours, €13/24 hours; electric bikes—€5/hour, €20/6 hours, €25/24 hours; daily May-Sept 9:00-19:00, Oct-April 9:00-17:00, Uus 33, mobile 511-1819, www.citybike.ee). They also do bike tours (see "Tours in Tallinn," later).

Parking: The Port of Tallinn has a cheap lot by D-Terminal (€5/day, www.portoftallinn.com). Old Town parking is very expensive; try parking in the lot underneath Freedom Square (Vabaduse väljak), at the southern tip of the Old Town, a short walk from the TI and Town Hall Square (€3/hour).

GETTING AROUND TALLINN

By Public Transportation: The Old Town and surrounding areas can be explored on foot, but use public transit to reach outlying sights (such as Kadriorg Park, Kumu Art Museum, or the Estonian Open-Air Museum). Tallinn has buses, trams, and trolley buses (buses connected to overhead wires)—avoid mistakes by noting that they reuse the same numbers (bus #2, tram #2, and trolley bus #2 are totally different lines). Maps and schedules are posted at stops, or visit http://soiduplaan.tallinn.ee. As you approach a station, you'll hear the name of the impeding stop, followed by the name of the next stop—don't get confused and hop off one stop too early.

You can buy a **single ticket** from the driver for €1.60 (exact change appreciated). If you'll be taking more than three rides in a day, invest in an **Ühiskaart smartcard.** You can buy one for €2 at any yellow-and-blue R-Kiosk convenience store (found all over town), and then load it up with credit, which is deducted as you travel (€1.10 for any ride up to 1 hour, €3/24 hours, €5/72 hours, €6/120 hours). The card is shareable by multiple people for single rides, but you'll need separate cards for the multiride options.

Bus #2 (Moigu-Reisisadam) is helpful on arrival and departure, running every 20-30 minutes between the ferry port's A-Terminal and the airport. En route it stops at D-Terminal; at A. Laikmaa, next to the Viru Keskus mall (a short walk south of the Old Town); and at the long-distance bus station.

By Taxi: Taxis in Tallinn are handy, but it's easy to get ripped off. The safest way to catch a cab is to order one by phone (or ask a trusted local to call for you)—this is what Estonians usually do.

Tulika is the largest company, with predictable, fair prices (€3.35 drop charge plus €0.69/kilometer, €0.80/kilometer from 23:00-6:00, tel. 612-0001 or 1200, check latest prices at www.

tulika.ee). **Tallink Takso** is another reputable option with similar fares (tel. 640-8921 or 1921). Cabbies are required to use the meter and give you a meter-printed receipt. If you don't get a receipt, it's safe to assume you're being ripped off and legally don't need to pay. Longer rides around the city (e.g., from the airport to the Old Town) should run around €8-10.

If you must catch a taxi off the street, go to a busy taxi stand where lots of cabs are lined up. Before you get in, take a close look at the yellow price list on the rear passenger-side door; the base fare should be €3-4 and the per-kilometer charge under €1. If it's not, keep looking. Glance inside—a photo ID license should be attached to the middle of the dashboard. Don't negotiate or ask for a price estimate; let the driver use the meter. Rates must be posted by law, but are not capped or regulated, so the most common scam—unfortunately widespread and legal—is to list an inflated price on the yellow price sticker (as much as €3/kilometer), and simply wait for a tourist to hop in without noticing. Singleton cabs lurking in tourist areas are usually fishing for suckers, as are cabbies who flag you down ("Taxi?")—give them a miss. It's fun to play spot-the-scam as you walk around town.

Tours in Tallinn

Bus and Walking Tour
This enjoyable, narrated 2.5-hour tour of Tallinn comes in two parts: first by bus for an overview of sights outside the Old Town, such as the Song Festival Grounds and Kadriorg Park, then on foot to sights within the Old Town (€20, pay driver, covered by Tallinn Card, in English; daily morning and early afternoon departures from A-Terminal, D-Terminal, and major hotels in city center; tel. 610-8616, www.traveltoestonia.com).

Local Guides
Mati Rumessen is a top-notch guide, especially for car tours inside or outside town (€35/hour driving or walking tours, price may vary with group size, mobile 509-4661, www.tourservice.ee, matirumessen@gmail.com). Other fine guides are **Antonio Villacis** (mobile 5662-9306, antonio.villacis@gmail.com) and **Miina Puusepp** (€20/hour, mobile 551-7028, miinap@hot.ee).

Tallinn Traveller Tours
These student-run tours show you the real city without the political and corporate correctness of official tourist agencies. Check www.traveller.ee to confirm details for their ever-changing lineup, and to reserve (or call mobile 5837-4800). The **City Introductory Walking Tour** is free, but tips are encouraged (around €5/person if you

Tallinn at a Glance

Central Tallinn

▲▲▲**Tallinn's Old Town** Well-preserved medieval center with cobblestoned lanes, gabled houses, historic churches, and turreted city walls. **Hours:** Always open. See page 204.

▲▲**Russian Orthodox Cathedral** Accessible look at the Russian Orthodox faith, with a lavish interior. **Hours:** Daily 8:00-19:00, icon art in gift shop. See page 211.

▲**Museum of Estonian History** High-tech exhibits explain Estonia's engaging national narrative. **Hours:** May-Aug daily 10:00-18:00, same hours off-season except closed Wed. See page 216.

▲**Museum of Occupations** Estonia's tumultuous, sometimes secret history under Soviet and Nazi occupiers from 1940 to 1991. **Hours:** June-Aug Tue-Sun 10:00-18:00, Sept-May Tue-Sun 11:00-18:00, closed Mon year-round. See page 218.

St. Nicholas Church Art museum displaying Gothic art in a restored old church. **Hours:** Wed-Sun 10:00-17:00, closed Mon-Tue. See page 209.

Town Hall and Tower Gothic building with history museum and climbable tower on the Old Town's main square. **Hours:** Museum—July-Aug Mon-Sat 10:00-16:00, closed Sun and rest of year; tower—May-mid-Sept daily 11:00-18:00, closed rest of year. See page 216.

TALLINN

enjoy yourself, daily at 12:00, 2 hours). They also typically offer a two-hour **Old Town Walking Tour** (€15, daily at 10:00, similar to the free tour but generally a much smaller group), a **ghost walk** (€15, 2/week at 20:00), and a **pub crawl** (€20, 1/week at 20:00), and can also arrange private tours. They have a variety of **bike tours**, including a 2.5-hour "Welcome to Tallinn" overview (€16, daily at 11:00). And they offer minibus excursions that get you into the Estonian countryside, including one to the **Coastal Cliffs** and the Soviet military town of Paldiski (€45, daily in summer at 10:00, 3/week off-season, 7 hours), and one to **Lahemaa National Park** (€49, daily at 10:00, 9 hours). If you're heading to **Rīga, Latvia,** consider the excellent value they provide: a 12-hour sightseeing shuttle trip between Tallinn and Rīga, with several stops on route to experience the Estonian and Latvian countrysides (€49). These excursions go year-round, but require at least two people to run. You can also book any one of these tours—or others, all well-described on their website—for your own small group for the same

Outside of the Core

▲▲**Kumu Art Museum** The best of contemporary Estonian art displayed in a strikingly modern building. **Hours:** May-Sept Tue-Sun 11:00-18:00, Wed until 20:00, closed Mon; same hours off-season except closed Mon-Tue. See page 220.

▲▲**Seaplane Harbor** Impressive museum of boats and planes—including a WWII-era submarine—displayed in a cavernous old hangar along the waterfront. **Hours:** May-Sept daily 10:00-19:00; same hours off-season except closed Mon. See page 223.

▲**Kadriorg Park** Vast, strollable oasis with the palace gardens, Kumu Art Museum, and a palace built by Czar Peter the Great. **Hours:** Park always open. See page 219.

▲**Song Festival Grounds** National monument and open-air theater where Estonians sang for freedom. **Hours:** Open long hours daily. See page 224.

▲**Estonian Open-Air Museum** Authentic farm and village buildings preserved in a forested parkland. **Hours:** Late April-Sept—park open daily 10:00-20:00, buildings open until 18:00; Oct-late April—park open daily 10:00-17:00 but many buildings closed. See page 228.

per-person price (4-person minimum). All tours start from in front of the main TI.

Hop-On, Hop-Off Bus Tours

Tallinn City Tour offers three different one-hour bus tours—you can take all three (on the same day) for one price. Aside from a stop near Toompea Castle, the routes are entirely outside the Old Town, and the frequency is low (just 6-8/day, May-Sept only—so you'll need to coordinate your sightseeing to the infrequent departures). But if you want to rest your feet and listen to a fairly good recorded commentary, the tours do get you to outlying sights such as Kadriorg Park and the towering Russalka Monument. You can catch the bus at the port terminals and near the Viru Turg clothing market (€19/24 hours, free with Tallinn Card, tel. 627-9080, www.citytour.ee). **CitySightseeing Tallinn** also runs three similar routes, with a similarly sparse frequency (€18 for all three lines, €15 for just one line, www.citysightseeing.ee).

City Bike Tours

City Bike offers a two-hour, nine-mile **Welcome to Tallinn** bike tour that takes you outside the city walls to Tallinn's more distant sights: Kadriorg Park, Song Festival Grounds, the beach at Pirita, and more (€16, 50 percent discount with Tallinn Card, daily at 11:00 year-round, departs from their office at Uus 33 in the Old Town). They can also arrange multiday, self-guided bike tours around Estonia (mobile 511-1819, www.citybike.ee).

Tallinn Walk

This self-guided walk, worth ▲▲▲, explores the "two towns" of Tallinn. The city once consisted of two feuding medieval towns separated by a wall. The upper town—on the hill, called Toompea—was the seat of government for Estonia. The lower town was an autonomous Hanseatic trading center filled with German, Danish, and Swedish merchants who hired Estonians to do their menial labor. Many of the Old Town's buildings are truly old, dating from the boom times of the 15th and 16th centuries. Decrepit before the 1991 fall of the Soviet Union, the Old Town has been slowly revitalized, though there's still plenty of work to be done.

Two steep, narrow streets—the "Long Leg" and the "Short Leg"—connect the upper town (Toompea) and the lower town. This two-part walk—"Part 1" focusing on the lower town, and "Part 2" climbing up to the upper town—goes up the short leg and down the long leg. Allow about two hours for the entire walk (not counting time to enter museums along the way).

PART 1: THE LOWER TOWN

• *The walk starts at the port—where cruise ships and ferries from Helsinki arrive. If you're coming from elsewhere in Tallinn, take tram #1 or #2 to the Linnahall stop, or just walk out to the Fat Margaret Tower from anywhere in the Old Town.*

❶ To Fat Margaret Tower and Start of Walk

From the port, hike toward the tall tapering spire, go through a small park, and enter the Old Town through the archway by the squat Fat Margaret Tower.

Just outside the tower, on a bluff overlooking the harbor, is half of a **black arch.** (The other half of the arch sits in the park just below the hill.) This is a memorial to 852 people who perished in September of 1994 when the *Estonia* passenger-and-car ferry sank

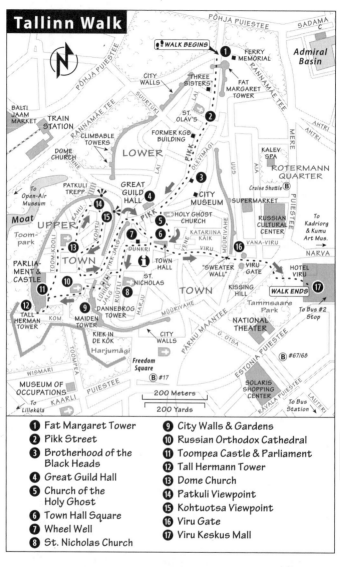

Tallinn Walk

1 Fat Margaret Tower
2 Pikk Street
3 Brotherhood of the Black Heads
4 Great Guild Hall
5 Church of the Holy Ghost
6 Town Hall Square
7 Wheel Well
8 St. Nicholas Church
9 City Walls & Gardens
10 Russian Orthodox Cathedral
11 Toompea Castle & Parliament
12 Tall Hermann Tower
13 Dome Church
14 Patkuli Viewpoint
15 Kohtuotsa Viewpoint
16 Viru Gate
17 Viru Keskus Mall

in stormy conditions during its Tallinn-Stockholm run. The ship's bow visor came off, and water flooded into the car deck, throwing the boat off-balance. Only 137 people survived. The crew's maneuvering of the ship after it began taking on water is thought to have caused its fatal list and capsizing.

Fat Margaret Tower (Paks Margareeta, so called for its thick walls) guarded the entry gate of the town in medieval times (the sea once came much closer to this point than it does today). The relief above the gate dates from the 16th century, during Hanseatic times, when Sweden took Estonia from Germany. The Estonian Maritime Museum in the tower is paltry—skip it.

• *Once through the gate, head up Tallinn's main drag...*

❼ Pikk Street

Literally "Long Street," the medieval merchants' main drag—leading from the harbor up into town—is lined with interesting

buildings. Many were warehouses, complete with cranes on the gables. Strolling here, you'll feel the economic power of those early German trading days.

One short block up the street on the right, the buildings nicknamed **"Three Sisters"** (now a hotel) are textbook examples of a merchant home/warehouse/office from the 15th-century Hanseatic Golden Age. The charmingly carved door near the corner evokes the wealth of Tallinn's merchant class.

After another, longer block, you'll pass **St. Olav's Church** (Oleviste Kirik, a Baptist church today), notable for what was once the tallest spire in the land. If the name didn't tip you off that this was once a Lutheran church,

then the stark, whitewashed interior guarantees it. Climbing 234 stairs up the tower rewards you with a great view. You can enter both the church and the tower around the back side (church—free entry, daily 10:00-18:00, July-Aug until 20:00; tower—€2, open April-Oct only; www.oleviste.ee).

While tourists see only a peaceful scene today, locals strolling this street are reminded of dark times under Moscow's rule. The KGB used the tower at St. Olav's Church to block Finnish TV signals. The once-handsome building at **Pikk #59** (the second house after the church, on the right) was, before 1991, the sinister local headquarters of the KGB. "Creative interrogation methods" were used here. Locals well knew that the road of suffering started here, as Tallinn's troublemakers were sent to Siberian gulags. The ministry building was called the "tallest" building in town (because "when you're in the basement, you can already see Siberia"). Notice the bricked-up wind ws at foot level and the commemorative plaque (in Estonian on̄l̄y).

• *A few short blocks farther up Pikk (after the small park), on the left at #26, is the extremely ornate doorway of the...*

❸ Brotherhood of the Black Heads

Built in 1440, this house was used as a German merchants' club for nearly 500 years (until Hitler invited Estonian Germans back

to their historical fatherland in the 1930s). Before the 19th century, many Estonians lived as serfs on the rural estates of the German nobles who dominated the economy. In Tallinn, the German big shots were part of the Great Guild (which we'll see farther up the street), while the German little shots had to make do with the Brotherhood of the Black Heads. This guild, or business fraternity, was limited to single German men. In Hanseatic towns, when a fire or

battle had to be fought, single men were deployed first, because they had no family. Because single men were considered unattached to the community, they had no opportunity for power in the Hanseatic social structure. When a Black Head member married a local woman, he automatically gained a vested interest in the town's economy and well-being. He could then join the more prestigious Great Guild, and with that status, a promising economic and political future often opened up.

Today the hall is a concert venue (and, while you can pay to tour its interior, I'd skip it—it's basically an empty shell). Its namesake "black head" is that of St. Maurice, an early Christian soldier-martyr, beheaded in the third century A.D. for his refusal to honor the Roman gods. Reliefs decorating the building recall Tallinn's Hanseatic glory days.

Keep going along Pikk street. Architecture fans enjoy several **fanciful facades** along here, including the boldly Art Nouveau #18 (on the left, reminiscent of the architectural bounty of fellow Baltic capital Rīga; appropriately enough, today this building houses one of Tallinn's leading cutting-edge architecture firms) and the colorful, eclectic building across the street (with the pointy gable).

On the left, at #16 (look for *Kalev* awnings), the famous and recommended **Maiasmokk** ("Sweet Tooth") coffee shop, in business since 1864, remains a fine spot for a cheap coffee-and-pastry break.

• *Just ahead, pause at the big yellow building on the right (at #17).*

❹ Great Guild Hall (Suurgildi Hoone)

With its wide (and therefore highly taxed) front, the Great Guild Hall was the epitome of wealth. Remember, this was the home of the most prestigious of Tallinn's Hanseatic-era guilds. Today it houses the worthwhile **Museum of Estonian History,** offering a concise, engaging, well-presented survey of this country's story (for details, see "Sights in Tallinn," later).

• *Across Pikk street from the Great Guild Hall is the...*

❺ Church of the Holy Ghost (Pühavaimu Kirik)

Sporting an outdoor clock from 1633, this pretty medieval church is worth a visit. (The plaque on the wall just behind the ticket desk is in Estonian and Russian, but not English; this dates from before 1991, when things were designed for "inner tourism"—within the USSR.) The church retains its 14th-century design. Flying from the back pillar, the old flag of Tallinn—the same as today's red-and-white Danish flag—recalls 13th-century Danish rule. (The name "Tallinn" means "Danish Town.") The Danes sold Tallinn to the German Teutonic Knights, who lost it to the Swedes, who lost it to the Russians. The windows are mostly from the 1990s (€1, Mon-Sat 9:00-18:00, closes earlier in winter, closed most of Sun to non-worshippers, Pühavaimu 2, tel. 646-4430, www.eelk.ee). The church hosts English-language Lutheran services Sundays at 15:00 (maybe earlier in summer).

• *If you were to go down the street to the left as you face the church, it's a three-minute walk to the* **Tallinn City Museum** *(described later, under "Sights in Tallinn").*

   Leading alongside the church, tiny Saiakang lane (meaning "White Bread"—bread, cakes, and pies have been sold here since medieval times) takes you to...

❻ Town Hall Square (Raekoja Plats)

A marketplace through the centuries, with a cancan of fine old buildings, this is the focal point of the Old Town. The square was the center of the autonomous lower town, a merchant city of Hanseatic traders. Once, it held criminals chained to pillories for public humiliation and knights showing off in chivalrous tournaments; today it's full of Scandinavians and Russians savoring cheap beer, children singing on the bandstand, and cruiseship groups following the numbered paddles carried high by their well-scrubbed local guides.

The 15th-century **Town Hall** (Raekoda) dominates the square; it's now a museum, and climbing its tower earns you a commanding view.

On the opposite side of the square, across from #12 in the corner, the **pharmacy** (Raeapteek) dates from 1422 and claims—as do many—to be Europe's oldest. With decor that goes back to medieval times, the still-operating pharmacy welcomes visitors with painted ceiling beams, English descriptions, and long-expired aspirin. Past the functioning counter is a room of display cases with historical exhibits (free entry, Tue-Sat 10:00-18:00, closed Sun-Mon).

Town Hall Square is ringed by inviting but touristy eateries, a few of which are still affordable, such as Troika and the Kehrwieder cafés. The TI is a block away (behind Town Hall).

• *Facing the Town Hall, head right up Dunkri street—lined with several more eateries—one long block to the* ❼ *wheel well, named for the "high-tech" wheel, a marvel that made fetching water easier.*

Turn left on Rataskaevu street (which soon becomes Rüütli) and walk two short blocks to...

❽ St. Nicholas Church (Niguliste Kirik)

This 13th-century Gothic church-turned-art-museum served the German merchants and knights who lived in this neighborhood 500 years ago. On March 9, 1944, while Tallinn was in German hands, Soviet forces bombed the city, and the church and surrounding area—once a charming district, dense with medieval buildings—were burned out; only the church was rebuilt.

The church's interior houses a fine collection of mostly Gothic-era ecclesiastical art (€3.50, Wed-Sun

10:00-17:00, last entry 30 minutes before closing, closed Mon-Tue; organ concerts Sat and Sun at 16:00 included in admission).

You'll enter the church through the modern cellar, where you can see photos of the WWII destruction of the building (with its toppled steeple). Then make your way into the vast, open church interior. Front and center is the collection's highlight: a retable (framed altarpiece) from 1481, by Herman Rode—an exquisite example of the northern Germanic late-Gothic style. Along with scenes from the life of St. Nicholas and an array of other saints, the altarpiece shows the skyline of Lübeck, Germany (Rode's hometown, and—like Tallinn—a Hanseatic trading city). The intricate symbolism is explained by a nearby touchscreen. Also look for another work by a Lübeck master, Bernt Notke's *Danse Macabre* ("Dance of Death"). Once nearly 100 feet long, the surviving fragment shows sinister skeletons approaching people from all walks of life. This common medieval theme reminds the viewer that life is fleeting, and no matter who we are, we'll all wind up in the same place.

• *As you face the church, if you were to turn left and walk downhill on Rüütli street, you'd soon pass near* **Freedom Square**—*for a taste of modern Tallinn.*

But for now, let's continue our walk into the upper town.

PART 2: THE UPPER TOWN (TOOMPEA)

• *At the corner opposite the church, climb uphill along the steep, cobbled, Lühike Jalg ("Short Leg Lane"), home to a few quality craft shops. At the top of the lane, pause at the giant stone tower, noticing the original oak door—one of two gates through the wall separating the two cities. This passage is still the ritual meeting point of the mayor and prime minister whenever there is an important agreement between town and country.*

Facing that tower and door, turn left and go through the café courtyard to its far end. You'll emerge into a beautiful view terrace in front of the...

❾ City Walls and Gardens

The imposing city wall once had 46 towers, of which 26 still stand. The gravel-and-grass strip that runs in front of the wall offers a fun stroll and fine views. If you have interest and energy, you can also climb some of the towers and ramparts. (While the views from the towers are nice, keep in mind that we'll be reaching some even more dramatic viewpoints—overlooking different parts of town—later on this walk.)

The easiest option is to simply scramble up the extremely steep and tight steps of the **Dannebrog restaurant tower;** you can buy a drink or a cheap meal here (€5 soups, €7 pastas), but they generally don't charge those who just want a quick look at the view.

To reach a higher vantage point—or if Dannebrog is charging admission—you can pay €3 to enter the nearby **Maiden Tower** (Neitsitorn). It has a few skippable exhibits, an overpriced café, and great views—particularly from the top floor, where a full glass wall reveals panoramic town views (tower and café open daily 10:30-22:00, exhibits open until 19:00, shorter hours Oct-April).

With more time, add a visit to the **Kiek in de Kök**—the stout, round tower that sits farther along the wall (with extremely tight,

twisty, steep stone staircases inside). While fun to say, the name is Low German for "Peek in the Kitchen"—so called because it's situated to allow guards to literally peek into townspeople's homes. This tower is bigger than the Maiden Tower, with more impressive exhibits—not a lot of real artifacts, but plenty of cannons, mannequins, model ships, movies, and models of the castle to give you a taste of Tallinn's medieval heyday. The €7 combo-ticket with the Maiden Tower lets you walk along the scenic rampart between the two towers (find the door marked *Väljapääs* on the second floor of the Maiden Tower, and open it with your wristband ticket; also possible to enter just Kiek in de Kök with €4.50 ticket; extra for tour of tunnels below the tower).

• *When you're finished with the towers and ramparts, go through the hole in the wall, and head uphill into the upper town.*

Circle around the left side of the big, onion-domed church; as you stroll, on your left is the so-called **"Danish King's Garden."** Tallinn is famous among Danes as the birthplace of their flag. According to legend, the Danes were losing a battle here. Suddenly, a white cross fell from heaven and landed in a pool of blood. The Danes were inspired and went on to win. To this day, their flag is a white cross on a red background.

• *Complete your circle around to the far side of the church (facing the pink palace) to enjoy a great view of the cathedral, and to find the entrance.*

❿ Russian Orthodox Cathedral

The Alexander Nevsky Cathedral—worth ▲▲—is a gorgeous building. But ever since the day it was built (in 1900), it has been a jab in the eye for Estonians. The church went up near the end of the two centuries when Estonia was part of the Russian Empire. And, as throughout Europe in the late 19th century, Tallinn's oppressed ethnic groups—the Estonians and the Germans—were caught up in national revival movements, celebrating their own culture, language, and history rather than their Russian overlords'. So the Russians flexed their cultural muscle by building this church in this location, facing the traditional Estonian seat of power, and over the supposed grave of a legendary Estonian hero, Kalevipoeg. They also tore down a statue of Martin Luther to make room.

The church has been exquisitely renovated inside and out. Step inside for a sample of Russian Orthodoxy (church free and open daily 8:00-19:00, icon art in gift shop). It's OK to visit discreetly during services (daily at 9:00 and 18:00), when you'll hear priests singing the liturgy in a side chapel. Typical of Russian Orthodox churches, it has glittering icons (the highest concentration fills the big screen—called an iconostasis—that shields the altar from the congregation), no pews (worshippers stand through the service), and air that's heavy with incense. All of these features combine to create a mystical, otherworldly worship experience. Notice the many candles, each representing a prayer; if there's a request or a thank-you in your heart, you're welcome to buy one at the desk by the door. Exploring this space, keep in mind that about 40 percent of Tallinn's population is ethnic Russian.

• *Across the street is the...*

⓫ Toompea Castle (Toompea Loss)

The pink palace is an 18th-century Russian addition onto the medieval Toompea Castle. Today, it's the Estonian Parliament (Riigigoku) building, flying the Estonian flag—the flag of both the first (1918-1940) and second (1991-present) Estonian republics. Notice the Estonian seal: three lions for three great battles in Estonian history, and oak leaves for strength and stubbornness. Ancient pagan Estonians, who believed spirits lived in oak trees, would walk through forests of oak to toughen up. (To this day, Estonian cemeteries are in forests. Keeping some of their pagan sensibilities, they believe the spirits of the departed live on in the trees.)

• *Facing the palace, go left through the gate into the park to see the...*

⓬ Tall Hermann Tower (Pikk Hermann)

This tallest tower of the castle wall is a powerful symbol here. For 50 years, while

Estonian flags were hidden in cellars, the Soviet flag flew from Tall Hermann. As the USSR was unraveling, Estonians proudly and defiantly replaced the red Soviet flag here with their own black, white, and blue flag.

• *Backtrack and go uphill, passing the Russian church on your right. Climb Toom-Kooli street to the...*

⓫ Dome Church (Toomkirik)

Estonia is ostensibly Lutheran, but few Tallinners go to church. A recent Gallup Poll showed Estonia to be the least religious country

in the European Union—only 14 percent of respondents identified religion as an important part of their daily lives. Most churches double as concert venues or museums, but this one is still used for worship. Officially St. Mary's Church—but popularly called the Dome Church—it's a perfect example of simple Northern European Gothic, built in the 13th century during Danish rule, then rebuilt after a 1684 fire. Once the church of Tallinn's wealthy German-speaking aristocracy, it's littered with more than a hundred coats of arms, carved by local masters as memorials to the deceased and inscribed with German tributes. The earliest dates from the 1600s, the latest from around 1900. For €5, you can climb 140 steps up the tower to enjoy the view (church entry free, daily 9:00-18:00, www.eelk.ee/tallinna.toom).

• *Leaving the church, turn left and hook around the back of the building. You'll pass a slanted tree, then the big, green, former noblemen's clubhouse on your right (at #1, vacated when many Germans left Estonia in the 1930s). Head down cobbled Rahukohtu lane (to the right of the yellow, pyramid-shaped house). Strolling the street, notice the embassy signs: Government offices and embassies have moved into these buildings and spruced up the neighborhood. Continue straight under the arch and belly up to the grand...*

⓬ Patkuli Viewpoint

Survey the scene. On the far left, the Neoclassical facade of the executive branch of Estonia's government enjoys the view. Below you, a bit of the old moat remains. The *Group* sign marks Tallinn's tiny train station, and the clutter of stalls

behind that is the rustic market. Out on the water, ferries shuttle to and from Helsinki (just 50 miles away). Beyond the lower town's medieval wall and towers stands the green spire of St. Olav's Church, once 98 feet taller and, locals claim, the world's tallest tower in 1492. Far in the distance is the 1,000-foot-tall TV tower, the site of a standoff between Soviet paratroopers and Estonian patriots in 1991.

During Soviet domination, Finnish TV was even more important, as it gave Estonians their only look at Western lifestyles. Imagine: In the 1980s, many locals had never seen a banana or a pineapple—except on TV. People still talk of the day that Finland broadcast the soft-porn movie *Emmanuelle*. A historic migration of Estonians purportedly flocked from the countryside to Tallinn to get within rabbit-ear's distance of Helsinki and see all that flesh onscreen. The TV tower was recently refurbished and opened to visitors.

• *Go back through the arch, turn immediately left down the narrow lane, turn right (onto Toom-Rüütli), take the first left, and pass through the trees to the...*

⓯ Kohtuotsa Viewpoint

Scan the view from left to right. On the far left is St. Olav's Church, then the busy cruise port and the skinny white spire of the Church

of the Holy Ghost. The narrow gray spire farther to the right is the 16th-century Town Hall tower. On the far right is the tower of St. Nicholas Church. Below you, visually trace Pikk street, Tallinn's historic main drag, which winds through the Old Town, leading from Toompea Castle down the hill (from right to left), through the gate tower, past the Church of the Holy Ghost, behind St. Olav's, and out to the harbor. Less picturesque is the clutter of Soviet-era apartment blocks on the distant horizon. The nearest skyscraper (white) is Hotel Viru, in Soviet times the biggest hotel in the Baltics, and infamous as a clunky, dingy slumbermill. Locals joke that Hotel Viru was built from a new Soviet wonder material called "micro-concrete" (60 percent concrete, 40 percent microphones). Underneath the hotel is the modern Viru Keskus, a huge shopping mall and local transit center, where this walk will end. To the left of Hotel Viru, between it and the ferry terminals, is the Rotermann

Quarter, where old industrial buildings are being revamped into a new commercial zone.

• *From the viewpoint, descend to the lower town. Go out and left down Kohtu, past the Finnish Embassy (on your left). Back at the Dome Church, the slanted tree points the way, left down Piiskopi ("Bishop's Street"). At the onion domes, turn left again and follow the old wall down Pikk Jalg ("Long Leg Lane") into the lower town. Go under the tower, then straight on Pikk street, and after two doors turn right on Voorimehe, which leads into Town Hall Square.*

⑯ Through Viru Gate

Cross through the square (left of the Town Hall's tower) and go downhill (passing the kitschy medieval Olde Hansa Restaurant, with its bonneted waitresses and merry men). Continue straight down Viru street toward Hotel Viru, the blocky white skyscraper in the distance. Viru street is old Tallinn's busiest and kitschiest shopping street. Just past the strange and modern wood/glass/stone mall, Müürivahe street leads left along the old wall, called the "Sweater Wall." This is a colorful and tempting gauntlet of women selling knitwear (anything with images and bright colors is likely machine-made). Katariina Käik, a lane with glassblowing shops, leads left, beyond the sweaters. Back on Viru street, pass the golden arches and walk through the medieval arches—Viru Gate—that mark the end of old Tallinn. Outside the gates, opposite Viru 23, above the flower stalls, is a small park on a piece of old bastion known as the Kissing Hill (come up here after dark and you'll find out why).

• *Use the crosswalk to your right to reach the...*

⑰ Viru Keskus Mall

Here, behind Hotel Viru, at the end of this walk, you'll find the real world: basement supermarket, ticket service, bookstore, and many bus and tram stops. If you still have energy, you can cross the busy street by the complex and explore the nearby Rotermann Quarter.

Sights in Tallinn

IN OR NEAR THE OLD TOWN

Central Tallinn has dozens of small museums, most suitable only for specialized tastes. The following sights are the ones I'd visit first.

TALLINN

▲Museum of Estonian History (Eesti Ajaloomuuseum)

The Great Guild Hall on Pikk street (described on my self-guided walk, earlier) houses this modern, well-presented-in-English exhibit. The museum's "Estonia 101" approach—combining lots of actual artifacts (from prehistory to today) and high-tech interactive exhibits—is geared toward educating first-time visitors about this obscure but endearing little country.

Cost and Hours: €5, May-Aug daily 10:00-18:00, same hours off-season except closed Wed, tel. 696-8690, www.ajaloomuuseum. ee.

Visiting the Museum: As you enter, download the free smartphone audioguide to navigate the collection. Pondering the question of what it means to be an Estonian, you'll view a coin collection of past currencies (including the Soviet ruble and the pre-euro krooni), then head into the whitewashed vaulted hall to see the "Spirit of Survival" exhibit, which traces 11,000 years of Estonian history. Steep steps lead down into the cellar, with an armory, ethnographic collection, items owned by historical figures, an exhibit about the Great Guild Hall itself, and a fun "time capsule" that lets you insert your face into videos illustrating episodes in local history.

Town Hall (Raekoda) and Tower

This museum facing Town Hall Square is open to the general public only in the summer. It has exhibits on the town's administration and history, along with an interesting bit on the story of limestone. The tower, the place to see all of Tallinn, rewards those who climb its 155 steps with a wonderful city view.

Cost and Hours: Museum—€5, entrance through cellar, July-Aug Mon-Sat 10:00-16:00, closed Sun and Sept-June; audioguide—€4.75; tower—€3, May-mid-Sept daily 11:00-18:00, closed rest of year; tel. 645-7900, www.tallinn.ee/raekoda.

Tallinn City Museum (Tallinna Linnamuuseum)

This humble museum, filling a 14th-century townhouse, features Tallinn history from 1200 to the 1950s. It displays everyday items through history. Even though there are basic English explanations, it's not enough; the museum is a loose collection of artifacts that offers a few intimate peeks at local lifestyles.

Cost and Hours: €3.20, March-Oct Wed-Mon 10:30-18:00, Nov-Feb Wed-Mon 10:00-17:30, closed Tue year-round, last entry 30 minutes before closing, Vene 17, at corner of Pühavaimu, tel. 615-5183, www.linnamuuseum.ee.

Visiting the Museum: You'll begin on the ground floor, at a model of circa-1825 Tallinn—looking much like it does today. Then you'll head up through three more floors, exploring exhibits on the port (with model ships), guilds (tools and products), advertising in the 1920s and 30s (chronicling the rise of modern local industries in pre-Soviet times), Tallinn's Estonian identity (with recreated rooms from the early 20th century), and the Soviet period (displaying propaganda, including children's art that celebrated the regime).

Freedom Square (Vabaduse Väljak)

Once a USSR-era parking lot at the southern tip of the Old Town, this fine public zone was recently revamped: The cars were moved underground, and now a glassy new plaza invites locals (and very few tourists) to linger. The recommended **Wabadus café,** with tables out on the square, is a popular hangout. The space, designed to host special events, feels a bit stern and at odds with the cutesy cobbles just a few steps away. But it's an easy opportunity to glimpse a contrast to the tourists' Tallinn.

The towering **cross** monument facing the square (marked *Eesti Vabadussõda 1918-1920*) honors the Estonian War of Independence.

Shortly after the Bolshevik Revolution set a new course for Russia, the Estonians took advantage of the post-WWI reshuffling of Europe to rise up and create—for the first time ever—an independent Estonian state. The "cross of liberty" on top of the pillar represents a military decoration from that war (and every war since). The hill behind the cross has more monuments, and fragments of past fortifications.

Across the busy street from the square, the hulking, red-brick building houses the **office of Tallinn's mayor.** Edgar Savisaar, a former prime minister, has been mayor of this city twice (most recently since 2007). Criticized by some for his authoritarian approach and his coziness with Russia, Savisaar is adored by others for his aggressive legislation. For example, in 2013, he made all public transit completely free to anyone living within the city limits—a move designed to cut commuting costs (and carbon emissions) and to lure suburbanites to move into the town center. Younger locals grumble about what they jokingly term *"Homo soveticus"*—a different species of Estonian who was raised in Soviet times and is accustomed to a system where everything is free. To this day, governmental giveaways are the easiest way to boost approval ratings.

If you're interested in Estonia's 20th- and 21st-century history, it's an easy five-minute walk from this square to the next sight.

TALLINN

▲Museum of Occupations (Okupatsioonide Muuseum)

Locals insist that Estonia didn't formally lose its independence from 1939 to 1991, but was just "occupied"—first by the Soviets (for one year), then by the Nazis (for three years), and then again by the USSR (for nearly 50 years). Built with funding from a wealthy Estonian-American, this compact museum tells the history of Estonia during its occupations.

Cost and Hours: €5, June-Aug Tue-Sun 10:00-18:00, Sept-May Tue-Sun 11:00-18:00, closed Mon year-round, skip the amateurish €4 audioguide, Toompea 8, at corner of Kaarli Puiestee, tel. 668-0250, www.okupatsioon.ee.

Visiting the Museum: Entering, you'll walk past a poignant monument made of giant suitcases—a reminder of people who fled the country. After buying your ticket, pick up the English descriptions and explore. (The ticket desk also sells a well-chosen range of English-language books on the occupation years.)

The exhibit is organized around seven TV monitors screening 30-minute **documentary films** (with dry commentary, archival footage, and interviews)—each focusing on a different time period. At each screen, use the mouse to select English. Surrounding each monitor is a display case crammed with artifacts of the era. The footage of the Singing Revolution is particularly stirring.

Before settling into the film loop, take a quick clockwise spin from the ticket desk to see the larger **exhibits,** which illustrate how the Soviets kept the Estonians in line. First you'll see a rustic boat that a desperate defector actually rowed across the Baltic Sea to the Swedish island of Gotland. Look for the unsettling surveillance peephole, which will make you want to carefully examine your hotel room tonight. Surrounded by a lot more of those symbolic suitcases, the large monument with a swastika and a red star is a reminder that Estonia was occupied by not one, but two different regimes in the 20th century. You'll also see vintage cars, phone boxes, and radios that give a flavor of that era. Near the center of the exhibit, somber prison doors evoke the countless lives lost to detention and deportation.

Near those prison doors, take the red-velvet staircase down to the **basement.** There, near the WCs, is a collection of Soviet-era statues of communist leaders—once they lorded over the people, now they're in the cellar guarding the toilets.

Nearby: One of Tallinn's most famous recent sights *can't* be seen in its original location, in front of the National Library (just south of the Museum of Occupations). Called simply **The Bronze Sol-**

dier, this six-foot-tall statue of a Soviet solider marked the graves of Russians who died fighting to liberate Tallinn in 1944. In 2007, the Estonian government exhumed those graves and moved them—along with the statue—from this very central location to the Tallinn Military Cemetery, on the city's southern outskirts. Estonia's sizeable Russian minority balked at this move, and—through a series of protests and clashes—grabbed the world's attention. The Kremlin took note, furious protestors surrounded the Estonian embassy in Moscow for a week (essentially laying siege to the building), and mysterious "cyberattacks" from Russian IP addresses crippled Estonian governmental websites. When the dust settled, The Bronze Soldier stayed in its new home—but Estonians of all stripes were confronted with a bitter reminder that even a generation after independence, tensions between ethnic Russians and ethnic Estonians have not been entirely resolved.

▲Rotermann Quarter (Rotermanni Kvartal)

Sprawling between Hotel Viru and the port, just east of the Old Town, this 19th-century industrial zone is being redeveloped into

shopping, office, and living space. Characteristic old brick shells are being topped with visually striking glass-and-steel additions. For those interested in the gentrification of an aging city—and even for those who aren't—it's worth a quick stroll to see the cutting edge of old-meets-new Nordic architecture. While construction is ongoing, and the area still feels a bit soulless (only a few shops and restaurants are open), developers are setting the stage for the creation of a vital new downtown district. I've recommended two good restaurants that give you an excuse to walk five minutes across the street from the Old Town to take a look around; see "Eating in Tallinn," later. To see the first completed section, start at Hotel Viru, cross busy Narva Maantee and walk down Roseni street. At #7 you'll find the hard-to-resist Kalev chocolate shop, selling Estonia's best-known sweets (Mon-Sat 10:00-20:00, Sun 11:00-18:00).

KADRIORG PARK AND THE KUMU MUSEUM
▲Kadriorg Park

This expansive seaside park, home to a summer royal residence and the Kumu Art Mu-

st a five-minute tram ride or a 25-minute walk from
After Russia took over Tallinn in 1710, Peter the Great
built the cute, pint-sized Kadriorg Palace for Czarina Catherine
(the palace's name means "Catherine's Valley"). Stately, peaceful,
and crisscrossed by leafy paths, the park has a rose garden, duck-
filled pond, playground and benches, and old czarist guardhouses
harkening back to the days of Russian rule. It's a delightful place
for a stroll or a picnic. If it's rainy, duck into one of the cafés in the
park's art museums (described below).

Getting There: Reach the park on tram #1 or #3 (direction:
Kadriorg; catch at any tram stop around the Old Town). Get off
at the Kadriorg stop (the end of the line, where trams turn and
head back into town), and walk 200 yards straight ahead and up
Weizenbergi, the park's main avenue. Peter's summer palace is on
the left; behind it, visit the formal garden (free). At the end of the
avenue is the Kumu Art Museum, the park's most important sight.
A taxi from Hotel Viru to this area should cost €5 or less. If you're
returning from here directly to the port to catch your cruise ship or
boat to Helsinki, use tram #1—it stops at the Linnahall stop near
the main cruise port and Terminals A, B, and C (a bit father from
Terminal D).

Visiting Kadriorg Park: The palace's manicured **gardens** (free
to enter) are a pure delight; on weekends, you'll likely see a steady
parade of brides and grooms here, posing for wedding pictures. The
summer palace itself is home to the **Kadriorg Art Museum** (Kadri-
oru Kunstimuuseum), with very modest Russian and Western European galleries (€4.80; May-Sept Tue-Sun 10:00-17:00, Wed
until 20:00, closed Mon; same hours off-season except closed Mon-
Tue; Weizenbergi 37, tel. 606-6400, www.kadriorumuuseum.ee).

The fenced-off yard directly behind the garden is where you'll
spot the local "White House" (although it's pink)—home of **Estonia's president.** Walk around to the far side to find its main entrance, with the seal of Estonia above the door, flagpoles flying
both the Estonian and the EU flags, and stone-faced guards.

A five-minute walk beyond the presidential palace takes you
to the Kumu Art Museum, described next. For a longer walk from
here, the rugged park rolls down toward the sea.

▲▲Kumu Art Museum
(Kumu Kunstimuuseum)

This main branch of the Art Museum
of Estonia brings the nation's best art
together in a striking modern building designed by an international
(well, at least Finnish) architect,
Pekka Vapaavuori. The entire collec-

tion is accessible, well-presented, and engaging, with a particularly thought-provoking section on art from the Soviet period. The museum is well worth the trip for art lovers, or for anyone intrigued by the unique spirit of this tiny nation—particularly when combined with a stroll through the nearby palace gardens (described earlier) on a sunny day.

Cost and Hours: €5.50, or €4.20 for just the permanent collection; May-Sept Tue-Sun 11:00-18:00, Wed until 20:00, closed Mon; same hours off-season except closed Mon-Tue; audioguide-€3.20; trendy café, tel. 602-6000, www.kumu.ee.

Getting There: To reach the museum, follow the instructions for Kadriorg Park, explained earlier; Kumu is at the far end of the park. To get from the Old Town to Kumu directly without walking through the park, take bus #67 or #68 (each runs every 10-15 minutes, #68 does not run on Sun); both leave from Teatri Väljak, on the far side of the pastel yellow theater, across from the Solaris shopping mall. Get off at the Kumu stop, then walk up the stairs and across the bridge.

Visiting the Museum: Just off the ticket lobby (on the second floor), the **great hall** has temporary exhibits; however, the permanent collection on the third and fourth floors is Kumu's main draw. While you can rent an audioguide, I found the free laminated sheets in most rooms enough to enjoy the collection. The maze-like layout on each floor presents the art chronologically.

The **third floor** displays a concise "Treasury of Estonian Art" through the mid-20th century. It starts with 18th-century por-

traits of local aristocrats, then moves through 19th-century Romanticism (including some nice views of Tallinn, scenes of Estonian nature, and idealized images of Estonian peasant women in folk costumes). Eduard von Gebhardt's engaging *Sermon on the Mount* (1904) includes a wide variety of Estonian portraits—some attentive, others distracted—listening to Jesus' most famous address. You'll see the Estonian version of several Modernist styles: Pointillism (linger over the lyrical landscapes of Konrad Mägi and the recently rediscovered works of Herbert Lukk), Cubism, and Expressionism. In the 1930s, the Pallas School provided a more traditional, back-to-nature response to the wild artistic trends of the time. By the dawn of World War II, you can see the art growing even more conservative, and the final canvases, from the war years, convey an unmistakable melancholy. In the corner, one very high-ceilinged room has a wall lined with dozens of expressive busts by sculptor Villu Jaanisoo.

The **fourth-floor exhibit,** called "Difficult Choices," is a fasci-

TALLINN

nating survey of Estonian art from the end of World War II until "re-independence" in 1991. Some of the works are mainstream (read: Soviet-style), while others are by dissident artists.

Estonian art parted ways with Western Europe with the Soviet takeover in 1945. The Soviets insisted that artworks actively promote the communist struggle, and to that end, Estonian artists were forced to adopt the Stalinist formula, making paintings that were done in the traditional national style but that were socialist in content—in the style now called **Socialist Realism.**

Socialist Realism had its roots in the early 20th-century Realist movement, whose artists wanted to depict the actual conditions of life rather than just glamour and wealth—in America, think of John Steinbeck's novels or Walker Evans' photographs of the rural poor. In the Soviet Union, this artistic curiosity about the working class was perverted into an ideology: Art was supposed to glorify labor and the state's role in distributing its fruits. In a system where there was ultimately little incentive to work hard, art was seen as a tool to motivate the masses, and to support the Communist Party's hold on power.

In the collection's first room, called "A Tale of Happiness," you'll see syrupy images of what Soviet leadership imagined to be the ideal of communist Estonia. In *Agitator Amongst the Voters* (1952), a stern portrait of Stalin in the hazy background keeps an eye on a young hotshot articulating some questionable ideas; his listeners' reactions range from shudders of horror to smirks of superiority. *The Young Aviators* (1951) shows an eager youngster wearing a bright-red neckerchief (indicating his membership in the Pioneers, the propaganda-laden communist version of Scouts) telling his enraptured schoolmates stories about a model airplane.

The next room shows canvases of miners, protesters, speechifiers, metalworkers, tractor drivers, and more all doing their ut-

most for the communist society. You'll also see paintings of industrial achievements (like bridges) and party meetings. Because mining was integral to the Estonian economy, miners were portrayed as local heroes, marching like soldiers to their glorious labor. Women were depicted toiling side by side with men, as equal partners. (Though they're not always on display here, posters were a natural fit, with slogans exhorting laborers to work hard on behalf of the regime.)

While supposedly a reflection of "real" life, Socialist Realism art was formulaic and showed little creative spirit. Though some Estonian artists flirted with social commentary and the avant-garde, a few ended up in Siberia as a result. Stroll through a few more rooms, noticing a handful of artists who attempted some bolder compositions. Also keep an eye out for a sly portrait of the "great leader"—Stalin.

Later, in the Brezhnev years, Estonian artists managed to slip Surrealist, Pop, and Photorealist themes into their work (for example, Rein Tammik's large painting *1945-1975*, which juxtaposes an old tractor with the flower children of the Swingin' Sixties). Estonia was the only part of the USSR that recognized Pop Art. As the Soviets would eventually learn, change was unstoppable.

The rest of the museum is devoted to temporary exhibits, with contemporary art always on the **fifth floor** (where there's a nice view back to the Old Town from the far gallery). It's also worth admiring the mostly successful **architecture**—the building is partly dug into the limestone hill, and the facade is limestone, too (for the big picture, look for the model of the building, just inside the main doors).

ALONG THE HARBORFRONT
▲▲Seaplane Harbor (Lennusadam)

One of Tallinn's newest and most ambitious sights, this nautical, aviation, and military museum fills a gigantic old hangar along the waterfront north of downtown. It has loads of hands-on activities for kids, and thrills anyone interested in transportation, while others find it off-puttingly militaristic. (The many Russian tourists who enjoy posing with its machine-gun simulators don't help matters.)

Cost and Hours: €10; May-Sept daily 10:00-19:00; same hours off-season except closed Mon; last entry one hour before closing, Vesilennuki 6, tel. 620-0550, www.seaplaneharbour.com.

Getting There: It's along the waterfront, about a mile north of the Old Town. It's a long but doable **walk,** made more enjoyable if you follow the red-gravel "Culture Kilometer" (Kultuurikilomeeter) seaside path from near the cruise terminals. While there's no handy tram or bus to the museum, a one-way **taxi** from the town center shouldn't cost much more than €5. The **hop-on, hop-off buses** also stop here.

Visiting the Museum: When you buy your ticket, you'll be issued an electronic card, which you can use at terminals posted throughout the exhibit to email yourself articles on topics that interest you. The entire collection is enlivened by lots of interactive screens, giant movies, and simulators (such as huge-scale shoot-'em-up video games with life-sized artillery). Touchscreens explain everything in three languages: Estonian, Russian, and English...in that order.

The cavernous old **seaplane hangar** cleverly displays exhibits on three levels: the ground floor features items from below the sea (such as a salvaged 16th-century shipwreck, plus a cinema that shows films subtitled in English); catwalks halfway up connect exhibits dealing with the sea surface (the impressive boat collection—from buoys to sailboats to the massive *Lembit* sub); and airplanes are suspended overhead. Touchscreens provide more information in English; just take your time exploring the collection. The star of the show is the 195-foot-long *Lembit* submarine from 1937: Estonian-commissioned and British-built, this vessel saw fighting in World War II and later spent several decades in the service of the USSR's Red Fleet. You can climb down below decks to see how the sailors lived, peek through the periscope, and even stare down the torpedo tubes. A cool café on the top level (above the entrance) overlooks the entire space, which feels endless.

Outside, filling the old harbor, is the maritime museum's collection of **historic ships,** from old-fashioned tall ships to modern-day military boats. The highlight is the steam-powered icebreaker *Suur Tõll,* from 1914. Sometimes you can pay to go out on a brief trip on one of the sailboats (ask at the ticket desk when you enter).

On the opposite side of the building, facing the main entrance, is a collection of **military vehicles.**

OUTER TALLINN
▲Song Festival Grounds (Lauluväljak)

At this open-air theater, built in 1959 and resembling an oversized Hollywood Bowl, the Estonian nation gathers to sing. Every five years, these grounds host a huge national song festival with 25,000 singers and 100,000 spectators. During the festival, the singers rehearse from Monday through Thursday, and then, on Friday morning, dress up in their traditional outfits and march out to the Song Festival Grounds from Freedom Square. While it hosts big pop-music acts, too, it's a national monument for the compelling role it played in Estonia's fight for independence.

Since 1988, when locals sang patriotic songs here in defiance of Soviet rule, these grounds have taken on a symbolic importance to the nation. Locals vividly recall putting on folk costumes knitted by their grandmothers (some of whom later died in Siberia) and coming here with masses of Estonians to sing. Overlooking the grounds from the cheap seats is a statue of Gustav Ernesaks, who directed the Estonian National Male Choir for 50 years through the darkest times of Soviet rule. He was a power in the drive for independence, and lived to see it happen.

TALLINN

Estonia's Singing Revolution

When you are a humble nation of just a million people lodged between Russia and Germany (and tyrants such as Stalin and Hitler), simply surviving is a challenge. Estonia was free from 1920 to 1939. The country then had a 50-year Nazi/Soviet nightmare. Estonians say, "We were so few in numbers that we had to emphasize that we exist. We had no weapons. Being together and singing together was our power." Singing has long been a national form of expression in this country; the first Estonian Song Festival occurred in 1869, and has been held every five years since then.

Estonian culture was under siege during the Soviet era. Moscow wouldn't allow locals to wave their flag or sing patriotic songs. Russians and Ukrainians were moved in, and Estonians were shipped out in an attempt to dilute the country's identity. But as cracks began to appear in the USSR, the Estonians mobilized—by singing.

In 1988, 300,000 Estonians—imagine...a third of the population—gathered at the Song Festival Grounds outside Tallinn to sing patriotic songs. On August 23, 1989—the 50th anniversary of a notorious pact between Hitler and Stalin—the people of Latvia, Lithuania, and Estonia held hands to make "the Baltic Chain," a human chain that stretched 360 miles from Tallinn to Vilnius in Lithuania. Some feared a Tiananmen Square-type bloodbath, but Estonians kept singing.

In February of 1990, the first free parliamentary elections took place in all three Baltic states, and pro-independence candidates won majorities. In 1991, hardline communists staged a coup against Soviet leader Mikhail Gorbachev, and Estonians feared a violent crackdown. The makeshift Estonian Parliament declared independence. Then, the coup in Moscow failed. Suddenly, the USSR was gone, and Estonia was free.

Watch the documentary film *The Singing Revolution* before your visit (www.singingrevolution.com) to tune into this stirring bit of modern history and to draw inspiration from Estonia's valiant struggle for freedom.

TALLINN

Cost and Hours: Free, open long hours, bus #1A, #5, #8, #34A, or #38 to Lauluväljak stop.

▲Pirita Neighborhood

Several gently fascinating sights cluster in the Pirita neighborhood, just a few miles northeast of the Song Festival Grounds. If you have a car (or a local guide with a car), or have the time to lace things together with public transportation, this can be a fun way to escape the city and see some different facets of Estonia.

Getting There: It's easy to lace these sights together: You'll take the waterfront Pirita Tee highway north (passing behind the Song Festival Grounds, described earlier) to Pirita, then turn right to cut through the forest to the TV Tower. Buses #34A and #38 follow exactly this same route—departing from the underground bus platforms at Viru Keskus mall—and conveniently link all of the places listed here.

Sights in Pirita: Coming from central Tallinn on Pirita Tee, you'll pass two starkly different memorials. First, as you skirt behind Kadriorg Park, watch on the left for the **Russalka Monument** (Russalka Mälestusmärk). An angel on a pedestal commemorates the 1893 sinking of the Russian warship *Russalka* ("Mermaid"). Farther along—after passing the Song Festival Grounds—look on the right for the towering **World War II Memorial** (Maarjamäe Memoriaal)—a 115-foot-tall obelisk erected to honor those who died defending the Soviet Union, and now the centerpiece of Estonia's war memorial.

Just after crossing the Pirita River and the little marina (with the yachting center built for the 1980 Olympics), watch on the right for the **ruins of St. Bridget's Convent** (Pirita Klooster; bus stop: Pirita). This early 15th-century convent, which housed both monks and nuns (in separate quarters, of course), was destroyed in 1577 by Ivan the Terrible. Its stones were quarried to build Baltic manor houses, but today you can pay a small fee to tour the evocative Gothic ruins (www.piritaklooster.ee).

Down along the water from here, **Pirita Beach** is one of the most popular in Tallinn. On a sunny summer day, Estonians are out enjoying sand, sun, and the Baltic Sea.

At the first traffic light after the convent ruins, turn right

on Kloostrimetsa Tee, which cuts through a forest—and through the **Forest Cemetery** (Metsakalmistu), offering a poignant look at unique Estonian burial customs (bus stop: Metsakalmistu, then continue about 200 yards down the road, following *Teletorn* signs to the gate). Traditionally, Estonians bury the departed not in fields or parks, but in forests—thanks to a deeply rooted belief that their spirit will live on in the trees. This particular cemetery is one of Estonia's best-known, and is the eternal resting place both of commoners and of VIPs—athletes, chess champions, musicians, writers, and politicians. Exploring here, find the "Hill of Celebrities" (Kuulsuste Küngas). Among the illustrious Estonians buried here is Konstantin Päts (1847-1956), the first president of independent Estonia, who later died in a Siberian mental institution. After freedom, his remains were located and moved here to be re-interred. Lydia Koidula (1843-1886, marked by a red stone) was Estonia's premier 19th-century poet and wrote the first play in Estonian.

Just past the Forest Cemetery, the **TV tower** (Teletorn)—with its antenna copping 1,000 feet tall—was built for the 1980 Moscow Olympics (the sailing regatta took place in Tallinn). You can ride up to the 550-foot-high observation deck for sweeping views over Estonia (and, on a clear day, all the way to Finland) and the endearing "Estonian Hall of Fame," celebrating Estonian contributions to the world (www.teletorn.ee).

In front of the tower, you'll see a monument to the brave Estonians who faced off against a potential Soviet counterattack. On August 19, 1991, a coup by generals in Moscow created confusion and panic across the USSR. The next day, on August 20—still celebrated today as Estonia's national holiday—the Declaration of Independence was signed. On August 21, Russian military forces moved to take this national broadcast tower and cut off Estonian communications. But two policemen and some radio operators cleverly prevented them from entering the tower's control station, by jamming the door and threatening to engage the fire-exhaust system. Eventually a ragtag gang of Estonian civilians showed up to defend the tower and stare down the troops. By late afternoon, it became clear that Boris Yeltsin had gained control in Moscow, and the Russian troops were told to stand down. Estonia had its tower—and a few weeks later, Russia recognized this little country's right to exist.

TALLINN

Lasnamäe Neighborhood

In its attempt to bring Estonia into the Soviet fold, Moscow moved tens of thousands of Russian workers into Tallinn, using the prom-

ise of new apartments as an incentive. Today, two generations later, Tallinn has a huge Russian minority (about 40 percent of the city's population) and three huge, charmless suburbs of ugly, Soviet-built apartments: Mustamäe, Õismäe, and Lasnamäe.

Sights in Lasnamäe: Today, about one of every two Tallinners lives in one of these Brezhnev-era suburbs of massive, cookie-cutter apartment blocks (many now privatized). About eighty percent of the residents who live in Las-namäe are Russian-speaking. Some parts are poor, rough, and edgy (not comfortable after dark), with blue lights in the public toilets so that junkies can't see their veins. Other sections are nicer, and by day, you can visit here without fear. Some zones are finally being upgraded with a spare-no-expense local pride; a new Russian Orthodox cathedral opened here in 2013 (built with the support of Tallinn's mayor to curry favor with ethnic-Russian voters). Some "social apartment" buildings—owned by the city—were also recently built in this area.

Forging Russians and Estonians into a single society, with the Estonian language dominant, was an optimistic goal in the early 1990s. Ethnic Russians grumbled, but knew they probably had a brighter economic future in Estonia than in Russia. Now, with a new generation of children learning both languages in school and most enjoying reasonable prosperity, peaceful ethnic coexistence (like between Swedes and Finns in Helsinki) may be achievable.

Getting There: For a quick look at Lasnamäe, hop on bus #67 or #68 (each runs every 10-15 minutes); both leave from Teatri Väl-jak, on the far side of the pastel yellow theater from the Old Town, across from the Solaris shopping mall. You'll see carefully dressed young women, track-suited men, grass that needs mowing, cracked paving stones, grandmothers pushing strollers, and lots of new, boxy shops. Ride to the last stop (about 25 minutes), then return to town.

▲Estonian Open-Air Museum (Vabaõhumuuseum)

Influenced by their ties with Nordic countries, Estonians are enthusiastic advocates of open-air museums. For this one, they sal-vaged farm buildings, windmills, and an old church from rural areas and transported them to a park-like setting just outside town (4 miles west of the Old Town). The goal: to both save and share their heritage. Attendants are posted in many houses, but to really visualize life in the old houses, rent the audioguide (€7/3 hours). The park's Kolu Tavern serves traditional dishes. You can rent a bike (€3/hour) for a breezy roll to quiet, far-away spaces in the park.

Cost and Hours: Late April-Sept: €7, park open daily 10:00-20:00, historic buildings until 18:00; Oct-late April: €5, park open daily 10:00-17:00 but many buildings closed; tel. 654-9100, www.evm.ee.

Getting There: Take bus #21 or #21B from the train station to the Rocca al Mare stop. Because buses back to Tallinn run infrequently, check the departure schedule as soon as you arrive, or ask staff how to find the Zoo stop, with more frequent service, a 15-minute walk away.

Lahemaa National Park (Lahemaa Rahvuspark)
This vast, flat, forested coastal preserve on the Gulf of Finland is only a one-hour drive east of Tallinn. While it is a popular tour destination and the nature is pristine, the park's charms are modest. I had a great guide, and it was a fascinating day out. But with an average guide, it could be a snore. Highlights include the thick forest (including cemeteries, because Estonians bury their dead in the woods), bog walks, rich berry and mushroom picking, rebuilt manor homes, and peaceful fishing villages surrounded by the evocative ruins of Soviet occupation. Tallinn Traveller Tours organizes day trips to the national park. For hiking and cycling trail descriptions, check online (www.keskkonnaamet.ee) or stop at the park's visitor center when you arrive (open daily in summer, Mon-Fri off-season, tel. 329-5555).

Shopping in Tallinn

With so many cruise-ship tourists inundating Tallinn, the Old Town is full of trinkets, but it is possible to find good-quality stuff. Wooden goods, like butter knives and juniper-wood trivets, are a good value. Marvel at the variety of booze on sale in Tallinn's liquor stores, popular with visiting Scandinavians. Tucked into the Old Town are many craft and artisan shops where prices are lower than in Nordic countries.

The **"Sweater Wall"** is a fun place to browse sweaters and woolens, though few are hand-knitted by grandmothers these

days. Find the stalls under the wall on Müürivahe street (daily 10:00-17:00, near the corner of Viru street). From there, explore **Katariina Käik,** a small alley between Müürivahe and Vene streets, which has several handicraft stores and workshops selling pieces that make nice souvenirs.

The cheery **Navitrolla Gallerii** is filled with work by the well-known Estonian artist who goes just by the name Navitrolla. His whimsical, animal-themed prints are vaguely reminiscent of *Where the Wild Things Are* (Mon-Fri 10:00-18:00, Sat 10:00-17:00, Sun 10:00-16:00, Sulevimägi 1, tel. 631-3716, www.navitrolla.ee).

The **Rahva Raamat** bookstore in the Viru Keskus mall (floors 3-4, high up in the glass atrium) has English-language literature on the main floor, and a huge wall of travel books upstairs (daily 9:00-21:00).

Balti Jaam Market, Tallinn's bustling traditional market, is behind the train station and has little of touristic interest besides

wonderful photo ops. That's why I like it. It's a great time-warp scene, fragrant with dill, berries, onions, and mushrooms. You'll hear lots of Russian. The indoor sections sell meat, clothing, and gadgets. You could also assemble a very rustic picnic here. To find the market from the train station, just walk across the head of the train platforms (following *Jaama Turg* signs) and keep going (Mon-Fri 8:00-18:00, Sat-Sun 8:00-17:00, better early).

For something tamer, the **Viru Turg outdoor market,** a block outside the Old Town's Viru Gate, has a lively, tourist-oriented collection of stalls selling mostly clothing, textiles, and flowers (daily May-Sept 9:00-17:00, Oct-April 10:00-16:00, north of Viru street at Mere Puiestee 1).

Entertainment in Tallinn

Music

Tallinn has a dense schedule of classical music performances, especially during the annual Old Town Days, generally at the beginning of June (www.vanalinnapaevad.ee). Choral singing became a symbol of the struggle for Estonian independence after the first Estonian Song Festival in 1869 (still held every five years—next one in 2019).

Even outside of festival times, you'll find many performances in Tallinn's churches and concert halls, advertised on posters around town or at the TI. Tickets are usually available at the door or through the Piletilevi booth in the Viru Keskus mall (daily 9:00-21:00, www.piletilevi.ee). Watch for performances by Hortus Musicus, one of Estonia's finest classical ensembles, or concerts featuring the work of Arvo Pärt, Veljo Tormis, or Erkki-Sven Tüür, who are among Estonia's best modern choral composers and arrangers. Estonian groups have put out a lot of good CDs; you'll find a good music shop on the top floor (A5) of the Kaubamaja department store (daily 9:00-21:00, behind Viru Keskus mall).

Swimming

The indoor water park and 50-meter pool at the **Kalev Spa** is lots of fun. Many Finns come here on fitness travel packages. It's centrally located, between the Old Town and the modern shopping zone (€11.90/2.5 hours, €9.90/1.5 hours, cheaper on weekday mornings; open Mon-Fri 6:45-21:30, Sat-Sun 8:00-21:30; swimsuit rental available, Aia 18, tel. 649-3370, www.kalevspa.ee).

Sleeping in Tallinn

In general, real hotel options are surprisingly sparse and expensive, particularly in the Old Town; many people prefer rental apartments found online (such as at Booking.com or Airbnb.com). While I've focused my listings on places in or near the Old Town, you'll have more options and pay less if you're willing to stay a short walk or bus ride away.

As in Scandinavia, it's important to start your search on hotel websites. Room prices vary with current demand. Many hotels, especially the bigger ones, list their best price on the website and offer walk-in individuals only the inflated rack rates—the bulk of their business comes from agencies anyway.

Summer is high season (Tallinn has more tourists than business travelers), and prices almost always drop from October to April, except around Christmas and New Year's. I've listed high-season, summer prices here. When I give a range, expect the higher rate during busy times (typically Friday and Saturday nights) and the lower price on slow days. All of my listings offer free Wi-Fi.

Use a taxi to get to your hotel when you arrive, and then figure out public transportation later.

IN AND NEAR THE OLD TOWN

$$$ **Baltic Hotel Imperial** is a fine four-star hotel set in a lovely park-like spot under the Old Town wall. Its 32 rooms are modern and small, while the public spaces have a spacious, professional ambience. Though it feels like a chain (and is), when it's discounted, it's the best Old Town, top-end value I've found (inflated official rates—Sb-€140, Db-€180; deals are often cheaper—website shows best rates; elevator, air-con, pay sauna, kids' playroom, Nunne 14, tel. 627-4800, www.imperial.ee, imperial@baltichotelgroup.com).

$$$ **My City Hotel** fills a handsome 1950s building on the south edge of the Old Town with 68 rooms and a spacious, classy lobby lounge. Along with the Sõprus cinema across the street, it's done in the Stalinist Classical style—Soviet stars and sheaves of wheat still adorn the facade (typically Db-€90 on weekdays— a great deal—or €140 on weekends, more for larger "superior" room, extra bed-€25, children 12 and under free in parents'

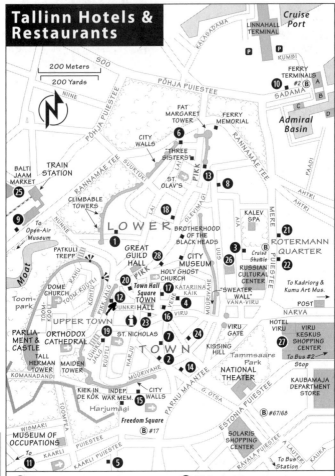

Tallinn Hotels & Restaurants

TALLINN

1 Baltic Hotel Imperial

2 My City Hotel

3 Hotel Bern

4 Villa Hortensia & Pierre Chocolaterie

5 St. Barbara Hotel

6 Meriton Old Town Hotel

7 Old Town Maestro's

8 Old House Guesthouse/Hostel

9 Hotel Shnelli

10 Tallink Express Hotel

11 To Valge Villa

12 Restaurant Aed, Vanaema Juures & Von Krahli Baar

13 Leib Restaurant

14 Mekk Restaurant

15 Wabadus Restaurant

16 Olde Hansa Restaurant & Peppersack Restaurant

17 Troika Restaurant

18 Hell Hunt Pub

19 Põrgu Pub

20 Kompressor Pub

21 Sfäär

22 Retoran Ö

23 Road Food

24 Eat Dumpling Café

25 Balti Jaama Kohvik

26 Rimi Supermarket

27 Viru Keskus Supermarket

28 Kolmjag "Everything" Grocery & Maiasmokk Café

room, elevator, air-con, guest computer, sauna-€20-30/hour, Vana-Posti 11/13, tel. 622-0900, www.mycityhotel.ee, booking@ mycityhotel.ee).

$$$ Hotel Bern, tucked at the edge of the Old Town, is an endearing place with 50 businesslike rooms in a new brick building (Db-€98, but can be less in slow times, air-con, elevator, Aia 10, tel. 680-6630, www.tallinnhotels.ee, bern@tallinnhotels.ee).

$$ Villa Hortensia rents six simple, creaky-floored rooms with kitchenettes above a sophisticated little café in a courtyard close to Town Hall Square. The three twin-bed rooms and one single-bed room are furnished sparsely, with beds in a sleeping loft. The "de-luxe" room comes with a double bed and a small balcony. The suite is on two floors, with a double bed upstairs and a foldout sofa bed in the living room. Named after the home of a group of down-and-outs in a famous Estonian novel, the hotel is creatively run by jewelry designer Jaan Pärn. It's a decent, inexpensive choice if you don't mind the ramshackle feeling and the fact that the rooms aren't serviced every day. Jaan's jewelry shop, across the courtyard, serves as the reception (Sb-€45, Db-€65, deluxe Db-€90, suite Db-€120 or Tb-€140, no breakfast, no elevator, 50 yards from the corner of Vene and Viru streets at Vene 6, look for *Masters' Courtyard* sign, mobile 504-6113, www.hoov.ee, jaan.parn@gmail.com).

$$ St. Barbara Hotel, a stylish and affordable choice, fills a former hospital from 1904 just beyond the ring road from Tal-linn's Freedom Square (at the edge of the Old Town)—about a 10-minute walk from Town Hall Square. This old building is filled with 53 modern, fairly simple rooms and an atmospheric beer cel-lar that gives the place a Germanic vibe (Db-€79 on weekdays or €87 on weekends—but prices are flexible, elevator, free parking, Roosikrantsi 2A—just take the pedestrian underpass from Free-dom Square under the busy road, tel. 640-0040, www.stbarbara. ee, reservations@stbarbara.ee).

TALLINN

\$\$ Meriton Old Town Hotel sits grandly (for a hotel in its egory) at the tip of the Old Town, near Fat Margaret Tower and not far from the ferry terminals. Its 41 small, slightly dated rooms are mostly doubles with twin beds and showers, and—as it faces a busy street—some could be noisy if you sleep with the window open. But the price is right and the location convenient. Don't let them move you to the nearby, similarly named, more expensive Meriton Old Town Garden Hotel (very fluid rates, Db-€85-110 depending on demand, much less off-season, can be cheaper if you skip breakfast, elevator, guest computer, Lai 49, tel. 614-1300, www.meritonhotels.com, reservations@meritonhotels.com).

\$\$ Old Town Maestro's is a simple budget choice with 23 modern rooms tucked in the heart of the Old Town. While the prices are right, it comes with a catch: It sits along one of Tallinn's rowdiest nightlife streets, so try requesting a quieter courtyard room (Sb-€55, Db-€65, elevator, Suur-Karja 10, tel. 626-2000, www.maestrohotel.ee, maestro@maestrohotel.ee).

\$ Old House Guesthouse and Hostel is your small-and-snug, cheap-and-basic option, split between two buildings halfway between Town Hall Square and the ferry terminals. There's street noise in many rooms, so bring earplugs (bed in 6-person dorm-€15, S-€30, twin D-€44, D with one big bed-€48, T-€63, Q-€84, see their website for deals, includes sheets and towel, breakfast-€4, no lockout, shared shower and WC, kitchen facilities, unsecured free parking—reserve ahead, Uus 26, tel. 641-1464, www.oldhouse. ee, info@oldhouse.ee). They also rent apartments around the Old Town.

SLEEPING MORE AFFORDABLY, AWAY FROM THE OLD TOWN

Near the Train Station: **\$\$ Hotel Shnelli,** a big, high-rise "efficiency hotel" adjacent to the sleepy little train station (a 5-minute walk from the Old Town in a neighborhood that feels a bit seedy at night), rents 137 Ikea-mod rooms. It fronts a noisy street, so request a quiet room in the back—these overlook the tracks, but no trains run at night (Db-€60-65, sometimes €10-20 more on weekends, connecting family rooms, apartment-€130, you can save a few euros if you skip breakfast, elevator, Toompuiestee 37, tel. 631-0100, www.gohotels.ee, reservations@gohotels.ee).

Near the Port: Given how compact Tallinn is (and how inexpensive honest taxis are), there's little reason to sleep near the ferry terminals—other than low prices. But if you're in a pinch, **\$\$ Tallink Express Hotel** is a few steps from the A, B, and C ferry terminals, close to Linnahall terminal, and a short walk from the Old Town. It's a modern, cheery Motel 6-type place with excellent prices and 163 comfortable, colorful, cookie-cutter rooms. The rooms can be stuffy in hot weather, as windows don't open very far and there's no air-conditioning. Walk-in rates are much higher than the website prices I give here (Sb/Db-€70-80 but can vary dramatically—less in winter and more on busy weekends, extra bed-€25, children under 17 sleep free on sofa beds in family rooms, elevator, free guest computer, free parking, Sadama 9, tel. 630-0808, www.hotels.tallink.com, hotelbooking@tallink.ee).

In Lilleküla, Outside the Center: Lilleküla is a quiet, green, and peaceful residential area of single-family houses, small Soviet-era apartment blocks, and barking dogs. For a clearer understanding of Estonian life, stay here. You'll save money without sacrificing comfort. The downside: It's a 15-minute, €1.10 bus ride into the center.

$ Valge Villa ("White Villa"), a homey guesthouse set in a great garden run by Anne and Andres Vahtra and their family, does everything right. It's worth the commute for its competitive prices and 10 spacious, wood-paneled, well-furnished rooms. They like you to book and pay a 10 percent advance deposit on their website (Sb-€39, Db-€45, small suite-€60, larger suite-€70, suite-apartments-€80, extra bed-€16, every fifth night free, guest computer, free parking, bikes-€15/day, sauna-€20, laundry-€12/load; take bus #17 to Rääbu stop, or trolley bus #2, #3, or #4 to Tedre stop; Kännu 26/2, between Rästa and Rääbu streets—tel. 654-2302, www.white-villa.com, villa@white-villa.com). I'd take a taxi here to check in (about €15 from the ferry port), and figure out the public-transit options later.

Eating in Tallinn

Tallinn's Old Town has a wide selection of largely interchangeable, mostly tourist-oriented eateries. Don't expect bargains here—you'll pay near-Scandinavian prices (average main dishes can cost €15-20). For a better value, roam at least a block or two off the main drags, where you can find great food at what seems like fire-sale prices. At most of my listings, you can assemble a three-course meal for around €20. Some restaurants have good-value lunch specials on weekdays (look for the words *päeva praad*). As a mark of quality, watch for restaurants with an *Astu Sisse!* label in the window; this Estonian equivalent of a Michelin star is awarded to just 50 restaurants each year. Tipping is not required, but if you like the service, round your bill up by 5-10 percent when paying. Reserving ahead for dinner is a smart idea.

A few years ago it was hard

to find authentic local cuisine, but now Estonian food is trendy—a hearty Northern mixture of meat, potatoes, root vegetables, mushrooms, dill, garlic, bread, and soup. Pea soup is a local specialty. You usually get a few slices of bread as a free, automatic side dish. A typical pub snack is Estonian garlic bread *(küüslauguleivad)*—deep-fried strips of dark rye bread smothered in garlic and served with a dipping sauce. Estonia's Saku beer is good, cheap, and on tap at most eateries. Try the nutty, full-bodied Tume variety.

ESTONIAN CUISINE IN THE OLD TOWN

Restorant Aed is an elegant, almost gourmet, health-food eatery calling itself "the embassy of pure food." While not vegetarian, it is passionate about serving organic, seasonal, modern Estonian cuisine in a woody, romantic setting. Take your pick from four dining options: under old beams, in the cellar, out front on the sidewalk, or out back on the garden terrace (€10-15 main dishes, daily 12:00-23:00, Rataskaevu 8, tel. 626-9088, www.vonkrahl.ee/aed).

Vanaema Juures ("Grandma's Place"), an eight-table cellar restaurant, serves homey, traditional Estonian meals, such as pork roast with sauerkraut and horseradish. This is a fine bet for local cuisine, and dinner reservations are strongly advised. No tacky medieval stuff here—just good food at fair prices in a pleasant ambience, where you expect your waitress to show up with her hair in a bun and wearing granny glasses (€8-17 main dishes, daily 12:00-22:00, Rataskaevu 10/12, tel. 626-9080, www.vonkrahl.ee/vanaemajuures).

At **Leib** ("Back Bread"), just outside the walls at the seaside end of the Old Town, you enter up steps into a fun garden under the medieval ramparts, and can sit indoors or out. Peruse the classy and engaging menu, which changes with the seasons—their food has Estonian roots, but with international influences (€10-16 main courses, daily 12:00-15:00 & 18:00-23:00, Uus 31, tel. 611-9026, www.leibresto.ee/en).

Mekk is a small, fresh, upscale place whose name stands for "modern Estonian cuisine." While their à la carte prices are a bit higher than at my other listings, they offer artful weekday lunch specials for just €7 (not available July-Aug), and a €35 four-course fixed-price meal for serious eaters. Young, elegant locals take their lunch breaks here (€12-25 main dishes, Mon-Sat 12:00-23:00, closed Sun, Suur-Karja 17/19, tel. 680-6688, www.mekk.ee).

Modern Cuisine on Freedom Square: **Wabadus,** facing the vast and modern square, turns its back on old Tallinn. This sleek, urbane café/restaurant—which has been the town meeting place since 1937—serves coffee, cocktails, and international fare. To escape the cobbles and crowds of the Old Town, walk a few minutes to enjoy a moment of peace—ideally at one of the terrace tables on the square, if the weather's good (€5 weekday lunch specials,

€7-10 salads, €7-18 main courses, Mon-Tue 11:00-19:00, Wed-Thu 11:00-21:00, Fri-Sat 11:00-24:00, closed Sun, Vabaduse Väljak 10, tel. 601-6461, www.wabadus.ee).

TOURIST TRAPS ON AND NEAR TOWN HALL SQUARE

Tallinn's central square is a whirlpool of tacky tourism, where aggressive restaurant touts (some dressed as medieval wenches or giant *matryoshka* dolls) accost passersby to lure them in for a drink or meal. While a bit off-putting, some of these restaurants have surprisingly good (if expensive) food. Of the many options ringing the square and surrounding streets, these are the ones most worth considering.

"Medieval" Estonian Cuisine: Two well-run restaurants just below Town Hall Square specialize in re-creating medieval food (from the days before the arrival of the potato and tomato from the New World). They are each grotesquely touristy, complete with gift shops where you can buy your souvenir goblet. Both have street seating, but you'll get all the tourists and none of the atmosphere.

Olde Hansa, filling three creaky old floors and outdoor tables with tourists, candle wax, and scurrying medieval waitresses, can be quite expensive. And yet, the local consensus is that the food here is far better than it has any right to be (€14-30 main dishes, daily 10:00-24:00, musicians circulate Tue-Sun after 18:00, a belch below Town Hall Square at Vana Turg 1, reserve in advance, tel. 627-9020, www.oldehansa.ee).

Peppersack, across the street, tries to compete in the same price range, and feels marginally less circus-like (Vana Turg 6, tel. 646-6800).

Russian Food: As more than a third of the local population is enthusiastically Russian, there are plenty of places serving Russian cuisine (see also "Budget Eateries," described later). **Troika** is my choice for Russian food. Right on Town Hall Square, with a folkloric-costumed waitstaff, they serve €7-11 *bliny* (pancakes) and *pelmeni* (dumplings), and €11-20 main dishes. Sit out on the square (reserve for dinner); in the more casual, Russian-village-themed tavern; or under a fine vault in the trendy, atmospheric cellar (which has slightly cheaper prices). A balalaika player usually strums and strolls after 19:00 (open daily 10:00-23:00, Raekoja Plats 15, tel. 627-6245, www.troika.ee).

PUBS IN THE OLD TOWN

Young Estonians eat well and affordably at pubs. In some pubs, you go to the bar to look at the menu, order, and pay. Then find a table, and they'll bring your food out when it's ready.

Hell Hunt Pub ("The Gentle Wolf") was the first Western-style pub to open after 1991, and it's still going strong, attracting a mixed expat and local crowd with its tasty food. Five of their own microbrews are on tap. Consider making a meal from the great pub snacks (€3-6) plus a salad (€5-6). Choose a table in its convivial, rustic-industrial interior or on the garden terrace across the street (€6 pastas, €10 main dishes, daily 12:00-24:00, Pikk 39, tel. 681-8333).

Von Krahli Baar serves cheap, substantial Estonian grub—such as potato pancakes *(torud)* stuffed with mushrooms or shrimp—in a big, dark space that doubles as a center for Estonia's alternative theater scene; there's also seating in the tiny courtyard where you enter. It started as the bar of the theater upstairs, then expanded to become a restaurant, so it has a young, avant-garde vibe. You'll feel like you're eating backstage with the stagehands (€6-7 main dishes, Mon-Sat 12:00-24:00, Sun 12:00-15:00, Rataskaevu 10/12, a block uphill from Town Hall Square, near Wheel Well, tel. 626-9090).

Põrgu is particularly serious about its beer, with a wide variety of international and Estonian brews on tap—including some microbrews. Its simple, uncluttered cellar feels like less of a tourist trap than the others listed here (€3-7 bar snacks and salads, €8-13 main dishes, Mon-Sat 12:00-24:00, closed Sun, Rüütli 4, tel. 644-0232).

Kompressor, a big, open-feeling beer hall, is in all the guidebooks for its cheap, huge, and filling €5 pancakes—savory or sweet (daily 11:00-24:00, Rataskaevu 3, tel. 646-4210).

IN THE ROTERMANN QUARTER

This modern, up-and-coming district, just across the busy road from Tallinn's Old Town, is well worth exploring for a jolt of cutting-edge architecture and hipster edginess. It's an antidote to the central area's ye-olde aura. As more and more buildings in this zone are being renovated, this is a fast-changing scene. But these two choices, in a long brick building facing the Old Town, are well-established and a good starting point.

Sfäär (Sphere), which combines an unpretentious bistro with a design shop, is a killing-two-birds look at the Rotermann Quarter. In this lively, cheery place, tables are tucked between locally designed clothes and home decor. The menu is bold but accessible and affordable, featuring Estonian and international fare with a hint of molecular flair (€6-10 starters and pastas, €12-16 main dishes, Mon-Wed 8:00-22:00, Thu-Fri 8:00-24:00, Sat 10:00-24:00, Sun 10:00-22:00, shop open daily 12:00-21:00, Mere Puiestee 6E, mobile 5699-2200, www.sfaar.ee).

Retoran Õ (Swedish for "Island"), just a few doors down in the same building, is your Rotermann Quarter splurge. The dressy, trendy, retrofitted-warehouse interior feels a sophisticated world away from the Old Town's tourist traps. The cuisine tries to highlight an Estonian approach to "New Nordic" cooking—small dishes carefully constructed with seasonal, local ingredients. Res-

ervations are smart (€19-24 main courses, €70 ta
Sat 18:00-23:00, closed Sun, Mere Puiestee 6E
parking lot around back, tel. 661-6150, www.res

BUDGET EATERIES

Road Food, tucked on a tiny lane immediately behind the Town Hall Tower, has some of the best cheap eats in the city. A branch of the Olde Hansa food empire, this sandwich shop serves up an excellent, quick taste of Estonia, stuffing its €4-5 sandwiches with local meats and sauces. It's attached to a well-stocked beer and wine shop, making it easy to browse for the perfect drink to wash things down (daily 11:00-24:00, shorter hours off-season, Vanaturo kael 8).

Eat, a laid-back, cellar-level student hangout with a big foosball table and a book exchange, serves the best-value lunch in town. Its menu is very simple: three varieties of *pelmeenid* (dumplings), plus sauces, beet salad, and pickles. You dish up what you like and pay by weight (€2-3/big bowl). Ask for an education in the various dumplings and sauces and then go for the complete experience. Enjoy with abandon—you can't spend much money here, and you'll feel good stoking their business (Mon-Sat 11:00-21:00, closed Sun, Sauna 2, tel. 644-0029).

At the Outdoor Market: **Balti Jaama Kohvik,** at the end of the train station near the Balti Jaam Market, is an unimpressive-looking 24-hour diner with no real sign (look for a faded red awning and *Kohvik avatud 24 tundi*—"café open 24 hours"—on the door; it's actually built into the train-station building). The bustling stainless-steel kitchen cranks out traditional Russian/Estonian dishes—the cheapest hot food in town. While you won't see or hear a word of English here, the glass case displays the various offerings and prices (€3 meals, €1.60 soups, dirt-cheap-yet-wonderful savory pancakes for less than €1, and tasty *beljaš*—a kind of pierogi). Unfortunately, the area feels sketchy after dark.

Supermarkets: For picnic supplies, try the **Rimi** supermarket just outside the Old Town at Aia 7, near the Viru Gate (daily 8:00-22:00). A larger, more upscale supermarket in the basement of the **Viru Keskus** mall (directly behind Hotel Viru) has convenient, inexpensive takeaway meals (daily 9:00-21:00). The handy little **Kolmjag "Everything"** grocery is a block off Town Hall Square (daily 24 hours, Pikk 11, tel. 631-1511).

BREAKFAST AND PASTRIES

The **Maiasmokk** ("Sweet Tooth") café and pastry shop, founded in 1864, is the grande dame of Tallinn cafés—ideal for dessert or breakfast. Even through the Soviet days, this was *the* place for a good pastry or a glass of herby Tallinn schnapps ("Vana Tallinn"). Point to what you want from the selection of classic local pastries counter, and sit down for breakfast (€3 omelets) or coffee the other side of the shop. Everything's reasonable (Mon-Fri 8:00-21:00, Sat 9:00-21:00, Sun 9:00-20:00, Pikk 16, across from church with old clock, tel. 646-4079). They also have a marzipan shop (separate entrance).

Pierre Chocolaterie at Vene 6 has scrumptious fresh pralines, sandwiches, and coffee in a courtyard filled with craft shops (also €5-8 light meals, daily 8:30-late, tel. 641-8061).

Tallinn Connections

BY BUS OR TRAIN

The bus is usually the best way to travel by land from Tallinn (for domestic bus schedules, see www.tpilet.ee). The largest operator, with the most departures, is Lux Express (tel. 680-0909, www. luxexpress.ee); there's also Ecolines (tel. 614-3600 or mobile 5637-7997, www.ecolines.net) and the spiffy Hansabuss (with onboard Wi-Fi, tel. 627-9080, www.hansabuss.ee). The bus station *(auto-bussijaam)* is at Lastekodu 46, a short taxi ride from the Old Town, or a few stops on trams #2 or #4 to the Autobussijaam stop (direction: Ülemiste). Not much English is spoken at the station; reserving online is recommended.

From Tallinn to: Rīga (12 buses/day, 4.5 hours, no train option; consider Tallinn Traveller Tours' "sightseeing shuttle" between these cities, a full-day, 12-hour journey with sightseeing stops en route—see "Tours in Tallinn," earlier), **Vilnius** (3 buses/day departing in the morning, plus 3/day overnight, 10 hours), **St. Petersburg** (buses nearly hourly, 6.5-8 hours; also possible by overnight cruise—about 1/week, 14.5 hours, www.stpeterline.com), **Moscow** (take the overnight train—daily at 17:20, 16-hour trip, www.gorail.ee—or fly). Americans and Canadians must obtain a visa to travel to Russia and need to plan long in advance (www. russianembassy.org or www.rusembassy.ca).

For the latest bus and train schedules, see the helpful binders at the TI or consult *Tallinn in Your Pocket*.

BY BOAT

You have two basic options: A slow overnight boat ride from Stockholm, or a fast daytime boat from Helsinki.

Sailing Overnight Between Stockholm and Tallinn

Tallink Silja's overnight cruise ships leave Stockholm at 17:30 or 17:45 every evening and arrive in Tallinn at 10:00 or 10:45 the next morning. Return trips leave Tallinn at 18:00 and arrive in Stockholm at 10:00 or 10:15. All times are local (Tallinn is an hour ahead of Stockholm). As with hotels, these cruises use "dynamic pricing" that flexes with demand. Fares vary by the day and season. The highest rates are typically for Friday and Saturday nights, and for the peak of summer (July-mid-Aug); outside of peak season, Sunday through Thursday nights tend to be cheaper. A one-way berth in a four-person, sex-segregated cabin with a private bath costs around €50; couples can travel in a private cabin for about €150-200. The *smörgåsbord* dinner and buffet breakfast cost extra (prebook these meals and reserve a table when buying your ticket). Book online (www.tallinksilja.com); booking by phone or in person may come with an extra charge, but they can answer questions for free (Swedish tel. 08/222-140, Estonian tel. 640-9808). Note that travelers below age 20 are not allowed on this cruise without a parent or guardian (for details, see the website).

Terminals: In **Stockholm,** Tallink Silja ships leave from the Värtahamnen harbor. To get there from downtown Stockholm, take the Tallink Silja shuttle bus from the train station (50 kr, departs according to boat schedule), or take the T-bana (subway) to the Gärdet station, then walk 10 minutes to the harbor. On Mondays through Saturdays, public bus #76 (direction: Ropsten) takes you directly to the terminal (leaves from several downtown locations, including Kungsträdgården; get off at Färjeterminalen stop). For Stockholm public transit information, see www.sl.se. In **Tallinn,** Tallink Silja ships dock at D-Terminal (see "Arrival in Tallinn," earlier).

Speeding Between Helsinki and Tallinn

Four different companies—shown in the table on the next page—offer ferry trips between Helsinki and Tallinn. Fares run €20-55 one-way (evening departures from Helsinki and morning departures from Tallinn tend to be cheaper; student and senior discounts available). Their websites have all the latest information and prices. Advance reservations aren't essential, but usually save a little money, ensure your choice of departure, and provide peace of mind. If you travel round-trip on the same day, your ticket will cost barely more than a one-way fare, but you'll have just a few hours on shore. Prices differ only slightly from company to company—base your choice on the most convenient departure times and ferry terminal locations. Make sure you know which terminal your boat leaves from and how to get to it (for descriptions of Tallinn's terminals, see "Arrival in Tallinn," earlier).

Unless you're bringing a car, the Linda and Viking lines are usually the most convenient, as their docks in Helsinki and Tallinn are easy to reach by foot or public transport. **Linda Line** uses 400-passenger, Australian-made catamarans that zip across the Gulf of Finland in just 1.5 hours (6-7/day March-Oct, 3-5/day Nov-Feb). Boats leave from the Makasiini terminal in Helsinki's

Helsinki/Tallinn Connections

Company	Website	Terminal in Helsinki	Terminal in Tallinn
Tallink Silja	www.tallinksilja.com	Länsi	D
Linda Line (fast catamarans)	www.lindaline.ee	Makasiini	Linnahall
Eckerö Line	www.eckeroline.fi	Länsi	A/B
Viking Line	www.vikingline.fi	Katajanokan	A/B

Note: All of these lines also have phone numbers and brick-and-mortar offices, both in Estonia and in Finland (find them on the websites); but in most cases, you'll pay an extra fee to book by phone or in person. Booking online is easy and free.

South Harbor (Eteläsatama), just five minutes' walk from Market Square, and arrive in Tallinn at the Linnahall terminal. Catamarans lack the spacious party atmosphere of larger boats, and are slightly more expensive. Cancellations, which can occur in stormy conditions, rarely happen in summer; still, if you have a plane to catch, play it safe and take a regular ferry. **Viking Line** leaves from the other side of Helsinki's South Harbor (Katajanokan terminal), and arrives at Tallinn's A/B-Terminal. Viking offers a more traditional experience on a big ferry with restaurants and shops (2/day, 2.5-hour crossing, generally a few euros less than Linda Line).

Tallink Silja and **Eckerö Line** leave from the relatively inconvenient Länsi terminal at Helsinki's West Harbor (Länsistama), which you can reach on tram #9 (catch it at Kamppi mall in downtown Helsinki; the terminal is the end of the line). At the other end of the journey, Tallink Silja uses Tallinn's D-Terminal—the farthest from the Old Town, making it a bit less convenient but still walkable. On the other hand, Tallink Silja's ferries are frequent and fast (6-7/day, 2-hour crossing). Eckerö Line has just two slow, inexpensive sailings per day (3.5-hour crossing).

Slower boats—all except Linda Line—have *smörgåsbord* buffets. The slower the boat, the more likely it is to be filled with "four-legged Finns" crazy about cheap booze, slot machines, and karaoke.

TALLINN

PRACTICALITIES

This section covers just the basics on traveling in St. Petersburg, Helsinki, and Tallinn (for additional information on traveling in Scandinavia, see *Rick Steves Scandinavia*). You'll find free advice on specific topics at www.ricksteves.com/tips.

TRAVELERS TO RUSSIA NEED A VISA

If you're going to St. Petersburg, you will need to arrange for a visa well in advance of your trip (unless you're arriving on a cruise ship or the St. Peter Line ferry, and are planning to pay for an excursion). Getting a visa is expensive (figure around $350 per person) and a hassle (filling out long bureaucratic forms, then mailing your application—and your passport—to the Russian embassy several weeks before your trip). Your first step is to carefully read the "Russian Visa Requirements" sidebar on page 12.

MONEY

Russia uses the ruble (abbreviated R or RUB). The value of the ruble has been unpredictable lately. Depending on the economy—and the price of oil—you could see higher prices (in rubles) than those listed here. In some listings I've given prices in US dollars, especially for personal services and smaller vendors. Check www.oanda.com for the latest exchange rates. Finland and Estonia use the euro.

The standard way for travelers to get rubles or euros is to withdraw money from ATMs, which are called *bankomat* in all of these countries; ATMs are often labeled **банкомат** in Russia and *Otto* in Finland and Estonia. Use a debit or credit card, ideally with a Visa or MasterCard logo. Before departing, call your bank or credit-card company: Confirm that your card(s) will work overseas, ask about international transaction fees, and alert them that you'll be making withdrawals in Europe. Also ask for the PIN number for your credit card in case it'll help you use Europe's "chip-and-PIN" payment machines (see below); allow time for your bank to mail your PIN to you. To keep your valuables safe, wear a money belt.

Dealing with "Chip and PIN": Much of Europe is adopting a "chip-and-PIN" system for credit cards, and some merchants—particularly in Finland—rely on it exclusively. European chip-and-PIN cards are embedded with an electronic chip, in addition to the magnetic stripe used on our American-style cards. This means that your credit (and debit) card might not work at automated payment machines, such as those at train and subway stations, toll roads, parking garages, luggage lockers, and self-serve gas pumps. Memorizing your credit card's PIN lets you use it at some chip-and-PIN machines—just enter your PIN when prompted. If a machine won't take your card, look for a machine that takes cash or see if there's a cashier nearby who can process your transaction. Often the easiest solution is to pay for your purchases with cash you've withdrawn from an ATM using your debit card (Europe's ATMs still accept magnetic-stripe cards).

PHONING

Smart travelers use the telephone to reserve or reconfirm rooms, reserve restaurants, get directions, research transportation connections, confirm tour times, phone home, and lots more.

Russia: Russia's country code is 7, and St. Petersburg's area code is 812. To call from another country to Russia, dial the international access code (011 from the US/Canada, 00 from Europe, or + from a mobile phone), then 7, followed by the area code and local number. For calls within Russia, dial just the number if you are calling locally; if you're calling long distance, dial 8 (you may need to wait a second on older phones), then the area code and the number. To call the US or Canada from Russia, dial 8, wait for a tone if needed, then dial 10, then 1, then your area code and phone number.

Finland: Finland's country code is 358; to call from another country to Finland, dial the international access code (011 from the US/Canada, 00 from Europe, or + from a mobile phone), then 358, followed by the area code (without initial zero) and the local number. For calls within Finland, dial just the number if you are calling locally, and add the area code if calling long distance. To place an international call from Finland, dial 999 or another 900 number (depending on the phone service you're using), the code of the country you're calling (1 for US and Canada), and the phone number.

Estonia: Estonia's country code is 372; to call from another country to Estonia, dial the international access code (011 from the US/Canada, 00 from Europe, or + from a mobile phone), then 372, followed by the local number. For calls within Estonia, just dial the number as it appears in this book—whether you're calling across the street or across the country. To place an international call from Estonia, dial 00, the code of the country you're calling (1 for US and Canada), and the phone number.

Tips on Phoning: A mobile phone—whether an American one that works in Europe, or a European one you buy when you arrive—is handy, but can be pricey. If traveling with a smartphone, consider getting an international plan from your provider and try to switch off data-roaming until you have free Wi-Fi. With Wi-Fi, you can use your smartphone to make free or inexpensive domestic and international calls by taking advantage of a calling app such as Skype, FaceTime, or Google+ Hangouts. Note that there are no pay phones in St. Petersburg or Estonia.

For much more on phoning, see www.ricksteves.com/phoning.

MAKING HOTEL RESERVATIONS

To ensure the best value, I recommend reserving rooms in advance, particularly during peak season. Email the hotelier with the following key pieces of information: number and type of rooms; number of nights; date of arrival; date of departure; and any special requests. (For a sample form, see the sidebar.) Use the European style for writing dates: day/month/year. Hoteliers typically ask for your credit-card number as a deposit.

Some hotels are willing to deal to attract guests—try emailing several to ask their best price. Many business hotels use "dynamic pricing," which means they change the room rate depending on demand—just like the airlines change their fares. This makes it

From:	rick@ricksteves.com
Sent:	Today
To:	info@hotelcentral.com
Subject:	Reservation request for 19-22 July

Dear Hotel Central,

I would like to reserve a room for 2 people for 3 nights, arriving 19 July and departing 22 July. If possible, I would like a quiet room with a double bed and a bathroom inside the room.

Please let me know if you have a room available and the price.

Thank you!
Rick Steves

extremely difficult to predict what you will pay. For many hotels, I list a range of prices. If the rate you're offered is at or near the bottom of my printed range, it's likely a good deal.

In general, hotel prices can soften if you do any of the following: offer to pay cash, stay at least three nights, or mention this book. You can also try asking for a cheaper room or a discount, or offer to skip breakfast.

EATING

Russia, Finland, and Estonia all have quite different cuisines. But as northern (and therefore chilly) destinations, they share many of the same ingredients and flavors: Potatoes, cabbage, beets, dill, cream, salmon, berries, and vodka are just a few of the staples you'll find here. I've noted specific culinary tips in each destination's "Eating" section. While not exorbitant, menu prices can be high; to save money, consider assembling a picnic at a local market and finding a scenic perch.

Service: Good service is relaxed (slow to an American). When you want the bill, you'll have to ask for it. A base gratuity is already included in your bill; if you're pleased with the service, you can round up. In most restaurants, 5 percent is adequate and 10 percent is considered a big tip. Rounding up for good service is especially common in Estonia (though never more than 10 percent). Tip only at restaurants with waitstaff; skip the tip if you order food at a counter. Servers prefer to be tipped in cash even if you pay with your credit card.

TRANSPORTATION

St. Petersburg, Helsinki, and Tallinn are all connected by boat; St. Petersburg is also linked to both cities by bus, and to Helsinki by a speedy rail line. The details are described in the "Connections" section at the end of each destination chapter.

HELPFUL HINTS

Emergency Help: To summon the **police** in **Russia** and **Finland,** call 112; in Estonia, call 110. For **medical emergencies** in all three countries, dial 112. For passport problems, call the **US Embassy or Consulate**—in St. Petersburg: tel. 331-2600, http://stpetersburg.usconsulate.gov; in Helsinki: tel. 40/140-5957, emergency tel. 09/616-250, http://finland.usembassy.gov; in Tallinn: tel. 668-8128, emergency tel. 668-8100, http://estonia.usembassy.gov. For other concerns, get advice from your hotelier.

Theft or Loss: To replace a passport, you'll need to go in person to an embassy or consulate (see above). Cancel and replace your credit and debit cards by calling these 24-hour US numbers collect: Visa—tel. 303/967-1096, MasterCard—tel. 636/722-7111,

American Express—tel. 336/393-1111. In Russia, to make a collect call to the US, dial 8, wait for a second dial tone, then dial 10-800-110-1011. Press zero or stay on the line for an operator. In Finland, dial 0-800-11-0015. In Estonia, call 800-12001. File a police report either on the spot or within a day or two; you'll need it to submit an insurance claim for lost or stolen railpasses or electronics, and it can help with replacing your passport or credit and debit cards. Precautionary measures can minimize the effects of loss—back up your digital photos and other files frequently. For more information, see www.ricksteves.com/help.

Time: Europe uses the 24-hour clock. It's the same through 12:00 noon, then keep going: 13:00, 14:00, and so on. Finland and Estonia are one hour ahead of most of continental Europe, and seven/ten hours ahead of the East/West Coasts of the US. St. Petersburg is one hour ahead of Finland and Estonia; two hours ahead of continental Europe; and eight/eleven hours ahead of the East/West Coasts of the US. For a handy online time converter, see www.timeanddate.com/worldclock.

Holidays and Festivals: The three cities in this book celebrate many holidays, which can close sights and attract crowds (book hotel rooms ahead). For information on holidays and festivals, check the national websites: www.russia-travel.com, www.visit finland.com, and www.visitestonia.com. For a simple list showing major—though not all—events, see www.ricksteves.com/festivals.

Numbers and Stumblers: What Americans call the second floor of a building is the first floor in Europe. Europeans write dates as day/month/year, so Christmas 2016 is 25/12/16. Commas are decimal points and vice versa—a dollar and a half is 1,50, and there are 5.280 feet in a mile. Europe uses the metric system: A kilogram is 2.2 pounds; a liter is about a quart; and a kilometer is six-tenths of a mile.

RESOURCES FROM RICK STEVES

This Snapshot guide is excerpted from the latest editions of *Rick Steves Scandinavia* and *Rick Steves Northern European Cruise Ports,* which are two of more than 30 titles in my series of guidebooks on European travel. I also produce a public television series, *Rick Steves' Europe,* and a public radio show, *Travel with Rick Steves.* My website, www.ricksteves.com, offers free travel information, a forum for travelers' comments, guidebook updates, my travel blog, an online travel store, and information on European railpasses and our tours of Europe. If you're bringing a mobile device on your trip, you can download my free Rick Steves Audio Europe app, featuring podcasts of my radio shows, audio tours of major sights in Europe, and travel interviews about Russia, Finland, and Estonia. You can get Rick Steves Audio Europe via Apple's App

PRACTICALITIES

Store, Google Play, or the Amazon Appstore. For more information, see www.ricksteves.com/audioeurope. You can follow me on Facebook and Twitter.

ADDITIONAL RESOURCES
Tourist Information: www.russia-travel.com, www.visitfinland.com, www.visitestonia.com
Passports and Red Tape: www.travel.state.gov
Packing List: www.ricksteves.com/packing
Travel Insurance: www.ricksteves.com/insurance
Cheap Flights: www.kayak.com
Airplane Carry-on Restrictions: www.tsa.gov
Updates for This Book: www.ricksteves.com/update

HOW WAS YOUR TRIP?
If you'd like to share your tips, concerns, and discoveries after using this book, please fill out the survey at www.ricksteves.com/feedback. Thanks in advance—it helps a lot.

INDEX

Our website enhances this book and turns

Explore Europe

At ricksteves.com you can browse through thousands of articles, videos, photos and radio interviews, plus find a wealth of money-saving travel tips for planning your dream trip. And with our mobile-friendly website, you can easily access all this great travel information anywhere you go.

TV Shows

Preview the places you'll visit by watching entire half-hour episodes of Rick Steves' Europe (choose from all 100 shows) on-demand, for free.

your travel dreams into affordable reality

Radio Interviews

Enjoy ready access to Rick's vast library of radio interviews covering travel

tips and cultural insights that relate specifically to your Europe travel plans.

Travel Forums

Learn, ask, share! Our online community of savvy travelers is a great resource for first-time travelers to Europe, as well as seasoned pros. You'll find forums on each country, plus travel tips and restaurant/hotel reviews. You can even ask one of our well-traveled staff to chime in with an opinion.

Travel News

Subscribe to our free Travel News e-newsletter, and get monthly updates from Rick on what's happening in Europe.

Rick's Free Travel App

Get your FREE **Rick Steves Audio Europe**™ app to enjoy…

- Dozens of self-guided tours of Europe's top museums, sights and historic walks
- Hundreds of tracks filled with cultural insights and sightseeing tips from Rick's radio interviews
- All organized into handy geographic playlists
- For iPhone, iPad, iPod Touch, Android

With Rick whispering in your ear, Europe gets even better.

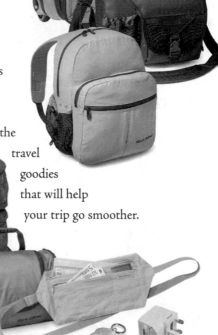

Gear up for your next adventure at ricksteves.com

Light Luggage

Pack light and right with Rick Steves' affordable, custom-designed rolling carry-on bags, backpacks, day packs and shoulder bags.

Accessories

From packing cubes to moneybelts and beyond, Rick has personally selected the travel goodies that will help your trip go smoother.

Shop at ricksteves.com

Experience maximum Europe

Save time and energy

This guidebook is your independent-travel toolkit. But for all it delivers, it's still up to you to devote the time and energy it takes to manage the preparation and logistics that are essential for a happy trip. If that's a hassle, there's a solution.

Rick Steves Tours

A Rick Steves tour takes you to Europe's most interesting places with great

with minimum stress

guides and small groups of 28 or less. We follow Rick's favorite itineraries, ride in comfy buses, stay in family-run hotels, and bring you intimately close to the Europe you've traveled so far to see. Most importantly, we take away the logistical headaches so you can focus on the fun.

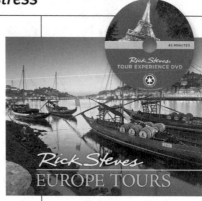

customers—along with us on 40 different itineraries, from Ireland to Italy to Istanbul. Is a Rick Steves tour the right fit for your travel dreams? Find out at ricksteves.com, where you can also get Rick's latest tour catalog and free Tour Experience DVD.

Join the fun

This year we'll take 18,000 free-spirited travelers— nearly half of them repeat

Europe is best experienced with happy travel partners. We hope you can join us.

See our itineraries at ricksteves.com

EUROPE GUIDES

Best of Europe
Eastern Europe
Europe Through the Back Door
Mediterranean Cruise Ports
Northern European Cruise Ports

COUNTRY GUIDES

Croatia & Slovenia
England
France
Germany
Great Britain
Ireland
Italy
Portugal
Scandinavia
Spain
Switzerland

CITY & REGIONAL GUIDES

Amsterdam, Bruges & Brussels
Barcelona
Budapest
Florence & Tuscany
Greece: Athens & the Peloponnese
Istanbul
London
Paris
Prague & the Czech Republic
Provence & the French Riviera
Rome
Venice
Vienna, Salzburg & Tirol

SNAPSHOT GUIDES

Basque Country: Spain & France
Berlin
Bruges & Brussels
Copenhagen & the Best of
    Denmark
Dublin
Dubrovnik
Hill Towns of Central Italy
Italy's Cinque Terre
Krakow, Warsaw & Gdansk
Lisbon
Madrid & Toledo
Milan & the Italian Lakes District
Munich, Bavaria & Salzburg
Naples & the Amalfi Coast
Northern Ireland
Norway
Scotland
Sevilla, Granada & Southern Spain
Stockholm

POCKET GUIDES

Amsterdam
Athens
Barcelona
Florence
London
Paris
Rome
Venice

Rick Steves guidebooks are published by Avalon Travel,
a member of the Perseus Books Group.

NOW AVAILABLE:
eBOOKS, DVD & BLU-RAY

TRAVEL CULTURE

Europe 101
European Christmas
Postcards from Europe
Travel as a Political Act

eBOOKS

Nearly all Rick Steves guides are available as ebooks. Check with your favorite bookseller.

RICK STEVES' EUROPE DVDs

11 New Shows 2013–2014
Austria & the Alps
Eastern Europe
England & Wales
European Christmas
European Travel Skills & Specials
France
Germany, BeNeLux & More
Greece, Turkey & Portugal
Iran
Ireland & Scotland
Italy's Cities
Italy's Countryside
Scandinavia
Spain
Travel Extras

BLU-RAY

Celtic Charms
Eastern Europe Favorites
European Christmas
Italy Through the Back Door
Mediterranean Mosaic
Surprising Cities of Europe

PHRASE BOOKS & DICTIONARIES

French
French, Italian & German
German
Italian
Portuguese
Spanish

JOURNALS

Rick Steves Pocket Travel Journal
Rick Steves Travel Journal

PLANNING MAPS

Britain, Ireland & London
Europe
France & Paris
Germany, Austria & Switzerland
Ireland
Italy
Spain & Portugal

RickSteves.com @RickSteves

Rick Steves books and DVDs are available at bookstores
and through online booksellers.

Photo © Patricia Feaster

Avalon Travel
a member of the Perseus Books Group
1700 Fourth Street
Berkeley, CA 94710

ISBN 978-1-63121-063-1

For the latest on Rick's lectures, guidebooks, tours, public radio show, and public television series, contact Rick Steves' Europe, 130 Fourth Avenue North, Edmonds, WA 98020, 425/771-8303, www.ricksteves.com, rick@ricksteves.com.

Rick Steves' Europe
Managing Editor: Risa Laib
Editorial & Production Manager: Jennifer Madison Davis
Editors: Glenn Eriksen, Tom Griffin, Cameron Hewitt, Suzanne Kotz, Cathy Lu, Carrie Shepherd
Editorial & Production Assistant: Jessica Shaw
Editorial Intern: Stacie Larsen
Researchers: Glenn Eriksen, Cameron Hewitt
Maps & Graphics: David C. Hoerlein, Sandra Hundacker, Lauren Mills, Mary Rostad

Avalon Travel
Senior Editor & Series Manager: Madhu Prasher
Editor: Jamie Andrade
Associate Editor: Maggie Ryan
Copy Editor: Patrick Collins
Proofreader: Jennifer Malnick
Indexer: Stephen Callahan
Production & Typesetting: Tabitha Lahr, Christine DeLorenzo
Cover Design: Kimberly Glyder Design
Maps & Graphics: Kat Bennett, Mike Morgenfeld

Photo Credits
Front Cover: Church of the Savior on Blood © graphixel/Getty Images
Additional Photography: Dominic Arizona Bonuccelli, Tom Griffin, Sonja Groset, Cameron Hewitt, David C. Hoerlein, Lauren Mills, Moesgaard Museum, Rick Steves, Ian Watson, Chris Werner (photos are used by permission and are the property of the original copyright owners).

ABOUT THE AUTHORS

RICK STEVES

Since 1973, Rick Steves has spent 100 days every year exploring Europe. Along with writing and researching a bestselling series of guidebooks, Rick produces a public television series *(Rick Steves' Europe)*, a public radio show *(Travel with Rick Steves)*, a blog (on Facebook), and an app and podcast *(Rick Steves Audio Europe)*; writes a nationally syndicated newspaper column; organizes guided tours that take more than 20,000 travelers to Europe annually; and offers an information-packed website (www.ricksteves.com). With the help of his hardworking staff of 100 at Rick Steves' Europe—in Edmonds, Washington, just north of Seattle—Rick's mission is to make European travel fun, affordable, and culturally enlightening for Americans.

Connect with Rick:

facebook.com/RickSteves twitter: @RickSteves

CAMERON HEWITT

Cameron Hewitt grew up listening to the Polish nursery rhymes of his grandfather, Jan Paweł Dąbrowski. Today he ventures to Eastern Europe often—to simmer in Budapest's thermal baths, twist through the Julian Alps on corkscrew roads, commune with his Polish roots, laugh at a good Czech joke, and set sail on the glimmering Adriatic. Cameron, who also writes and edits other guidebooks for Rick Steves, lives in Seattle with his wife Shawna.